METAPHYSICS . COSMOLOGY . TRADITION . SYMBOLISM

STUDIES IN COMPARATIVE RELIGION

The First English Journal on Traditional Studies — established 1963

T0306476

Studies in Comparative Religion is devoted to the exposition of the teachings, spiritual methods, symbolism, and other facets of the religious traditions of the world, together with the traditional arts and sciences which have sprung from those religions. It is not sectarian and, inasmuch as it is not tied to the interests of any particular religion, it is free to lay stress on the common spirit underlying the various religious forms.

One of our primary aims is to meet the need for accurate information created by the now world-wide interest in the question of "ecumenical relations" between the great religions, by providing a forum where writers of proven authority can exchange views on various aspects of religious life, doctrinal, historical, artistic and mystical, not forgetting the element of personal experience and reminiscence.

By collecting accurate information about the great religions under their many aspects and rendering them available to interested readers we feel we are fulfilling a very pressing need of our time and also contributing in a practical manner to the cause of inter-religious understanding. If there is to be an effective measure of this understanding at any level this can only be on the basis of accurate presentation both of teachings and facts. An ill-informed benevolence is no substitute for genuine insight, based on information that is neither willfully distorted nor confined to the surface of things.

In this manner we think that we are best serving the interest of our readers in their search for truth.

(*Excerpt from the Introduction to our first publication, almost fifty years ago*)

World Wisdom

Education in the Light of Tradition

Studies in Comparative Religion

Edited by
Jane Casewit

World Wisdom

Education in the Light of Tradition:
Studies in Comparative Religion
© 2011 World Wisdom, Inc.

All rights reserved.
No part of this book may be used or reproduced
in any manner without written permission,
except in critical articles and reviews.

Library of Congress Cataloging-in-Publication Data

Education in the light of tradition / edited by Jane Casewit.
p. cm. -- (Studies in comparative religion)
Includes bibliographical references.
ISBN 978-1-935493-99-0 (pbk. : alk. paper) 1. Education--Religious aspects. 2. Education--Sociological aspects. 3. Education--Aims and objectives. I. Casewit, Jane, 1952-
LB1027.2.E38 2011
379.2'8--dc23
2011038883

Printed on acid-free paper in USA.

For information address World Wisdom, Inc.
P.O. Box 2682, Bloomington, Indiana 47402-2682
www.worldwisdom.com

CONTENTS

Education in the Light of Tradition

Editorial

Relative — like the whole world —
Is the phenomenon of man, and absolute
Is God alone.
What counts is not the bustle
Of science and education, with which one struggles —
It is only our relationship with the One
That is all — of which men say
It is mere dream.
If thou holdest fast to God,
It is indifferent what thy pursuits are —
Whether thou venturest forth with lofty science
Or huntest bisons on the prairie.
(Frithjof Schuon, *Autumn Leaves*, "The Relationship")

This profound poem by Frithjof Schuon tells us what the fundamental goal of educating young souls should be—enhancing their relationship with God. Modern educators study extensively "how" children learn or should learn; yet the underlying aim of learning is rarely brought under serious scrutiny because the meaning of life itself and the human condition is no longer understood in most modern education systems.

Almost every country in the modern world is undergoing "reform" of its education system. Yet despite the enormous efforts and resources being invested in public teaching and learning, modern ministries of education continually revise curricula in an attempt to decide what their nation's children need to learn. However, a clear understanding of human nature itself has been forgotten, along with a loss of a sense of a sacred center and a connection to the Divine Principle. A child's sense of the sacred and the concept of his/her being a servant of God, or devotee of one of His Qualities, has been replaced by the urgent need to solidify young allegiances to nation states through education for upright "citizenship."

As long as the Divine Principle has been eliminated from the foundation of children's upbringing, those truths that children essentially need to learn for their good in this world and for the ultimate benefit of their final ends will be neither communicated nor understood.

He knoweth nothing as he ought to know, who thinks he knoweth anything
Without seeing its place and the manner how it relateth to God, angels and men,
And to the creatures in earth, heaven and hell, time and eternity.
(Thomas Traherne)[1]

If we therefore begin with the premise that our main objective in life should be our relationship with God and to return to our Creator with purified souls prepared for Eternity, it follows naturally that young people therefore should initially learn to understand the Divine

[1] English cleric, mystic, and poet (1636/7-1674).

Principle and its reflection in manifestation and all that this understanding implies for their own lives, that is, how to cultivate a relationship with God and their neighbors.

Within this perspective, we can understand why the sacred was ever present in education in traditional societies and instruction addressed a youthful soul as well as the body and mind, the latter being considered an extension of both body and soul. Knowledge and understanding of metaphysical and symbolic truths were formulated to address the higher reaches of the intelligence, creating a vibration in that part of young souls which begins to overlap with the Heart, seat of the Divine spark in all of us. Teachers, therefore, were held in the highest respect and occupied revered positions in society because they were the transmitters of this precious knowledge.

Indeed, the original goal of education was to understand and approach the Real, and distinguish between the Real and the illusory, equipped with tools of learning such as a knowledge of sacred texts enshrined into one's memory and a thorough understanding of the grammar of a sacred or liturgical language, as well as the ability to express oneself through rhetoric and debate. Physical sciences, mathematics, and geography were also taught within the perspective of their reflection of the Divine Principle. Children also learnt myths, magical tales, and stories which evolved out of their respective traditions.

Most schools are criticized today for not teaching "values." Parents blame schools for no longer instilling a moral compass and discipline into students, and schools blame parents for abdicating their roles as "first educators." C.S. Lewis remarked, "Education without values, as useful as it is, seems rather to make man a more clever devil."

Undoubtedly, the transmission of moral values is problematic within a secular education curriculum. "Values" can only be taught within an education system that safeguards a liaison with the Divine, thus providing a framework for values which reflect Divine Qualities and encourage young people to be "viceregents" of God on earth. True values and ensuing ethics can only be understood against a backdrop of tradition and a revealed religion, encompassing a sacred law which places certain limitations on individuals and societies in order to promote virtue and preserve social equilibrium.

Most modern schools formulate "rules" and a "dialogue" about students' rights and responsibilities towards themselves and others which are generally carried out at some stage of the curriculum. However, shorn of their sacred foundation, these rules (and the subsequent dialogue) are liable to seem arbitrary and self-justifying, the product of yet another self-appointed adult authority, to which students feel no allegiance, and against which they frequently rebel. Taken to its logical conclusion, "ethics and values education" in schools cannot but instill in young minds a distrust of adult authority and an identification of tradition with a sort of oppressive tyranny of the aged. And indeed, this is precisely the message that the media and popular culture incessantly "markets" to young minds. The result is (another) generation of young people in despair, with few hopes or aspirations for their lives, provoking even further social disequilibrium through their unprecedented, negative behaviour.

Although objections could justifiably be made that, in earlier times in traditional worlds, equal opportunities for education were not offered to everyone in society, nevertheless, an appropriate form of training suited to one's destined role in life ensured the transmission of handicrafts, artistic traditions, domestic expertise, animal husbandry, agricultural skills and the like, and allowed most people to learn how to perform well the tasks bestowed upon them through their destined caste, social standing, and gender. The underlying principle of education in the light of tradition could be illustrated in another poem by Frithjof Schuon:

It may be good to bring a child into the world,
And to educate him with love and care —
But when he grows up, the world will take the trouble
To do the opposite: to draw the child's soul,
Which is still wavering, into the realm of deception.
Therefore, give the child a right soul at an early age,
So that, with courage, he may choose the True.

The objective of this collection of articles on education in the light of tradition is to offer a glimmer of the traditional view of education from within living traditions and to open a space for criticism of modern, national education programs which have been designed based on modern philosophies of education. As we experience it today, education is inevitably fraught with insoluble challenges, as programs are constructed upon flattened, uniform curricula and a philosophy which expounds "education for all"—that panacea for social ills which ends up being instruction aimed at the lowest common denominator of human capabilities and ignores the infinite diversity of human souls, while attempting to push as many young people as possible through a public education system.

Some of the articles are philosophical and express traditional principles of education, while others are direct or indirect criticisms of public education systems or offer alternative approaches. Yet other contributions describe the transmission of knowledge and values from within a traditional society.

Sincere gratitude is owed to all those who responded to our request for articles and contributed to this special volume of Studies in Comparative Religion. I would like to especially thank Michael Fitzgerald, Clinton Minnaar, Edin Lohja, Tayeb Al-Tayeb, and Scott Macky for their continued support during the preparation of this special issue.

Jane Casewit

I.

Education and the Human Condition

The Triple Nature of Man

Frithjof Schuon

Human intelligence is essentially objective, hence total: it is capable of disinterested judgment, reasoning, assimilating and deifying meditation, with the help of grace. The quality of objectivity also belongs to the will—it is what makes it human—and this is why our will is free, in other words capable of self-transcendence, sacrifice, and asceticism: our willing is not inspired by our desires alone; fundamentally it is inspired by the truth, which is independent of our immediate interests. The same is true for our soul, our sensibility, our capacity for loving: since it is human, it is by definition objective, hence disinterested in its essence or in its primordial and innocent perfection; it is capable of goodness, generosity, compassion. This means that it is able to find its happiness in the happiness of others and at the expense of its own satisfactions; in the same way it is capable of finding its happiness above itself in its celestial personality, which is not yet completely its own. From this specific nature, made of totality and objectivity, come the vocation, rights, and duties of man.

To say that the prerogative of the human state is a capacity for objectivity is to recognize that the quintessential content and ultimate purpose of this capacity is the Absolute: for the intelligence is objective insofar as it perceives not only what is but also all that is; an intelligence that rejects the Absolute does not take account of the total Reality to which it is proportioned; it is no longer human, and since it cannot be that of an animal—for it is in fact the intelligence of a man—it has no other choice than to be satanic. As for the will, it is objective insofar as it has as its aim not only an attainable and useful end or some genuine good but also and even above all the Sovereign Good and insofar as it envisions things in their connection, near or distant, with this Good. And the soul is objective insofar as it loves what is worthy of being loved, the transcendent essence of which is divine Beauty and divine Love.

The human subject necessarily seeks the contingent because it itself is contingent and to the extent it is so; and it seeks the Absolute because it derives from the Absolute in its capacity for objectivity, precisely, and because this capacity shows it that every positive reality, and thus all we call good, belongs to the Absolute.

It is obvious that objectivity is nothing other than the truth, in which subject and object coincide as far as possible and in which the essential takes precedence over the accidental—or the necessary over the contingent—either by extinguishing it in some fashion or on the contrary by reintegrating it, according to the various ontological aspects of relativity itself.

It has been said that man is a rational animal; while this formulation is insufficient and ill-sounding, it nonetheless points to an undeniable truth, though in an elliptical fashion, for the rational faculty actually serves to underscore the transcendence of man in relation to the animal. Man is rational because he possesses the Intellect, which by definition has a capacity for the absolute and therefore a sense of the relative as such; and he possesses the Intellect because he is made "in the image of God", which he demonstrates—it is hardly necessary to add—by his physical form, his gift of speech, and his ability to produce and construct. Man is a theophany in his form as well as in his faculties; to deny this is an indirect way of denying God. Without an opening toward transcendence, human intelligence would be a luxury as inexplicable as it would be useless.

* * *

The soul loves beauty and is thereby obliged to be virtuous, for virtue is the soul's beauty and happiness; beauty, and a love of beauty, give the soul the happiness to which it aspires by its nature. The soul loves beauty, desires happiness, and practices goodness; to say that the soul is fundamentally happy only through beauty amounts to saying that it is happy only in virtue.

Sensible beauties are situated outside the soul, and its encounters with them are more or less accidental; if the soul wishes to be happy in an unconditional and permanent fashion, it must carry the beautiful within itself. This inward beauty is nothing other than a consciousness of the Source of all harmony; it is a sense of the sacred as well as faith, the "yes" of the soul to the meeting with God. From this inward source spring the virtues, which communicate beauty of soul and more fundamentally that of the Sovereign Good.

Virtue is the message of that beauty which is goodness. But goodness is extrinsically differentiated according to circumstance: upon contact with whatever may oppose it, it must sometimes become adamantine and other times lightning-like; but it is always goodness that is clothed in these veils. Good combats evil not by ceasing to be good but because it is good.

Virtue consists in allowing free passage within the soul to the Beauty of God.

*　　*　　*

Sat, Chit, Ānanda: Being, Consciousness, Felicity. Being, hence Power; Consciousness, hence Wisdom; Felicity, hence Beauty. This divine ternary is mirrored in the human microcosm in the corresponding ternary of will, intelligence, sentiment, or activity, knowledge, love.

This doctrine of the three human dimensions can be expressed in a very simple and immediately plausible way as follows: the good that a man is capable of knowing must also be willed insofar as it can be an object of the will; he must also love this good, and at the same time he must love the knowledge of it as well as the will toward it, just as he must will and love the earthly and contingent reflections of this good in a way that reflects what their nature requires or permits. It is no more possible to devote oneself to knowledge without loving and willing it than to will something without knowing it and loving its fulfillment; and one cannot love without knowing an object and wishing to love it. This interdependence shows that the immortal soul is one and that each of its modes has the same meaning, to manifest God while realizing Him.

There can be no knowledge of God without a knowledge of eschatological truths; it is not possible to will God without willing the good things that bring us close to God and shunning the evils that separate us from Him; and there can be no love of God without love for one's neighbor and for whatever bears witness to God and brings us close to Him, both in us and around us.

*　　*　　*

Man can know, will, love; and to will is to act. We know God by distinguishing Him from whatever He is not and by recognizing Him in whatever bears witness to Him; we will God by accomplishing whatever leads us to Him and by abstaining from whatever removes us from Him; and we love God by loving to know and will Him and by loving whatever bears witness to Him, both around us and in us.

These three elements correspond respectively to understanding, which is intellective, concentration, which is volitive, and conformity, which is affective; now, the last of these elements is distinguished by the fact that it attaches itself to both will and intelligence by amplifying them in a certain fashion[1] and because, when we consider it in itself, we can see that it is inspired by these two sister-faculties. As a result this third element, whether we call it conformity, love, or sentiment, contains two poles: faith, which refers to intelligence and knowledge, and virtue, which refers to will and practice; neither pole can simply be reduced to the intelligence or will, however, for both of them—virtue as well as faith—have as their substance our living soul and not some particular faculty.

In a certain sense man's virtue responds to the divine quality that gives him life and overwhelms him with blessings, and his faith responds to the divine quality that saves and liberates him.

But let us return to the intelligence and the will: symbolically speaking, the first pertains to the brain and the second to the heart; this complementarity has its basis in the fact that the mental faculty opens to the object, which presents itself to discernment, whereas the heart is identified with the subject, which exercises volition; but the mental faculty is merely the organ of recording and formulation—of trial and error—and not of intellection, whose seat is the subtle center of which the heart is the vital manifestation. This center—the Intellect—is simultaneously the source of discernment, will, and love.[2]

In Islamic terms, the divine roots of the spiritual dimensions of man are the hypostases of "Power" (*Qudrah*), "Wisdom" (*Hikmah*), and "Clemency" (*Rahmah*), the last of which is polarized into the two Divine Names: "the infinitely Good in Himself" (*Rahmān*) and the "infinitely Merciful" (*Rahīm*). We can interpret these Names by saying that "Beauty", which is intrinsic, and "Goodness", which is extrinsic, constitute "Beatitude" (*Rahmah*, the equivalent of the Vedantic *Ānanda*).[3]

* * *

The third dimension of man, as we have said, is love or conformity of soul, or what amounts to the same thing: faith and virtue. To these elements could be added another discipline, albeit subsidiary, that of the style of one's surroundings, and this includes not only the company of men of ascending tendency—this is the Hindu *satsanga*—but also in a wider sense the search for a congenial framework. This in turn brings us to the field of liturgy, sacred art, traditional craftsmanship, and the role of nature—in short to the problem, if there is a problem, of the function of theophanic appearances, whether direct or indirect. As we have said, all this pertains to the principle of *satsanga*, "association with saints", as well as to *darshan*, "contemplation", whether of a saint as such or of the sacred in all its forms, for a sense of the sacred is the life-giving sap of both virtue and faith.

[1] Thus the feelings of certitude and serenity, for instance, amplify intellectual operations, just as the feelings of decisiveness and satisfaction, or fulfillment, amplify the operations of the will.

[2] Pure intellection is independent of will and sentiment; and likewise pure volition and pure sentiment are sufficient in themselves. Nonetheless it is impossible to think without willing to do so and without finding some satisfaction in it, just as it is impossible to will something without thinking, unless one considers the case of a sudden intuition or reflex, and other such similar possibilities.

[3] Speaking analogically, the invincible substance of the sun is *Qudrah*, "Power"; its perfect form is *Hikmah*, "Wisdom"; its radiance is *Rahmah*, "Beatitude". And within this radiance light is *Rahmān*, "Beauty", while heat is *Rahīm*, "Goodness". This interpretation of the terms *Rahmah*, *Rahmān*, and *Rahīm* expresses the intention of the hypostatic constellation.

But leaving aside this more or less extrinsic, and indeed accidental, dimension—accidental when compared to conditions that are *sine qua non*—we may sum up the spiritual functions in the following terms: discernment, union, faith, virtue. Discernment extends from metaphysical principles to earthly things: "discernment of spirits" is incumbent on all; and even on the most contingent of planes, our intelligence on the one hand and the nature of things on the other make discrimination unavoidable, whether in the intuitive and direct form of intellection or in the discursive and indirect form of reasoning, as the case may be.

The application of the will to the spiritual path culminates in contemplative concentration or in the practice that supports this concentration: namely, prayer in all its forms or meditation, in short "the remembrance of God"; this is why we may give the name "union" to this supreme function of the will, although what is in question is not a union of grace, such as ecstasy or the station of unity. Beneath this summit of contemplative concentration—which corresponds to the intrinsic will insofar as it is united to its immanent source—the will necessarily applies itself to a thousand things that help us to advance toward our goal, even if only by contributing to the balance and stability without which it is impossible for us to take flight.

If a man seeks to realize what in fact immensely transcends him, he must *a priori* conform to this end or model, for otherwise he will fail either simply by collapsing or else by being broken; and this conformity, which is like an anticipated realization *hic et nunc*, is faith combined with virtue, for the one is never without the other. Faith is a "yes" from the whole of our soul to the Divinity and to divine things, and if this "yes" is sincere it will produce, develop, or stabilize virtue: "Be ye therefore perfect, even as your Father which is in Heaven is perfect." We could also say that the soul is made of love and that its substance coincides with faith, for love in itself is the love of God; and just as the good tends to communicate itself—quasi-ontologically—the radiance of faith is the totality of attitudes that manifest beauty of soul and culminate in generosity.

* * *

The function of the intelligence—whether we call it knowledge, understanding, or something else—includes a passive mode, which is contemplative, and an active mode, which is discriminative. The intelligence cannot be anything other than passive in relation to the Divine Object that determines it, but it is active when it distinguishes the relative from the Absolute and in proceeding to all the other distinctions resulting from this initial discrimination; and, not to be forgotten, this activity is that of the Divine Intellect within us, and our certitude is a trace of this immanence.

Will or activity, considered in relationship to its loftiest object, is synonymous with spiritual concentration, which refers ultimately to the mystery of identity; now this concentration is either fully effective in the present or underlying in duration. In other words realizational and unitive concentration must in itself be perfect or total—it must be everything that its nature requires—but it must also be persevering, for the perfection of the moment would be ineffective without fixation in time and thus without the reduction of duration to the instant of God.

Sentiment or love, or the conformity of our person and thus our sensibility to the Divine Reality, which both determines and attracts us, is inward or outward, devotional or generous; it is faith, devotion, or piety with regard to God, and virtue, moral beauty, or generosity with regard to other creatures. In faith, resignation is combined with fervor; and in virtue, patience is combined with generosity.

One could also say that to know God is to see Him "here" and "everywhere": to see Him in Himself and in His manifestations. In a similar fashion one could say that to will God—to act in accordance with Him and for Him—is to will God "now" and "always": in the act, which coincides with the present, and in the disposition, which guarantees duration and allows us to reduce it to the present. And likewise in the case of the sensible soul: to love God is to love Him "solely" and "totally": to love Him more than creatures but at the same time to love creatures in Him.

* * *

In searching for especially adequate or suggestive terms for the spiritual dimensions of man, we could suggest the following quaternity: objectivity, inwardness, faith, and virtue.

Objectivity is the perfect adaptation of the intelligence to objective reality; and inwardness is the persevering concentration of the will on that particular "Inward" which, according to Christ, coincides with the heart, the door of which it is fitting to lock after one has entered—a door that opens onto the "Kingdom of God", which is indeed "within you".

And this inwardness needs a foundation of faith and virtue, of intensity and radiance, without which man, in the eyes of God, would not be man.

* * *

Given that the Divine Principle is tri-polarized into Being-Power, Consciousness-Wisdom, and Beatitude-Mercy, it may be asked what the hierarchical relationship is among these three hypostases. Without wishing to resort to an unrealistic schematization, we would note that there are sufficient reasons for saying that Being-Power and Consciousness-Wisdom are two undifferentiated aspects of the Absolute—undifferentiated but distinguishable on the already relative plane of creative Being—whereas Beatitude-Mercy coincides with the Infinitude of the Principle. Beatitude—*Ānanda*—also possesses two aspects: projecting *Māyā*, which refers to Being-Power, and reabsorbing *Māyā*, which refers to Consciousness-Wisdom.

The question of whether Power or Consciousness comes first is subjectively insoluble because objectively it cannot be asked. When it is said that *Sat*, pure Being, is the Root-Principle, one assumes that Being comes before Knowing; when on the contrary *Ātmā*, the Self, is said to be the Supreme Reality, one sets out from the truth that the Divine Principle is essentially Light, Spirit, and Consciousness and that Power and Goodness are its principal aspects or functions.[4] This truth or reality unquestionably appears in man, of whom it can be said that he is an intelligence prolonging itself in—or by—the will and the sentiments; nonetheless voluntarists place all the emphasis on the will and appear to be saying that by choosing God the will determines both the sensibility and the intelligence. This way of envisioning things appears in any case in the axiom "God is Love", which gives rise in turn to a perspective that actually diverges from voluntarism in that it locates sentiment and not will at the summit of the triangle; this is the point of view of *bhakti*, which subordinates both will and intelligence, not indeed to sentiment pure and simple, but to a love that coincides with the whole soul—a love imbued, when it meets divine Love, with a supernatural and liberating Presence.

[4] In Sufism as elsewhere there have been many controversies regarding the priority of the objective and the subjective *in divinis*.

Since the Intellect contains all three elements and prefigures them in its unity, it is always possible to reduce one or another of the elements—as they appear in man—to the Intellect and then to subordinate the two remaining elements to this synthesis: in other words it is always possible to subordinate the will and love to the Intellect-Intelligence, intelligence and love to the Intellect-Will, and intelligence and will to the Intellect-Love.

Translated by Mark Perry

The Bugbear of Literacy

Ananda K. Coomaraswamy

It was possible for Aristotle,[1] starting from the premise that a man, being actually cultured, may *also* become literate, to ask whether there is a necessary or merely an accidental connection of literacy with culture. Such a question can hardly arise for us, to whom illiteracy implies, as a matter of course, ignorance, backwardness, unfitness for self-government: for us, unlettered peoples are uncivilized peoples, and vice versa—as a recent publisher's blurb expresses it: "The greatest force in civilization is the collective wisdom of a literate people."

There are reasons for this point of view; they inhere in the distinction of a people, or folk, from a proletariat, that of a social organism from a human ant heap. For a proletariat, literacy is a practical and cultural necessity. We may remark in passing that necessities are not always goods in themselves, out of their context; some, like wooden legs, are advantageous only to men already maimed. However that may be, it remains that literacy is a necessity *for us*, and from both points of view; (1) because our industrial system can only be operated and profits can only be made by men provided with at least an elementary knowledge of the "three R's"; and (2) because, where there is no longer any necessary connection between one's "skill" (now a timesaving "economy of motion" rather than a control of the product) and one's "wisdom," the possibility of culture depends so much on our ability to read the best books. We say "possibility" here because, whereas the literacy actually produced by compulsory mass education often involves little or no more than an ability and the will to read the newspapers and advertisements, an actually cultured man under these conditions will be one who has studied many books in many languages, and this is not a kind of knowledge that can be handed out to everyone under "compulsion" (even if *any* nation could afford the needed quantity and quality of teachers) or that could be acquired by everyone, however ambitious.

We have allowed that in industrial societies, where it is assumed that man is made for commerce and where men are cultured, if at all, in spite of rather than because of their environment, literacy is a necessary skill. It will naturally follow that if, on the principle that misery loves company, we are planning to industrialize the rest of the world, we are also in duty bound to train it in Basic English, or words to that effect—American is already a language of exclusively external relationships, a tradesman's tongue—lest the other peoples should be unable to compete effectively with us. Competition is the life of trade, and gangsters must have rivals.

In the present article we are concerned with something else, viz., the assumption that, even for societies not yet industrialized, literacy is "an unqualified good and an indispensible condition of culture."[2] The vast majority of the world's population is still unindustrialized

[1] *Metaphysics*, VI:2, 4, and XI:8, 12. "Reading, for a man devoid of prior-understanding, is like a blind man's looking in a mirror" (*Garuda Purāna*, XVI:82).

[2] Walter Shewring, "Literacy," in the *Dictionary of World Literature*, 1943. "We are becoming culturally illiterate faster than all these agencies are managing to make us literate in the use of the potentialities of the culture" (Robert S. Lynd, in *Knowledge for What?*). Professor John U. Nef of Chicago, speaking at Hamline University in 1944, remarked: "In spite of the alleged great spread of literacy [in America] . . . the proportion of the population who can communicate with each other on a relatively high level of discourse is very much smaller than it was." A recent study sponsored by the Carnegie Foundation for the Advancement of Teaching found that "the average senior in

and unlettered, and there are peoples still "unspoiled" (in the interior of Borneo): but the average American who knows of no other way of living than his own, judges that "unlettered" means "uncultured," *as if* this majority consisted only of a depressed class in the context of his own environment. It is because of this, as well as for some meaner reasons, not unrelated to "imperial" interests, that when we propose not merely to exploit but also to educate "the lesser breeds without the [i.e. *our*] law" we inflict upon them profound, and often lethal, injuries. We say "lethal" rather than "fatal" here because it is precisely a destruction of their *memories* that is involved. We overlook that "education" is never creative, but a two-edged weapon, always destructive; whether of ignorance or of knowledge depending upon the educator's wisdom or folly. Too often fools rush in where angels might fear to tread.

As against the complacent prejudice we shall essay to show (1) that there is no necessary connection of literacy with culture, and (2) that to impose our literacy (and our contemporary "literature") upon a cultured but illiterate people is to destroy their culture in the name of our own. For the sake of brevity we shall assume without argument that "culture" implies an ideal quality and a good form that can be realized by all men irrespective of condition: and, since we are treating of culture chiefly as expressed in words, we shall identify culture with "poetry"; not having in view the kind of poetry that nowadays babbles of green fields or that merely reflects social behavior or our private reactions to passing events, but with reference to that whole class of prophetic literature that includes the Bible, the Vedas, the Edda, the great epics, and in general the world's "best books," and the most philosophical if we agree with Plato that "wonder is the beginning of philosophy." Of these "books" many existed long before they were written down, many have never been written down, and others have been or will be lost.

We shall have now to make some quotations from the works of men whose "culture" cannot be called in question; for while the merely literate are often very proud of their literacy, such as it is, it is only by men who are "not only literate but also cultured" that it has been widely recognized that "letters" at their best are only a means to an end and never an end in themselves, or, indeed, that "the letter kills." A "literary" man, if ever there was one, the late Professor G. L. Kittredge writes:[3] "It requires a combined effort of the reason and the imagination to conceive a poet as a person who cannot write, singing or reciting his verses to an audience that cannot read. . . . The ability of oral tradition to transmit great masses of verse for hundreds of years is proved and admitted. . . . To this oral literature, as the French call it, education is no friend. Culture destroys it, sometimes with amazing rapidity. *When a nation begins to read . . . what was once the possession of the folk as a whole, becomes the heritage of the illiterate only, and soon, unless it is gathered up by the antiquary, vanishes altogether.*" Mark,

six colleges recognized only 61 out of 100 words in familiar use by educated people"! In view of all the facts, it is indeed astonishing to find Lord Raglan saying: "By savage I mean illiterate" (in the *Rationalist Annual* [1946], p. 43). There was a time, indeed, when the English bourgeoisie thought of the Gaelic Highlanders as "savages"; but from an anthropologist one would expect a refutation of such "myths," rather than their revival!

3 F. G. Childe, *English and Scottish Popular Ballads*, Introduction by G. L. Kittredge. Cf. W.W. Comfort, *Chrétien de Troyes* (Everyman's Library), Introduction: Chrétien's poetry "was intended for a society that was still homogeneous, and to it at the outset doubtless all classes of the population listened with equal interest." Nothing of this kind is or can be achieved by the organized and compulsory education of today—"a province of its own, detached from life" with its "atmosphere of intense boredom that damps the vitality of the young" and of which "the result is: the young people do not know anything really well," or as "it would be more exact to say, they do not know what knowledge is," which "explains the dangerous gullibility which propaganda exploits" (Erich Meissner, *Germany in Peril* [1942], pp. 47, 48).

too, that this oral literature once belonged "to the whole people . . . the community whose intellectual interests are the same from the top of the social structure to the bottom," while in the reading society it is accessible only to antiquaries, and is no longer bound up with everyday life. A point of further importance is this: that the traditional oral literatures interested not only all *classes*, but also all *ages* of the population; while the books that are nowadays written expressly "for children" are such as no mature mind could tolerate; it is now only the comic strips that appeal alike to children who have been given nothing better and at the same time to "adults" who have never grown up.

It is in just the same way that music is thrown away; folk songs are lost to the people at the same time that they are collected and "put in a bag"; and in the same way that the "preservation" of a people's art in folk museums is a funeral rite, for preservatives are only necessary when the patient has already died. Nor must we suppose that "community singing" can take the place of folk song; its level can be no higher than that of the Basic English in which our undergraduates must be similarly drilled, if they are to understand even the language of their elementary textbooks.

In other words, "Universal compulsory education, of the type introduced at the end of the nineteenth century, has not fulfilled expectations by producing happier and more effective citizens; on the contrary, it has created readers of the yellow press and cinema-goers" (Karl Otten). A master who can himself not only read, but also *write* good classical Latin and Greek, remarks that "there is no doubt of the quantitative increase in literacy of a kind, and amid the general satisfaction that something is being multiplied it escapes enquiry whether the something is profit or deficit." He is discussing only the "worst effects" of enforced literacy, and concludes: "Learning and wisdom have often been divided; perhaps the clearest result of modern literacy has been to maintain and enlarge the gulf."

Douglas Hyde remarks that "in vain have disinterested visitors opened wide eyes of astonishment at schoolmasters who knew no Irish being appointed to teach pupils who knew no English. . . . Intelligent children endowed with a vocabulary in every day use of about three thousand words enter the Schools of the Chief Commissioner, to come out at the end with their natural vivacity gone, their intelligence almost completely sapped, their splendid command of their native language lost forever, and a vocabulary of five or six hundred English words, badly pronounced and barbarously employed, substituted for it. . . . Story, lay, poem, song, aphorism, proverb, and the unique stock in trade of an Irish speaker's mind, is gone forever, *and replaced by nothing*. . . . The children are taught, if nothing else, to be ashamed of their own parents, ashamed of their own nationality, ashamed of their own names. . . . It is a remarkable system of 'education.'"[4]—this system that you, "civilized and literate" Americans, have inflicted upon your own Amerindians, and that all imperial races are still inflicting upon their subjected peoples, and would like to impose upon their allies—the Chinese, for example.

The problem involved is both of languages and what is said in them. As for language, let us bear in mind, in the first place, that no such thing as a "primitive language," in the sense of one having a limited vocabulary fitted only to express the simplest external relationships, is known. Much rather, that is a condition to which, under certain circumstances and as the result of "nothing-morist" philosophies, languages tend, rather than one from which they originate; for

[4] Douglas Hyde, *Literary History of Ireland* (1903), p. 633.

example, 90 per cent of our American "literacy" is a two-syllabled affair.[5]

In the seventeenth century Robert Knox said of the Sinhalese that "their ordinary Plow-men and Husbandmen do speak elegantly, and are full of compliment. And there is no difference of ability and speech of a Country-man and a Courtier."[6] Abundant testimony to the like effect could be cited from all over the world. Thus of Gaelic, J.F. Campbell wrote, "I am inclined to think that dialect the best which is spoken by the most illiterate in the islands. . . . Men with clear heads and wonderful memories, generally very poor and old, living in remote corners of remote islands, and speaking only Gaelic,"[7] and he quotes Hector Maclean, who says that the loss of their oral literature is due "partly to reading . . . partly to bigoted religious ideas, and partly to narrow utilitarian views"—which are, precisely, the three typical forms in which modern civilization impresses itself upon the older cultures. Alexander Carmichael says that "the people of Lews, like the people of the Highlands and Islands generally, carry the Scriptures in their minds and apply them in their speech. . . . Perhaps no people had a fuller ritual of song and story, of secular rite and religious ceremony . . . than the ill-understood and so-called illiterate Highlanders of Scotland."[8]

St. Barbe Baker tells us that in Central Africa "my trusted friend and companion was an old man who could not read or write, though well versed in stories of the past. . . . The old chiefs listened enthralled. . . . Under the present system of education there is grave risk that much of

[5] American is already "a one-dimensional public language, a language oriented to the description of external aspects of behavior, weak in overtones. . . . Our words lack . . . the formal precision which comes from awareness of past and different usage" (Margaret Mead, *And Keep Your Powder Dry* [1942], p. 82). Any author who uses words precisely is liable to be misunderstood.

"Perhaps at no other time have men been so knowing and yet so unaware, so burdened with purposes and so purposeless, so disillusioned and so completely the victims of illusion. This strange contradiction pervades our entire modern culture, our science and our philosophy, our literature and our art" (W.M. Urban, *The Intelligible World* [1929], p. 172). Under such conditions, ability to read a printed page becomes a mere trick, and is no guarantee whatever of power to grasp or to communicate ideas.

[6] Robert Knox, *An Historical Relation of Ceylon* (1681; 1911 ed.), p. 168.

[7] J.F. Campbell, *Popular Tales of the West Highlands* (1890 ed.), pp. v, xxiii, cxxii.

[8] Alexander Carmichael, *Carmina Gadelica*, Vol. I, 1900, pp. xxiii, xxix. Cf. J. G. Mackay, *More West Highland Tales* (1940), General Preface: "The poorest classes generally speak the language admirably. . . . Some recited thousands of lines of ancient heroic poems. . . . Another cause of the fragmentary character of some tales is the obliterating effect of modern civilization"; and J. Watson, *ibid.*, Introduction: "This intellectual inheritance . . . this ancient culture extended over all the north and northerly midlands of Scotland. The people who possessed this culture may have been, and usually were, unlettered. They were far from being uneducated. It is sad to think that its decay has been partly due to the schools and the Church!" It is, in fact, precisely by "the schools and the Church" that the decay of cultures all over the world has been hastened in the last hundred years.

H.J. Massingham in *This Plot of Earth* (1944), p. 233, tells of "the old man, Seonardh Coinbeul, who could neither read nor write and carried 4,500 lines of his own bardic composition in his head, together with all manner of songs and stories."

A. Solonylsin in the *Asiatic Review* (NS. XLI, Jan., 1945), p. 86, remarks that the recording of the Kirghiz epic is still incomplete, although over 1,100,000 lines have already been taken down by the Kirghiz Research Institute—"Bards who recite the 'Manas'—or 'Manaschi'—have phenomenal memories in addition to poetic talent. Only this can explain the fact that hundreds of thousands of verses have been handed down orally." A writer reviewing *Manas, Kirghiski Narodni Epos* in the *Journal of American Folklore*, 58, 1945, p. 65, observes that "general education has already done much to remove the raison d'être of the minstrel's position in tribal life. . . . With acculturation becoming a rolling Juggernaut it is not surprising that what remains of epic singing may soon degenerate into an artificial and ostentatiously national publicity device."

this may be lost."[9] W.G. Archer points out that "unlike the English system in which one could pass one's life without coming into contact with poetry, the Uraon tribal system uses poetry as a vital appendix to dancing, marriages, and the cultivation of a crop—functions in which all Uraons join as a part of their tribal life," adding that "if we have to single out the factor which caused the decline of English village culture, we should have to say it was literacy."[10] In an older England, as Prior and Gardner remind us, "even the ignorant and unlettered man could read the meaning of sculptures that now only trained archeologists can interpret."[11]

The anthropologist Paul Radin points out that "the distortion in our whole psychic life and in our whole apperception of the external realities produced by the invention of the alphabet, the whole tendency of which has been to elevate thought and thinking to the rank of the exclusive proof of all verities, never occurred among primitive peoples," adding that "it must be explicitly recognized that in temperament and in capacity for logical and symbolical thought, there is no difference between civilized and primitive man," and as to "progress," that none in ethnology will ever be achieved "until scholars rid themselves, once and for all, of the curious notion that everything possesses an evolutionary history; until they realize that certain ideas and certain concepts are as ultimate for man"[12] as his physical constitution. "The distinction of peoples in a state of nature from civilized peoples can no longer be maintained."[13]

We have so far considered only the dicta of literary men. A really "savage" situation and point of view are recorded by Tom Harrisson, from the New Hebrides. "The children are educated by listening and watching. . . . Without writing, memory is perfect, tradition exact. The growing child is taught all that is known. . . . Intangible things cooperate in every effort of making, from conception to canoe-building. . . . Songs are a form of story-telling. . . . The layout and content in the thousand myths which every child learns (often word perfect, and one story may last for hours) are a whole library. . . . The hearers are held in a web of spun words"; they converse together "with that accuracy and pattern of beauty in words that we have lost." And what do they think of us? "The natives easily learn to write after white impact. They regard it as a curious and useless performance. They say: 'Cannot a man remember and speak?'"[14] They consider us "mad," and may be right.

When we set out to "educate" the South Sea Islanders it is generally in order to make them more useful to ourselves (this was admittedly the beginning of "English education" in India), or to "convert" them to our way of thinking; not having in view to introduce them to Plato. But if we or they should happen upon Plato, it might startle both to find that their protest, "Cannot a man *remember*?" is also his.[15] "For," he says, "this invention [of letters] will produce forgetfulness in the minds of those who learn to use it, because they will not exercise their memory. Their trust in writing, produced by external characters which are no part of themselves, will discourage the use of their own memory within them. You have invented an elixir *not of memory, but of reminding*; and you offer your pupils the appearance of wisdom,

[9] R. St. Barbe Baker, *Africa Drums* (1942), p. 145.

[10] W.G. Archer, *The Blue Grove* (1940), Preface; and in JBORS, Vol. XXIX, p. 68.

[11] Edward Schröder Prior and Arthur Gardner, *An Account of Medieval Figure-Sculpture in England* (1912), p. 25.

[12] Paul Radin, *Primitive Man as Philosopher* (1927).

[13] J. Strzygowski, *Spüren indogermanische Glaubens in der bildenden Kunst* (1936), p. 344.

[14] Tom Harrisson, *Savage Civilization* (1937), pp. 45, 344, 351, 353.

[15] Plato, *Phaedrus*, 275 f. Cf. H. Gauss, *Plato's Conception of Philosophy* (1937), pp. 262-265.

not true wisdom, for they will read many things without teaching, and will therefore seem to know many things [Professor E.K. Rand's "more and more of less and less"], when they are for the most part ignorant and hard to get along with, since they are not wise but only wiseacres." He goes on to say that there is another kind of "word," of higher origin and greater power than the written (or as we should say, the printed) word; and maintains that the wise man, "*when in earnest*, will not write in ink" dead words that cannot teach the truth effectively, but will sow the seeds of wisdom in souls that are able to receive them and so "to pass them on forever."

There is nothing strange or peculiar in Plato's point of view; it is one, for example, with which every cultured Indian unaffected by modern European influences would agree wholly. It will suffice to cite that great scholar of Indian languages, Sir George A. Grierson, who says that "the ancient Indian system by which literature is recorded not on paper but on the memory, and carried down from generation to generation of teachers and pupils, is still [1920] in complete survival in Kashmir. Such fleshly tables of the heart are often more trustworthy than birch bark or paper manuscripts. The reciters, even when learned Pandits, take every care to deliver the messages word for word," and records taken down from professional storytellers are thus "in some respects more valuable than any written manuscript."[16]

From the Indian point of view a man can only be said to *know* what he knows *by heart*; what he must go to a book to be reminded of, he merely knows of. There are hundreds of thousands of Indians even now who daily repeat from knowledge by heart either the whole or some large part of the *Bhagavad Gītā*; others more learned can recite hundreds of thousands of verses of longer texts. It was from a traveling village singer in Kashmir that I first heard sung the Odes of the classical Persian poet, Jalālu'd-Dīn Rūmī. From the earliest times, Indians have thought of the learned man, not as one who has read much, but as one who has been profoundly taught. It is much rather from a master than from any book that wisdom can be learned.

We come now to the last part of our problem, which has to do with the characteristic preoccupations of the oral and the written literature; for although no hard and fast line can be drawn between them, there is a qualitative and thematic distinction, as between literatures that were originally oral and those that are created, so to speak, on paper—"In the beginning was the WORD." The distinction is largely of poetry from prose and myth from fact. The quality of oral literature is essentially poetical, its content essentially mythical, and its preoccupation with the spiritual adventures of heroes: the quality of originally written literature is essentially prosaic, its content literal, and its preoccupation with secular events and with personalities. In saying "poetical" we mean to imply "mantic," and are naturally taking for granted that the "poetic" is a literary *quality*, and not merely a literary (versified) form. Contemporary poetry is essentially and inevitably of the same caliber as modern prose; both are equally opinionated, and the best in either embodies a few "happy thoughts" rather than any certainty. As a famous gloss expresses it, "Unbelief is for the mob." We who can call an art "significant," knowing not of what, are also proud to "progress," we know not whither.

Plato maintains that one who is *in earnest* will not write, but teach; and that if the wise man writes at all, it will be either only for amusement—mere "belles lettres"—or to provide reminders for himself when his memory is weakened by old age. We know exactly what Plato means by the words "in earnest"; it is not about human affairs or personalities, but about the eternal verities, the nature of real being, and the nourishment of our immortal part, that the

[16] Sir George A. Grierson, *Lallā Vākyāni* (1920), p. 3.

wise man will be in earnest. Our mortal part can survive "by bread alone," but it is by the Myth that our Inner Man is fed; or, if we substitute for the true myths the propagandist myths of "race," "uplift," "progress," and "civilizing mission," the Inner Man starves. The written text, as Plato says, can serve those whose memories have been weakened by old age. Thus it is that in the senility of culture we have found it necessary to "preserve" the masterpieces of art in museums, and at the same time to record in writing and so also to "preserve" (if only for scholars) as much as can be "collected" of oral literatures that would otherwise be lost forever; and this must be done before it is *too late*.

All serious students of human societies are agreed that agriculture and handicraft are essential foundations of any civilization; the primary meaning of the word being that of making a home for oneself. But, as Albert Schweitzer says, "We proceed as if not agriculture and handicraft, but reading and writing were the beginning of civilization," and, "from schools which are mere copies of those of Europe they ["natives"] are turned out as 'educated' persons, that is, who think themselves superior to manual work, and want to follow only commercial or intellectual callings. . . . Those who go through the schools are mostly lost to agriculture and handicraft."[17] As that great missionary, Charles Johnson of Zululand, also said, "the central idea [of the mission schools] was to prize individuals off the mass of the national life."

Our literary figures of thought, for example, the notions of "culture" (analogous to agriculture), "wisdom" (originally "skill"), and "asceticism" (originally "hard work"), are derived from the productive and constructive arts; for, as St. Bonaventura says, "There is nothing therein which does not bespeak a true wisdom, and it is for this reason that Holy Scripture very properly makes use of such similes."[18] In normal societies, the necessary labors of production and construction are no mere "jobs," but also rites, and the poetry and music that are associated with them are a kind of liturgy. The "lesser mysteries" of the crafts are a natural preparation for the greater "mysteries of the kingdom of heaven." But for us, who can no longer think in terms of Plato's divine "justice" of which the social aspect is vocational, that Christ was a carpenter and the son of a carpenter was only an historical accident; we read, but do not understand that where we speak of primary matter as "wood," we must also speak of Him "through whom all things were made" as a "carpenter." At the best, we interpret the classical figures of thought, not in their universality but as figures of speech invented by individual authors. Where literacy becomes an only skill, "the collective wisdom of a literate people" may be only a collective ignorance—while "backward communities are the oral libraries of the world's ancient cultures."[19]

The purpose of our educational activities abroad is to assimilate our pupils to our ways of thinking and living. It is not easy for any foreign teacher to acknowledge Ruskin's truth, that there is one way only to help others, and that that is, not to train them in our way of living (however bigoted our faith in it may be), but to find out what they have been trying to do, and were doing before we came, and if possible help them to do it better. Some Jesuit missionaries in China are actually sent to remote villages and required to earn their living there by the practice of an indigenous craft for at least two years before they are allowed to teach at all. Some such condition as this ought to be imposed upon all foreign teachers, whether in

[17] Albert Schweitzer, *On the Edge of the Primeval Forest*.

[18] *De reductione artium ad theologiam*, 14.

[19] N. K. Chadwick, *Poetry and Prophecy* (1942), Preface, further, "The experience of exclusively literate communities is too narrow." "Ever learning, and never able to come to the knowledge of the truth" (II Timothy 3:7)!

mission or government schools. How dare we forget that we are dealing with peoples "whose intellectual interests are the same from the top of the social structure to the bottom," and for whom our unfortunate distinctions of religious from secular learning, fine from applied art, and significance from use have not yet been made? When we have introduced these distinctions and have divided an "educated" from a still "illiterate" class, it is to the latter that we must turn if we want to study the language, the poetry, and the whole culture of these peoples, "before it is too late."

In speaking of a "proselytizing fury" in a former article I had not only in view the activities of professed missionaries but more generally those of everyone bent by the weight of the white man's burden and anxious to confer the "blessings" of our civilization upon others. What lies below this fury, of which our punitive expeditions and "wars of pacification" are only more evident manifestations? It would not be too much to say that our educational activities abroad (a word that must be taken to include the American Indian reservations) are motivated by an *intention* to destroy existing cultures. And that is not only, I think, because of our conviction of the absolute superiority of our *Kultur*, and consequent contempt and hatred for whatever else we have not understood (all those for whom the economic motive is not decisive), but grounded in an unconscious and deep-rooted envy of the serenity and leisure that we cannot help but recognize in people whom we call "unspoiled." It irks us that these others, who are neither, as we are, industrialized nor, as we are, "democratic," should nevertheless be *contented*; we feel bound to discontent them, and especially to discontent their women, who might learn from us to work in factories or to find careers. I used the word *Kultur* deliberately just now, because there is not much real difference between the Germans' will to enforce their culture upon the backward races of the rest of Europe and our determination to enforce our own upon the rest of the world; the methods employed in their case may be more evidently brutal, but the kind of will involved is the same.[20] As I implied above, that "misery loves company" is the true and unacknowledged basis of our will to create a brave new world of uniformly literate mechanics. This was recently repeated to a group of young American workmen, one of whom responded, "And *are* we miserable!"

But however we may be whistling in the dark when we pride ourselves upon "the collective wisdom of a literate people," regardless of what is read by the "literates," the primary concern of the present essay is not with the limitations and defects of modern Western education *in situ*, but with the spread of an education of this type elsewhere. Our real concern is with the fallacy involved in the attachment of an absolute value to literacy, and the very dangerous consequences that are involved in the setting up of "literacy" as a standard by which to measure the cultures of unlettered peoples. Our blind faith in literacy not only obscures for us the significance of other skills, so that we care not under what subhuman conditions a man may have to earn his living, if only he can read, no matter what, in his hours of leisure; it is also one of the fundamental grounds of inter-racial prejudice and becomes a prime factor in the spiritual impoverishment of all the "backward" people whom we propose to "civilize."

[20] Modern "education" imposed upon traditional cultures (e.g. Gaelic, Indian, Polynesian, American Indian) is only less deliberately, not less actually, destructive than the Nazi destruction of Polish libraries, which was intended to wipe out their racial memories; the Germans acted consciously, but we who Anglicize or Americanize or Frenchify are driven by a rancor that we do not recognize and could not confess. This rancor is, in fact, our reaction to a superiority that we resent and therefore would like to destroy.

The Traditional Sciences in Fez[1]

Titus Burckhardt

Traditional science (*al- 'ilmu 't-taqlīdī*) and modern science have little or nothing in common; they do not have the same root and do not bear the same fruits. To say tradition is to say transmission; it is a question of essential transmission of non-human origin, one destined to ensure the continuity of a spiritual influence and of an integral science which, should they ever be lost, could not be reconstituted by human efforts. Completely different is the nature of modern science, which is founded on sensory experience, and thus on something which in principle is accessible to everyone, so that this science can always be reconstituted from scratch, provided that one can accumulate sufficient experimental data. This condition however is difficult to fulfill, since scientific data and the conclusions drawn from them are accumulated in such a progression that it has become impossible for anyone to grasp them all. Experimentation on the basis of the senses, practiced methodically and as if it were the only approach to reality, gets bogged down in the indefinite multitude of physical phenomena and thereby runs the risk of forgetting its own point of departure: man in his integral nature, man who is not only a physical datum but, at one and the same time, body, soul, and spirit (*jasad*, *nafs*, *rūh*).

If one should ask modern science, what is man? it will either remain silent through awareness of its own limits, or it will reply by saying that man is an animal with particularly well-developed cerebral faculties. And if one should raise the question as to the origin of this animal, it will speak to you about an infinitely long chain of coincidences, accidents, and chances. As much as to say that the existence of man has no meaning.

If on the other hand one should ask traditional science, what is man?, it will reply by means of metaphors—e.g. Biblical and Koranic stories about the creation of Adam—which one might be tempted to cast aside as outworn mythology, if one did not divine that these sacred accounts are the vehicle of a profound vision of man, too profound in fact to be encapsulated in rational definitions. The first thing we gather from accounts of this kind is that man has a unique cause, situated entirely beyond contingency, and that his existence on earth has a meaning. This meaning—or this vision of man—has nothing to do with an empirical science; one could not reconstitute it from experiments and reasonings, for it concerns man, not in respect of his spatial and temporal existence, but "in respect of eternity", if one may venture to express it thus.

Tradition in all its forms is essentially a remembrance (*dhikrā*) of this timeless vision of man and his origin—whether it be a question of the transmission of sacred laws and customs, or of their spiritual significance—to the extent that this can be transmitted from one man to another, in other words, to the extent that masters are authorized to expound it and disciples are ready to receive it.

These somewhat general observations were necessary in order to situate our theme and above all to make clear what is meant by "traditional science". Even in the earlier part of this century, many branches of Islamic science—which had reached its peak during the Middle Ages—were no longer part of the instruction offered in the great mosque of Al-Qarawīn. Already in the

[1] Editor's Note: This article is the text of an address given by the author to members of staff and former students at the University of Al-Qarawīn in Fez, Morocco, in Autumn 1972.

fourteenth century Ibn Khaldun had complained about a certain intellectual impoverishment in the field of the Islamic sciences, and the decline continued during the following centuries, up to the time of the arrival of the French in Morocco. However, the progressive reduction of the domains covered by traditional science was not uniquely due to decadence; it was the exclusive domination of Malikism[2] that had simplified the study of law, while Asharism[3] had eliminated Hellenistic philosophy. And, in a more general manner, there is in the genius of the Maghreb a tendency to reduce things to the essential and to the rigorously necessary. The teaching of history, for example, had come to be concerned only with sacred history, that of the origins of Islam, because it was considered that only sacred history—which expressed timeless truths (*haqā'iq*)—deserved to be retained. As for astronomy, it had been reduced to the calculations necessary for the establishment of the Muslim calendar and the hours of prayer. In spite of these reductions—and perhaps also because of them—the corpus of sciences taught at the great mosque of Al-Qarawīn in the 1930s constituted a perfectly homogeneous whole, whereas modern university instruction is divided into different disciplines which are often divergent among themselves. At Al-Qarawīn, all the branches of learning: language, logic, law, moral philosophy, and theology converged toward one and the same end; and it could also be said that they derived from one and the same source, namely the Koran and the *hadīth* (traditions of the Prophet), which are the foundation of both the spiritual order and the social order in Islam.

One might be astonished at the zeal of the grammarians who would hold forth for hours, or even days, on one single verb, or one single grammatical form. And yet it is perhaps not so astonishing that a language that had served as the vehicle of a divine revelation—and had thereby retained a depth and a fineness that profane languages had long since lost—should be cherished as the most precious of possessions.

One might also be astonished at the meticulousness with which the specialists in *hadīth* examined the "chain of transmission" (*isnad*) of every saying of the Prophet; their memory in this field was indeed prodigious. And yet it is hardly astonishing that, for sayings on which depend the very life of both the community and each individual soul, the proofs of authenticity had to be scrupulously weighed.

But there was something else that might understandably astonish or even dismay the uninformed observer, namely the apparently rationalistic and in any case frankly legalistic style generally attaching to instruction given in the great mosque. Sometimes the courses, which took the form of a dialogue between master and pupil, would resemble a legal discussion. It is true that juridical thought had its wholly legitimate place in this instruction, since the *sharī'ah* is a law, and the legal science that derives from it constituted the principal object of study for the majority of students. Nevertheless, in the theological domain (*kalam*), legalistic thought with its pros and its contras—its *law kāna*, *in kāna*, and *lam yakun*—could give the impression of rationalism, that is to say of a mode of thought exclusively made up of alternatives, and for this reason much too schematic to be adequate for its object: Infinite Reality. All the same, it was only a provisional rationalism, a rationalism on the surface, for undoubtedly none of the *'ulamā* who used this method of argumentation would have dreamt of making human

2 Editor's Note: one of the four schools of Islamic jurisprudence, named after its founder, Malik ibn Anas (716-795).

3 Editor's Note: the predominant school of theology (*kalām*) in Sunni Islam, named after its founder, al-Asharī (873-935); it is characterized by emphasis on the inscrutability of the Divine Will, whose operation should not be questioned (*bilā kayfa*, "without asking how"), as well as by its denial of secondary causes.

reason the measure of all things, as in fact modern science believes it can do. The difference between the two points of view, that of Islamic law (*fiqh*) and that of modern rationalism (be it philosophic or merely scientistic), is basically the following: for *fiqh*, reason does not include all reality, far from it, but represents it after its fashion and to the extent that it opens itself to divine revelation; on the other hand, for philosophic and scientific rationalism, everything must be explainable by reason, and by it alone, even though one does not know what this reason is, nor why it should possess this quasi-absolute right with regard to reality.

Let us note that, among the best of the learned men of Fez, the juridical routine was tempered by a lively awareness of human fragility, and thus by a sort of constant prudence, which conferred on them much dignity. And it was perhaps this virtue that had the greatest influence on their pupils, as well as on the simple men of the people who would come to listen to courses given at Al-Qarawīn, while remaining seated at a respectful distance from the man of learning who was surrounded by his regular students.

In a general manner, the open and generous character of the instruction had a benefic influence on the whole town. The relationship between professor and student was a human one: not impeded by regulations, but based on reciprocal trust. Very often both master and disciple worked only for the love of the science. Many of the professors received only a very modest salary or none at all; some of them lived from a trade which they would practice in addition to their teaching function, or from gifts made to them by rich citizens.

From time to time, classical works of Sufism (*at-Tasawwuf*) were read and commented on at Al-Qarawīn. One such work was "The Revivification of the Religious Sciences" (*Ihya 'ulūm ad-dīn*) of Al-Ghazālī, and it was not the first time in Morocco that this work played the role of conciliator between law (*fiqh*) and mysticism (*tasawwuf*), between outward science (*'ilm az-zāhir*) and inward science (*'ilm al-bātin*). In general, however, the professors at the university of Al-Qarawīn were very reserved regarding anything that had to do with Sufism. During the period of the French protectorate this attitude was reinforced by the political opposition between the university circles and the Sufi brotherhoods (*turuq*), an opposition which the colonial administration exploited to the limit. The brotherhoods do indeed derive from Sufism, of which they represent, in a sense, the popular form; nevertheless they constitute groups that are too large not to be subject to political pressures. This danger was all the greater in that many of these brotherhoods no longer had true spiritual masters at their head, but purely nominal leaders, mostly descendants of the founder of the brotherhood; physical heredity, however, is not a guarantee of spirituality. The true spiritual masters—and there still were such—remained aloof from politics and from the great collective movements and were surrounded by only a small number of disciples; it was in these more or less isolated circles that true *tasawwuf* was taught.

On the other hand, there were always scholars at Al-Qarawīn who, without necessarily adhering to Sufism, recognized its validity, for the simple reason that *fiqh* clearly did not embrace all the dimensions of religion (*ad-dīn*). We may recall in this connection the three dimensions of the Islamic religion—"submission" (*al-islām*), "faith" (*al-īmān*), and "virtue" or "excellence" (*al-ihsān*)—established by the famous "Gabriel *hadīth*".[4] The first two dimensions comprise

[4] The full form of this *hadīth*, reported by Umar, is as follows: "One day when we were with the Messenger of God, there came unto us a man whose clothes were of exceeding whiteness and whose hair was of exceeding blackness, nor were there any signs of travel upon him, although none of us had seen him before. He sat down knee unto knee opposite the Prophet, upon whose thighs he placed the palms of his hands, saying: 'O Muhammad, tell

respectively the prescribed actions and the dogmas—and these are precisely the domain of scholastic science—whereas the third dimension, spiritual virtue, refers to the contemplative life. According to the Prophet's own words, *al-ihsān* consists in the following: "That thou shouldst worship God as if thou sawest Him, for if thou seest Him not, verily He seeth thee." These few words summarize a far-reaching inward practice, one whose development is in principle unlimited, since its object is infinite, and which presupposes, not a more or less dialectical knowledge, but a "science of the heart".

The presence of man—body, soul, and spirit—in the act of worship opens onto the presence of God in man, if it be permitted to express in these terms a complete spiritual universe that is too subtle and too rich to be defined lightly. In a certain sense, the whole of Islamic mysticism (*tasawwuf*) is developed from the fundamental requirement for sincerity (*ikhlās*): "to worship God as if thou sawest Him" is to worship Him sincerely; now this effort logically leads to a "conversion" (*tawbah*) of the whole being, and this brings about a sort of reversal of the subject-object relationship in one's inward vision: until then man saw everything with the eye of his individual ego, his passional soul, and everything for him was inevitably colored by this; henceforward man sees his own ego with the eye of the spirit, which transcends it and judges it; as the *hadīth* teaches: "He who knows his own soul, knows his Lord" (*Man 'arafa nafsa-hu, fa-qad 'arafa Rabba-h*).

In order to express things as simply as possible, we could also put it as follows: in Islam, the believer is saved basically by the double testimony, that "there is no god but God", and that "Muhammad is the Messenger of God", the first testimony in a sense including the second. What Sufism (*tasawwuf*) does is to give to this testimony all the meaning that it can possibly have, and to demand at the same time that the believer be completely sincere. This amounts to saying that, for *tasawwuf* all things are finally effaced before the Absolute: the world, which is but its reflection, and the ego, which is both its reflection and its veil (*hijāb*); the reflection because, like all things, it has its existence from God, and the veil because it attributes to itself *a priori* an absolute character that belongs to God alone: "there is no god but God" (*la ilāha illā 'Llāh*).

As we have said, the brotherhoods represent the popular form of *tasawwuf*, a fact which does not exclude the existence, in their midst, of authentic spiritual treasures. Some fundamental classics of *tasawwuf* like the *Hikam* of Ibn 'Atā'i 'Llāh were read and commented on to the members of such brotherhoods (*fuqarā*, the "spiritually poor"), and the poems of Ibn al-Fārid, Shushtari and other great Sufis, which were sung at *majālis* (spiritual meetings for the "remembrance of God" [*dhikr*]), expound the highest spiritual truths; these are sometimes

me what is the surrender unto God (*al-islām*).' The Prophet answered: 'The surrender is that thou shouldst testify that there is no god but God and that Muhammad is God's Apostle, and that thou shouldst perform the prayer, bestow the alms, fast Ramadan and make, if thou canst, the pilgrimage to the Holy House.' He said: 'Thou hast spoken truly' and we were amazed that having questioned him he should corroborate him. Then he said: 'Tell me what is faith (*īmān*),' and the Prophet answered: 'It is that thou shouldst believe in God and His Angels and His Books and His Apostles and the Last Day, and that thou shouldst believe that no good or evil cometh but by His Providence.' 'Thou hast spoken truly,' he said, and then: 'Tell me what is excellence (*ihsān*).' The Prophet answered: 'It is that thou shouldst worship God as if thou sawest Him, for if thou seest Him not, verily He seeth thee.' Then the stranger went away, and I stayed there long after he had gone, until the Prophet said to me: 'O Umar, knowest thou the questioner, who he was?' I said 'God and His Prophet know best, but I know not at all.' 'It was Gabriel,' said the Prophet. 'He came to teach you your religion'" (translated by Martin Lings; see *A Sufi Saint of the Twentieth Century* [London: Allen & Unwin, 1971]).

better understood by simple and apparently uncultivated men than by the educated, because the intelligence of the heart and the intelligence of the brain are not the same thing.

Morocco has always been a land of Sufis; it received a rich heritage of spiritual masters who, in the twelfth and thirteenth centuries, came over from Spain and settled in North Africa. At the very time when Europe was undergoing the effects of the French revolution, a major victory for materialism, Morocco was enjoying a new flowering of the contemplative life: masters such as Al-'Arabī ad-Darqāwī and Al-Harrāq continued to represent the purest of classical Sufism.

Traditional medicine, which had been taught on the margin of the official courses at Al-Qarawīn, was banished by the French protectorate. The contempt of modern Europeans for "medieval" and "backward" sciences inevitably had its effect. Nevertheless, this medicine continued to be practiced clandestinely. Has it now entirely disappeared? It would be a matter for regret if it has, for this science—which the Arabs inherited from ancient Greece, but which they considerably enriched—possessed (over and above its long and rich experience) a synthetic vision of man, compared with which the impoverished viewpoint of modern science can be seen for what it is.

It was moreover this viewpoint of synthesis that constituted the link that attached Greco-Arab medicine to the intellectual world of Islam. Unity-totality-equilibrium: these are the reference points of Islamic thought, and it was equilibrium, precisely, that was the principle of this form of traditional medicine. According to its perspective, the whole of nature and *a fortiori* the human organism are ruled by the law of equilibrium. There are four radical humors which, analogous to the four elements, are subtly combined in the various vital functions; any rupture of equilibrium in the relationship of these humors causes an illness. The art of the doctor in Greek medicine was to help nature to recover its original equilibrium. Nature acts by complementary forces: it tempers heat with cold, and dryness with humidity; or expansion with contraction, and solution with coagulation; the doctor does the same, using whatever in nature corresponds to these forces. The *materia medica* generally consisted of vegetable substances, preferably plants which were also foodstuffs and which the body would absorb spontaneously. Many of these means are still to be found in popular medicine.

Having referred to traditional medicine, we must also mention alchemy, which is also a science or an art of pre-Islamic origin which has been spiritually integrated into Islam. False ideas regarding alchemy—which was practiced in Fez until relatively recently—are common. It is usually regarded as a superstitious practice that seeks—on a basis of complete self-deception—to transmute lead and other base metals into gold. In actual fact, true alchemy was often concealed behind this caricatural appearance. For true alchemy, the lead or other base metal that was to be transmuted into gold was only the symbol—a very adequate one—of the human soul sunk in the darkness and chaos of the passions, while gold represented the original nature of man, in which even the body is ennobled and transfigured by the life of the spirit. Every base metal, image of a certain state of the soul, is considered as a "sick gold", while gold itself corresponds to the perfect equilibrium of the natural forces; here we encounter once more the same principles as govern traditional Greek medicine. True alchemy might be described as a "medicine" of total man: body, soul, and spirit. But why did one use metallurgical symbols and descriptions of strange chemical procedures in order to express realities of a completely different order? Doubtless because the "professions using fire"—metallurgists, smelters, enamellers, potters, etc.—exist, and because their procedures lend themselves quite naturally, and providentially, to the expression of certain very intimate states and transformations of the soul.

We have seen that science and art are often the two faces of one and the same tradition;

medicine, for example, is both a science and an art; alchemy calls itself a "royal art", and *tasawwuf* is a spiritual art. Likewise, the traditional plastic arts—architecture, sculpture, mosaics, etc.—presuppose a certain knowledge which, without being explicit, nevertheless also pertains to the domain of traditional science.

It is particularly significant that proficiency in a traditional art concerns both the technical solution and the aesthetic solution of a given problem; thus, the procedure enabling one to trace the outline of an arch concerns both its stability and its elegance. In traditional art, beauty and use go hand in hand; they are two inseparable aspects of perfection, as envisaged by tradition: "God prescribed perfection for all things" (*Inna 'Llāha kataba 'l-ihsāna 'alā kulli shay*), according to the *hadīth*. Here again we encounter the term *ihsān*, which in Sufism may be translated as "spiritual virtue", or simply as "virtue", and which includes the ideas of beauty and perfection.

In art and craftsmanship—in a traditional context, the two are not distinguishable—it often happens that instruction is not transmitted by means of words. The apprentice sees his master at work, and imitates him. But it is not merely a case of methods of work; the good craftsman is distinguished by a whole cluster of human values: patience, discipline, sincerity. It is difficult to overestimate the pedagogic quality of art (or craft) in the traditional sense of the terms. In a Fez of not so long ago, we knew men well-versed in one or other of the sciences—for example law (*fiqh*) or spirituality (*tasawwuf*)—and more particularly men who saw in the most modest aspects of their profession a means of spiritual perfection (*ihsān*).

How can tradition, in a plastic art, be reconciled with creative freedom, without which art is not art? Through tradition, the artist has at his disposal a set of models or typical forms which he will use or adapt according to the circumstances, or more exactly, according to the particular goal of the work. In adapting, he creates, but this creation obeys certain laws: the models or typical forms are the elements of a language that possesses its grammar and syntax; mastery in a given art is to be able to express oneself freely while obeying the rules of the language—or rather: it is to be able to express oneself freely thanks to the resources of the language. If the expression is just and adequate to the goal of the work, it is nourished by a sort of inspiration that arises from the supra-individual depth of the tradition; for just as Islamic science has its roots in the Koran (on which it is a more or less direct commentary), so the typical forms of Islamic art are rooted in the spirit of Islam, of which they are as it were the visible traces; now Islam, like all the great spiritual traditions of humanity, was not "invented" by man.

Translated by William Stoddart

The Role of Culture in Education

William Stoddart

The spiritual life has been described as the "interiorization of the outward" (*khalwa*) and the "exteriorization of the inward" (*jalwa*).[1] Education is an aspect of the latter process; the very etymology of the word (*e-ducare*, "to lead out") is an indication of this. As a "leading-out", education is a rendering explicit of the immanent Intellect (*Intellectus* or *Nous*), the seat of which, symbolically speaking, is the heart. As Frithjof Schuon has said more than once: "The Intellect can know everything that is knowable". This is because "heart-knowledge" (*gnosis*) is innate, and thus already fully present within us, in a state of virtuality. This virtuality[2] has to be realized, and this realization is education. This corresponds to the Platonic doctrine of "recollection" (*anamnesis*), which in the last analysis is the "remembrance of God" (*memoria Dei*). "The Kingdom of Heaven is within you."

Man is constituted by the ternary: Spirit, soul, and body (*Spiritus*, *anima*, *corpus*); only the last two are exclusively individual or human, the first being supra-individual or universal. The Intellect (*Intellectus*) is identifiable with the Spirit: Intellect and Spirit are but two sides of the same coin, the former pertaining to the theoretical or doctrinal and the latter to the practical or realization. They pertain respectively to the objective (or discriminatory) and the subjective (or unitive) modes of knowing.

It is easy to see how education, both etymologically and philosophically, is an "exteriorization of the inward". But it is also an "interiorization of the outward", for an important function of education is precisely to ensure that the myriad of impressions coming from the outside be "inwardly digested" and reduced to unity. Thus education is both "exteriorization of the inward" (intellectuality) and "interiorization of the outward" (spirituality). It is both *jalwa* and *khalwa*.

The following summary of terminology may be useful:

English	Latin	Greek	Arabic
Spirit (Intellect)	*Spiritus* (*Intellectus*)	*Pneuma* (*Nous*)	*Rūh* (*'Aql*)
soul	*anima*	*psyche*	*nafs*
body	*corpus*	*soma*	*jism*

In modern parlance, "intellectual" is often wrongly taken as a synonym of "mental" or "rational". In fact, unlike the Intellect, which is "above" the soul, the mind or the reason is a content of the soul, as are the other human faculties: will, affect or sentiment, imagination, and memory. The spiritual or intellectual faculty, on the other hand—because of its higher level—

[1] These "alchemical" definitions come from Frithjof Schuon. In Arabic, *khalwa* means "spiritual retreat" and *jalwa* means "spiritual radiance", the former being logically prior to the latter. The two processes are symbolized respectively by the colors black and gold.

[2] Examples (immediately apparent, and built into the human substance) of this innate and objective knowledge are our sense of logic, our capacity for arithmetic, our sense of justice, and our sense of right and wrong.

can be categorized as "angelic". The operation of the Intellect is referred to as "intellectual intuition" or "intellection".

Let it be said right away that there is no impenetrable barrier between Intellect and mind: the relationship of the former to the latter is like the relationship of the pinnacle of a cone to its circumferential base. Metaphorically speaking, the majority of philosophers, since the end of the Middle Ages, have concerned themselves solely with the circumferential base, with little or no transcendent content in their thought. Henceforth the transcendent (previously known to be accessible either through revelation or intellection) has been regarded as mere "dogma", "superstition", or arbitrary imagining. The result has been the tumultuous *dégringolade*, from Descartes to the present day, known as the "history of philosophy"! One miraculous exception to this cascading downwards were the Cambridge Platonists of the 17th century. The words of Virgil were never more applicable: *Facilis descensus Averni; sed revocare gradum, hic labor est* ("The descent to hell is easy; but to retrace your steps, this is the task")!

In the light of the foregoing, we are also able to see that the error, in a nutshell, of psychologists such as Jung, is completely to confuse Spirit and soul and so, in the last analysis, entirely to "abolish" Spirit (the only truly supra-individual, "archetypal", or "objective" element). It is not difficult to see the chaos—and the damage—that results from this fatal and anti-Platonic act of blindness.

The linking of education with spirituality may cause some surprise; but the parable of the talents applies to the mind as well as to every other faculty. "Thou shalt love the Lord thy God with all thy heart and with all thy soul . . . and *with all thy mind*." It is at our peril that we neglect the need for "a well-stocked mind"; for it is surely obvious that, from a purely spiritual point of view, the mind cannot be allowed to lie fallow. This would allow it to become a playground for the devil, and *si monumentum requiris, circumspice* ("if you seek his monument, look around").

Use of the phrase "a well-stocked mind" makes it necessary immediately to specify (and never more so than in the "reign of quantity" that is the present age) that, as far as true education is concerned, it is nevertheless a question, not of quantity (however intoxicating), but of quality; not of shadows (however beguiling), but of substance; not of trivia (however intriguing), but of essentials. In the present age, more than in all previous ages, the grasping of a true and permanent principle is infinitely more precious than the piling up of a hundred undigested and un-understood contingencies. In addition, there is no greater joy.

Since education, by definition, is a thing of the *mind*, we can do no better than cite here the injunction of St. Paul:

> Whatsoever things are true, whatsoever things are honest, whatsoever things are just, whatsoever things are pure, whatsoever things are lovely, whatsoever things are of good report; if there be any virtue, and if there be any praise, *think* on these things (*Philippians*, 4, 8).

One might say: whatsoever things are true, good, and beautiful; or whatsoever things manifest or reflect the absolute, the infinite, and the perfect.

* * *

All civilizations—for example, the Chinese, Hindu, Greco-Roman, Christian, and Islamic—manifest the central or cardinal role of learning, at least for those classes or individuals capable of it. In this connection, it might be objected that the North American Indians—who possessed a daunting spiritual tradition if ever there was one—were not educated. In the light of the considerations expressed above, however, it is clear that the Red Indians too, in their own fashion, were "educated". To regard the Indians as uneducated because they were unlettered, would be like regarding the Buddhists as atheistic, because they envisage Ultimate Reality as a supreme State (*Nirvāna* or *Bodhi*) rather than as a supreme Being. Just as the Buddhists are manifestly different from the superficial and arrogant atheists of modern times, so the Indians are manifestly different from the technologically-trained but culturally-uneducated and mentally-immature people of modern times. The Indians' Book is Nature herself, and none have ever known this book better.

Education has many forms and, in any case, has in view only those classes and individuals who are capable of receiving it. Indeed the type of literacy resulting from the non-discriminating "universal" education of the last hundred years may even be inimical to culture, as Ananda Coomaraswamy has so trenchantly pointed out in his important work "The Bugbear of Literacy". Coomaraswamy demonstrates beyond any dispute how the new-found capacity of the immature mind to read modern printed material—now always to hand in such staggering quantity[3]—has killed the rich traditional culture (largely oral for the mass of the people) in many societies, including European ones. This is the opposite of true education, which is depth, subtlety, and finally, wisdom.

The European tradition consists of two currents: the Greek and the Christian, or the Classical and the Medieval. The Greek current is evoked by such names as Homer, Pythagoras, and Plato; the Christian current is evoked not only by such figures as St. Gregory Palamas and Meister Eckhart ("apophatic" and "gnostic" metaphysicians respectively), but also by St. Augustine and St. Thomas Aquinas (whose viewpoints represent two important strands, amongst others, of Western Christian thought). Christianity is also epitomized by that "second Christ", St. Francis of Assisi, and by the great epic poet of Christendom, Dante Alighieri. In practical terms, education in Europe has obviously to take account of both the Classical and the Medieval currents.

In English-speaking countries, a good education must start with the Christian catechism and attendance at Divine Worship, as well as the study of the Bible and the most celebrated Christian authors, such as the great names just mentioned. It must include the study of Greek and Latin, coupled with some Homer, Plato, Virgil, Cicero and other ancient authors. The "history of philosophy" (an understanding of the relative "stability" of Ancient and Medieval philosophy as contrasted with the innovative nature and "instability" of Modern philosophy) is obviously necessary. Likewise, some notion of the "philosophy of science"—especially as regards the differing conceptions of science on the part of Ancient and Medieval times on the one hand and Modern times on the other—is also desirable. In present circumstances, some "comparative religion" is no doubt essential, but this must be of high quality and taught from a conservative and believing point of view, which is not lethal to the student's faith in his own religion.

Also essential are subjects such as English and European (and perhaps world) history and

[3] As Lord Northbourne has said (referring to the industrialized countries): "We live in an age of plenty; but what use is plenty of rubbish?" (*Look to the Land* [London: Dent, 1940]).

literature—within the limits of the reasonable and the possible. It should be stressed that this proviso applies throughout, as does also the frequently forgotten principle that formal or "scholastic" education is only intended for those fit to profit by it. The need for the study of modern languages, above all French and German, is apparent. A study of these two languages, coupled with the study of Greek and Latin, has the additional merit of facilitating access to other modern European languages, such as Italian and Spanish. Obviously all aspects of mathematics must be available, and the essentials taught to all.

In the modern situation, modern science and technology are inescapable, since, in some branch or other, they will be indispensable for most, from the point of view of earning a livelihood. Modern science and technology, however, are alien to culture and consequently do not pertain to education as defined in this paper.

Education in the Light of Tradition:

A Metaphysical Perspective

M. Ali Lakhani

It is no longer enough to know the rules.
We have to understand what lies behind the rules.
Charles Le Gai Eaton[1]

Let no man deceive himself. If any man among you seemeth to be wise
in this world, let him become a fool, that he may be wise.
1 Corinthians, 3:18[2]

We use the term "education" in conventional parlance as though it were synonymous with the school system, so that to be "educated" often means no more than to be a university graduate or possess a college degree, or to be recognized as having been trained in a particular discipline, skill, or technique. There is also the broader sense in which the term "education" is equated with experience, carrying the connotation that learning involves more than passing exams or having a merely theoretical understanding of a subject: it also involves the practical dimension of a lived experience. After all, "only small fish swim in schools".[3] Both these aspects—the theoretical and the practical—form a part of the Traditional conception of education, but with some significant differences. The aim of this paper is to provide an overview of these differences from the perspective of Traditional metaphysics. But to do so, we will also need to debunk a few modernist preconceptions about Tradition.[4]

By way of an overview of our subject, we note that while conventional secular education is primarily aimed at training the individual to earn a living, Traditional education is aimed at training the individual in self-realization or the art of living. From a theoretical perspective, Tradition teaches the discernment of Reality ("*theoria*" signifying "seeing", not merely conceptualization), and from a practical perspective, it teaches the methodologies of Realization and self-transformation. Traditional teachings offer "an education in philosophy, in Plato's and Aristotle's sense of the word, for whom it means ontology and theology and the map of life, and a wisdom to be applied to everyday matters"[5]. While the outlook of a secular education—even

[1] Charles Le Gai Eaton, *Remembering God: Reflections on Islam* (Chicago, IL: ABC International, 2000), p. 233.

[2] St. Symeon's commentary on this passage is as follows: "Anyone who thinks himself intelligent because of his scholarly or scientific learning will never be granted insight into divine mysteries unless he first humbles himself and becomes a fool" (cited in volume 4 of *The Philokalia*, translated by G.E.H. Palmer, Philip Sherrard, and Kallistos Ware (London: Faber, 1995), pp. 46-47.

[3] Isaac Bashevis Singer.

[4] The term "Tradition" refers to the primordial and perennial wisdom and teachings found in all faith traditions, grounded in metaphysical "first principles" that are universal in their essence though they may differ in their articulation, and that have been handed down through time. "Traditional" is not synonymous with "conventional" or "of olden days". It refers to a doctrine by which reality is discerned as One, and a method of realization or union with that reality. Traditional metaphysics is the science of the Real.

[5] Ananda K. Coomaraswamy, *Why Exhibit Works of Art?*, *Studies in Comparative Religion*, Summer 1971

in the fields of the humanities and the liberal arts—is almost exclusively materialistic, that of Tradition—even in the utilitarian fields of teaching practical skills and crafts—extends into the vertical realm of Heaven, which is the source and prototype of Earthly purpose and endeavor.

At the outset we need to dispose of certain potential misunderstandings about Tradition. Any discussion regarding education immediately raises the concern of the possibilities of abuse and indoctrination, and provokes questions of the legitimacy of both educational content and pedagogical authority. We live in a world that largely takes for granted the wondrous miracle of existence, but at the same time is greatly impressed by the marvels and novelties of modern technologies. It is a world whose outlook is dominated by faith in science. Given this domination, it is important to clarify at the outset that Traditional metaphysics is itself an intellectually grounded science of reality. In this, it is not at odds with secular science, though Tradition has a broader cosmological perspective—that extends vertically and is not confined to the horizontal dimension that is the concern of modern science—and consequently it also has a broader epistemological foundation. Thus we see that Traditional metaphysics endorses scientific facts and all perceptions of reality premised upon reliable sensory observations and proper scientific reasoning and experimentation, so long as these facts and methodologies are understood to pertain to the materialistic worldview that is the focus of modern science, and do not encroach beyond these legitimate bounds. When they do, it is not authentic science that is guilty of the encroachment but ideological "scientism". The epistemology of "scientism" confines knowledge to outwardly verifiable physical realities and thereby improperly denies legitimacy to those metaphysical realities which, being of a transcendent order, cannot properly be made subject to its limited epistemology. In recognition of this transcendent dimension, Tradition teaches that man has been given eyes to see the Invisible, and it therefore carefully distinguishes between the irrational follies of the passive intelligence—which, according to Tradition, science is fully justified in criticizing—and the supra-rational or transcendent realities of the active intelligence in its receptive mode—which have been universally attested to by sages and by spiritual philosophers throughout time, and which science is not equipped to examine in the same way as it does material realities. To adapt a line from Shakespeare, there are more things in heaven and earth than are dreamt of in the philosophy of conventional science.

As scientism poses a barrier to understanding Tradition, so does the secularist bias of modernism. The meaning of several terms that we will be using in this paper—terms such as "tradition", along with a host of others, such as "religion", "faith", "revelation", and "orthodoxy"—have been devalued in modernist usage, and are viewed with skepticism, if not actually maligned by the modernist outlook in its assumptions and teachings. The underlying causes of this devaluation of meaning are the denial of transcendence that characterizes secular dogmatism, and the distortions of sacred language by religious fundamentalists. A critical function of Traditional education must therefore be to redeem this language from its modernist abuses and to recover its sacred etymology and the true meaning of sacred words.

Here, it is important to recognize that modernism has led to the deracination of religion. While it is beyond the scope of this paper to discuss how and why this has occurred, we can note that many misrepresentations of authentic religion are carried out in the name of conventional religion. These abuses, which are generally labeled as "fundamentalism", take a variety of forms, are marked by their excessive formalism (emphasizing the letter over the spirit), and their rigid exclusivism (emphasizing homogeneity and outward conformity over diversity and pluralism). These distortions are themselves a component of modernism, and are not a part of Traditional education or its respect for the divine gift of human intelligence, even if Traditional settings or texts are employed to promote such abusive teachings. They have contributed greatly to the devaluation of sacred meaning, and are, notwithstanding outward appearances, a reflection of the denial of transcendence within the sanctum of conventional religion itself.

The implications of the denial of transcendence—both in the secularist and fundamentalist senses of modernism—are catastrophic because of the resulting distortion of reality. When Earth is viewed in isolation from Heaven, man is cut adrift from his divine source, and becomes disoriented, both in terms of identity and purpose. All attempts to construct a sense of order or purpose in life become relativized and lack any objective foundation. Decentered man is perched perilously between the extremes of hypertrophic narcissism and existential nihilism. The only apparent hope for salvation within the secularist ethos of modernism is Reason. Yet, Reason alone cannot construct a foundation for the meaning of life that is not itself capable of rational challenge. It is only by transcending discursive Reason through the higher faculty of the universal Intellect—whose epistemological legitimacy can be experientially verified by Traditional techniques, and which is grounded in an intellectually-rooted understanding of "faith"[6]—that we can hope to recover the basis of objectivity. Though social contracts and rational consensus may yield truths that conform to the Intellect, consensually-based values are unreliable, particularly in an age of "manufactured consent", and are more likely to be manipulated and rationalized than to be grounded in objective metaphysical Truth. Also unreliable are the pseudo-religious alternatives of occultism and "New Age" experimentation with syncretic religion, which are not grounded in sound metaphysics, and all-too-frequently conflate the psyche and the spirit—and therefore are objectively unreliable.

All of this points to the conclusion that there is a critical role in Traditional education to expose the false premises of modernism—not only in secularism and scientism, but also especially in the abuses of religion—and to offer an alternative worldview based on the timeless and objective premises of Traditional metaphysics, which perceives all faith traditions as supra-formal expressions of that universal Reality which is Truth, Goodness, and Beauty.

Having addressed these preliminary barriers in modernity to viewing education in the light of Tradition, we will now examine what we mean by a Traditional education. The term "education" derives from the Latin roots "*ex*" ("from" or "out of") and "*ducere*" ("to lead" or "to guide") and signifies the meanings "to lead out of" or "to draw from", all of which presupposes a source. From the Traditional perspective, this source is the Absolute Reality or that transcendent font of Being in which we participate existentially, and which is therefore immanently accessible to us, both ontologically as the being we possess in life, and epistemologically as the innate Adamic "knowledge of naming"[7] that we can draw upon to "recognize" things. All education is a drawing-forth from this font of Truth, from our innermost Being, which can be the only legitimate criterion of knowledge. Thus, there is no learning without our recognition (or remembrance, in the Platonic sense of *anamnesis*) of the pre-existing and innate knowledge that is latent within our soul.

Traditional education therefore engages the art of directly accessing knowledge from the divine font of Truth that is the transcendent and immanent Source of all knowing and being.

[6] By "faith", we mean, cognitively, the active participation of the intelligence in the receptive mode of knowing, and, volitively, the conforming of the will to its guiding intelligence. See "The Secularization of Faith in the Modern World" by M. Ali Lakhani, published as the Editorial for volume 23 of *Sacred Web* (Vancouver, June 2009).

[7] *Qur'an* 2:31: "And He taught Adam the names of all things"; see also *Genesis* 2:19-20.

In Book IV of the *Mathnavi*, the Sufi mystical poet and metaphysician, Jalal ud-Din Rumi (1207-1273), distinguishes two kinds of intelligence: one is the conventionally acquired and fragmented "plumbing-learning"[8] of the lower intelligence, while the other is God-given and emerges from within us like a fountain. This latter is the direct Source-based learning of the superior Heart-centered Universal Intellect—which it is the object of a Traditional education to draw upon. Rumi states:

> The intellect is of two kinds: The first is acquired. You learn it like a boy at school,
> From books, teachers, reflection and rote, from concepts and from excellent and new sciences.
> Your intellect becomes greater than that of others, but you are heavily burdened because of your acquisition. . . .
> The other intellect is a gift of God. Its fountainhead lies in the midst of the spirit.
> When the water of knowledge bubbles up from the breast, it will never become stagnant, old, or discolored.
> If the way to the outside source should become blocked, there is no reason to worry since the water keeps on bubbling up from within the house.
> The acquired intellect is like a stream led into a house from outside.
> If its way should be blocked, it is helpless. Seek the fountain from within yourself![9]

Traditional education, then, is based on the direct apprehension of Truth by an intellectual quest of "seeking the fountain from within".[10] However, this search presupposes a certain relationship regarding authority, which has its roots in Traditional metaphysics. While the font of knowledge resides within, it is nevertheless a fool who would have himself for a master. This is because the unguided and undisciplined mind, prone to beguilement by the illusory and centrifugal aspects of the contingent world, will not necessarily discern or conform to the authority inherent in the hierarchic ordering of Reality. Traditional cosmology is based on a hierarchy that places the One above the many, Heaven over Earth, the vertical over the horizontal, and, on condition of this verticality, the right in ascendance over the left. Man is raised up above all creatures only by virtue of his willingness to bow before God, and those who hold authority do so only by virtue of the principle of *noblesse oblige.* Just as there is a legitimate outward hierarchy between the Outer Guide and the disciple, so there is a legitimate inward hierarchy among the faculties, among which the pre-eminent faculty is the Inner Guide or Intellect: this is depicted in the famous Hindu image of the Divine charioteer (representing the Heart-centered Intellect) who wields the reins (of discursive reason, the lower intelligence) that control the unruly steeds (of willfulness and unbridled passion) that propel the chariot (of the body) through life. Thus it is stated in the Upanishads:

[8] This term is from Coleman Barks' translation of the passage quoted below, from Book IV of Rumi's *Mathnavi*, lines 1960-1968.

[9] Translated by William C. Chittick, in *The Sufi Path of Love: The Spiritual Teachings of Rumi* (Albany, NY: SUNY, 1983), pp. 35-36.

[10] The precept inscribed in gold letters over the portico of the great temple at Delphi proclaims: "*gnothi seauton*" ("know thyself"). This basic command is central to Traditional epistemology, with its implication that nothing can be truly known until it has been authenticated within the Self.

> Know that the Self is like the Lord of the chariot, and the body is his chariot. Know that the intellect is the charioteer and the mind the reins. The senses, they say, are the horses, the objects of the senses their roads. When the Self is in union with the body, the senses and the mind, the wise call Him the enjoyer.[11]

The relationship between the Inner Guide and the Outer Guide defines the contours of authority in a master-disciple relationship. Because no one can be educated who is unwilling to learn, Traditional methodologies require the initiation of the disciple. The spiritual teacher will not normally initiate one who is unprepared to learn. Preparedness requires not only a sufficient indication of the disciple's willingness to submit to the teacher's authority as Outer Guide, but also of the disciple's readiness to orient to the innate powers of the Inner Guide. The role of the teacher is to teach according to the evolving levels of competence of the disciple and to guide his efforts, while the role of the student is to make the efforts demanded of him, to obey the teacher and to be receptive to his teachings and to the graces of the spiritual states bestowed on him as divine gifts,[12] but always in conformity to his faith and his critical Intellect. Within the parameters of sympathetic receptivity and spiritual courtesy—which require the disciple to love and honor the teacher—and of the Law—which is both "right thinking" (or "orthodoxy", in its strict etymological sense) and "right conduct" (or "orthopraxy")—Traditional education is premised upon the pre-eminence of the inner over the outer, and therefore of the Inner Guide over the Outer Guide. Hence the adage, "If you meet the Buddha on the path, slay him!"[13] Far from being a prescription for individualism or a licensing of exemption from the Law, this adage speaks to the liberating goal of spiritual education. Just as a parent directs and guides a child through the stages of its education until it reaches its maturity—whereafter the child, as an adult, becomes responsible for its own decisions, thereby in a sense outgrowing its dependence on the parent—so too the disciple is guided by the teacher to the threshold of spiritual maturity, whereafter the disciple crosses the threshold accompanied only by the Inner Guide whom the Outer Guide has fully awakened. Prior to such awakening, there remains the constant danger that the disciple will succumb to intellectual pride or the temptations of the will—both beguilements of the egoic self. It is to protect against these dangers, among others, that Tradition counsels the guidance of a spiritual teacher and requires the disciplines of initiation.

We referred earlier to the fact that, in general, Traditional learning encompasses a doctrine of Reality and a methodology for Realization. Beyond the various conventional forms of literacy, Tradition instructs us in the various dimensions of spiritual literacy. While conventional education offers us the understanding, training, and techniques to develop those skills that are necessary to operate the self and the world in a mechanistic and utilitarian sense, Traditional education aims to initiate us into the mysteries of life through the divine imagination, symbolic knowledge, and spiritual disciplines that will, by the divine Grace, awaken us to the depth and

[11] *Katha Upanishad* III.Up.3-4.

[12] In Traditional education, the efforts of the disciple enable him to attain certain "stations" (*maqamat* in Arabic), but these are distinct from the spiritual "states" (*ahwal* in Arabic) that are conferred by Grace.

[13] This paradoxical adage must not be misunderstood: it is only when the Inner Guide is functional—as active intelligence, rather than as passive conformity—that it will intelligently appreciate and properly accede to the legitimate authority of the Outer Guide. Obedience to the Law and submission of the egoic self to the greater Self (represented by the Outer Guide or Master) are vital components of any Traditional education.

height of our transcendent senses. Thereby, we can expand our awareness of things, discerning them with the "eyes of our eyes" and with the "ears of our ears". By perceiving the universe through these inner senses—which are aspects of the Intellect—we become aware of the underlying harmony of the divine theophany, the beauty of the "Face of God". This awareness and vision in turn reconnects us to the universe through a participative sympathy that is the root of all spiritual ethics. By living our lives integrally, in conformity with this theophanic vision and the awareness of our intrinsic harmony with all creatures, we are alchemically transformed into spiritually alive and engaged souls. This transformative vision is an antidote to the dehumanizing and soul-destroying influences of the materialistic world of modernism that René Guénon has famously referred to as "The Reign of Quantity".

By the gift of this transformative vision—which Traditional training teaches through a combination of contemplative and hermeneutic techniques that fall under the broad heading of "prayer"—we can come to see the world as a unified whole, rather than as the fragmentary world of mind and matter. Matter is just one dimension within a vertical and hierarchic continuum of reality that descends from the One Absolute Source through multiple contingent levels of reality that are transcendentally and supra-formally unified. The ever-renewing theophany can then be seen as a creative aspect of the Presence that mercifully reintegrates and replenishes creation within its divine womb. This discernment enables us to appreciate the fragility and bounty of the gift of life and of a world that is destroyed and remade in each moment as an act of divine compassion and love. Through the blessing of this vision, we can awaken to our individual purpose in life, to express those special qualities and attributes with which our souls are compassionately and uniquely endowed. We can situate our relationships within an ethical dimension that connects us with the rest of creation. We can understand our existential purpose within the context of the larger dynamic of life as a descent from our Place of Origin, and as an ascent to our Place of Return—both these abodes being the One ground of being which is Ever-Present and is our innermost Center. By appreciating our intrinsic poverty in relation to that transcendent Center, we are able to detach ourselves from the contingent aspects of reality, and at the same time to discover within that Center the source of our abiding joy, transcending the sufferings and illusions of this world. Thus we can awaken to our own existential purpose, and to our own creative gifts and powers, conscious of the blessings we have to offer other creatures, and that they have to offer us. We can embrace the world sympathetically, aware of its complementarity and interdependence, united in our diversity, seeing our reflection in it and its reflection in us.

To see the world in this special way, one must be trained to look with the Inner Eye of the Heart—the Eye of the Intellect. This requires a proper orientation—the search for the Center everywhere. To combat the centrifugal tendencies of the world, the Traditional teacher initiates the student in the hermeneutics and techniques of "prayer". In general, these involve the remembrance or witnessing of one's existential context, that God alone is, that creation is a theophany emerging continually from the infinite bounty and compassion of the divine, that all creatures are united in the hierarchical order of the divine matrix, which defines both their individual rights and their ethical responsibilities, and that man must therefore worship his Creator and must respect His Divine Face in all His creatures. Prayer, then, is more than a liturgy or the recitation of a prescribed formula. It is a perpetual hermeneutic, of which beauty and virtue, and all their complements such as love and wonder and gratitude, are the resonance. Prayer is an opening into mystery and intimacy, and, above all, an engagement with Presence. It is the central component of Traditional praxis, the practice of a quality of attention by which one can be fully engaged and present in life, in sympathetic participation with the Other as a part of our Self.

The development of an ethical sensibility is a vital component of a Traditional education. According to Traditional metaphysics, the cosmos is substantively "good" and its ongoing creation and integration within the divine womb are sustained acts of divine compassion. Mankind, who is formed in the divine image, is created to reflect these divine qualities of goodness and compassion. Virtue is the inner substance of reality, and so of beauty, which is its outward expression. By contrast with this Traditional view, modernist theories of ethical behavior reduce ethics to mechanistic prescriptions justified by utilitarian needs or consensual preferences that are not rooted in any principled notion of objective Truth. By contrast, the ethos of Tradition is predicated on a metaphysical structure of reality in which the Other is *seen* and, more importantly, *felt* as an aspect of the Self. It is through this participative connection of sympathy that metaphysical truth is embodied as virtue.

The counterpart of virtue is beauty. The development of an aesthetic sensibility is therefore another vital component of a Traditional education. In Traditional metaphysics, "beauty" is the radiant effulgence of the divine. It is the presence of the Center in the periphery. The aesthetic sense therefore corresponds to the sense of the sacred and to the wholeness and harmony that is implicit in the divine order. It is only by finding the Center within us that the underlying order and the criterion of relationships can be known. It is only by discerning the Center in all things that one can achieve harmony and the abiding peace that is its corollary. In any Traditional education, the sense of the sacred is honed through the discipline of *ascesis*, the detachment from contingency. By this discipline, one creates the conditions of detachment that will remove the veils of egoic illusion that cloud our perception and that tempt our baser senses. It is through clarifying and cleansing our perceptions that we can perceive the Real. As man is a microcosm of the universe, it is by "polishing the mirror of the Self" that one can perceive the reflection within it of the divine theophany of the macrocosm. It is only through the inward gaze that opens into "the deepest freshness deep down things" that one can discover how "Nature is never spent"[14] but is an ever-renewing theophany. It is this continually replenishing fountain of life that is the core of beauty. It is ungraspable and fluid, yet abidingly present and still. It is therefore simultaneously mysterious and intimate. The Traditional doctrine of beauty therefore engages us in the Traditional praxis of ascetic discipline, by which we are enabled to detach ourselves from contingent reality and to open into the substantive presence of beauty, harmony, and peace, which is the substance of our innermost Self. According to the Vedantic formula, *sat-chit-ananda*, the abiding and blissful peace of *ananda* is an attribute of *chit*, the ontologically participative consciousness of *sat*, the transcendent Absolute who is the Sole Existent and our innermost Center or Self.

To sum up, these are the elements of a Traditional education: an initiation into the mysteries of Truth as Presence; the doctrine of Reality and Unity, and the method of Realization and Union; the "saving barque"[15] of prayer; the cultivation of the ethical sensibility of "virtue", and the aesthetic sensibility of "beauty". This is the wisdom that Tradition seeks to impart. The knowledge it seeks to convey is not merely of outer things, but is ontological—a part of our being, out of which it is drawn. The lessons that it offers are an antidote to the limited vision

[14] These quotations are from Gerard Manley Hopkins' poem, "God's Grandeur".

[15] Frithjof Schuon, *The Play of Masks* (Bloomington, IN: World Wisdom Books, 1992), p. vii.

of reality that hubristically claims the part to be the whole, and that would deny us our noble birthright—the "kingdom of heaven", the divine treasure that lies buried within.

Moral Tuition and Education

Enes Karić

A famous parable noted by the ancient writings recounts how philosophers and the *ulama*, in a debate before the Caliph himself, argued over what would prevail in the human person, nature or education, stock or upbringing, the blood in the veins or the sweat of the school benches.

The philosophers asserted that nurture would prevail over nature. Throughout the debate they maintained the view that education tames the human complexion and character, and overcomes mere human nature. The *ulama*, for their part, claimed that even after education, passion and nature predominate in man, particularly in times of evil, war, disorder, and discord. Nature is always more powerful than mere education, especially at such times, simply because nature is inner, unalterable; it is what it is, it is in the blood. The *ulama* further averred that education is one thing and moral tuition quite another. Only good moral tuition, along with a thorough education, can be an adequate sluice-gate to hold back the surges of nature in the raw.

The Caliph listened attentively to the two groups and then called upon the contesting parties to submit their evidence. The following night the philosophers, by way of evidence that education is more important than nature, brought a cat which they had taught, or trained, to use its forepaws to set out cups of tea at gatherings. And indeed, the cat served the participants in the debate with their favorite beverage. It seemed that the *ulama* had suffered a complete defeat in the debate.

However, although the *ulama* were amazed, they requested the Caliph's permission to meet again the following night so the cat could show off once again what the philosophers had taught her. At the very moment when the cat was serving the cups of tea, the *ulama* pulled some mice out of the pockets of their robes and let them loose in front of the cat. At once the cat dropped the cups of tea and began to chase the mice.

* * *

Men are not as cats, of course, but this old illustration of the theory of moral tuition and education speaks volumes of the main issues that are encountered at the beginning and the end of every process of education and moral tuition. Is mankind merely to be taught, educated by family, school, and the teaching process, or is he at the same time to be nurtured, so as to arouse all that is noble in his nature? Every religion and culture in the world has not only asked the question, but has at the same time answered it.

In these times of globalization, this question is the very axis of many societies, particularly those that have emerged in ideologies of education. In the nineteenth and twentieth centuries, for the first time in history, education ceased to be a matter only for the *ulama*, priestly caste, tribal or ruling elite. Education has become, during these two centuries, available to almost everyone. There would be nothing wrong in that if education had not been emptied of moral tuition, if it had not been turned into mass education, that is, knowledge has been transmitted with the new clichés of education to pupils, students, people *en masse*, precisely so that not only are they seen as a mass, but have been taught as a mass. Since mass is itself a physical phenomenon, not only can one not see anyone's face in the mass, but every face, every individual characteristic, is lost in the mass. For this reason many ideologues of the nineteenth and twentieth centuries, both in the West and the East, especially those who came into power, included the "education of the masses" in their political programs. It is only a short step from the "education of the masses" to conditioning them. Where totalitarian regimes have succeeded in taking power, as is well known, they have taken that step.

However, not only have they reduced the recipients of knowledge to a mass with their mass education, they have made knowledge itself into a mass, transmitted as a mass of isolated, compartmentalized facts belonging to a given discipline. Physics, chemistry, biology—during the nineteenth and twentieth centuries, the sciences have been autonomized and atomized. Treating knowledge as a mass of facts which, on the one hand, are transmitted to millions of pupils, the student public, through the medium of mass education, and which, on the other hand, are fragmented and isolated into separate disciplines that with time have become completely divorced one from another, has led to a terrible outcome: more and more the world is not seen by modern education as a whole. The sciences have sundered the world, like beasts tearing at a carcass, each seizing its own portion.

This concept of mass education, developed during the past two centuries, has increasingly neglected the moral tuition of pupils, the moral tuition of the individual. Education has ceased to include moral tuition. The consequences have not only been ominous, but also inescapable. Little proof is required of this. The gas chambers of the holocaust were the creation of highly educated academics, who had not received moral tuition. Ethnic cleansing is the result of projects dreamed up by highly educated professors, who had not had moral tuition.

Too much is being written about this these days, as about the environmental catastrophe on the planetary scale. The ancient civilizations took root along rivers and in maritime bays and gulfs; modern education and the armies of people it has conditioned, but not given moral tuition, have poisoned those rivers and bays. No one with any sense can deny the fact that modern education, from which the element of moral tuition has been extracted, has trained armies of scientists who not only feel no humility in the face of nature, but do not even think of the possibility that, say, physics or chemistry could be concerned with the fact of scientific humility in the face of nature, its graciousness and virginal purity.

This tells us that mass education systems, depriving education of the element of moral tuition, have led to arrogantly irresponsible knowledge. The knowledgeable but irresponsible man resembles the cat from the start of this essay. A man who has been educated in this way, a humanity educated in this way, will always retreat, will always be defeated by the upsurge of raw nature. However, now that it has been armed with irresponsible education, the ungovernability of raw human nature is far more dangerous than it was in the case of the uneducated "savage."

It is sufficient here, in the context of this assertion, to recall the metaphor of man as the inhabitant of nature's own ready-made habitation, the cave. This is a favorite metaphor of religion, philosophy, history, art. Just as the shell is innate to the snail that carries it, so man has not forgotten the cave, carrying deep within him its character, or at least the distant memory of it. Although religion tells us that the counterpoint to the cave has always been the temple (in Islam one such temple is known as the Kaaba), as a symbol of faith and measure, order and symmetry, as a symbol of upbringing and as the boundary up to which one may step, the cave has for all that remained deeply entrenched in the depths of man's ancient memories. The cave, fire, smoke, the hunt, plunder—to all this man has returned in the cycles of history and only with difficulty does he resist the lure of plunder.

Modern education, from which moral tuition has been removed, has led to an absurd phenomenon: the wars of "cave men" are just an innocent joke compared with the wars of civilized man, armed with knowledge gained from education in the form of training. The wars that have broken out during the most recent centuries, despite the fact that mankind has never been so well educated as during the nineteenth and twentieth centuries, show that even with that very education, not only does educated man lack the power to resist the old call of the cave, fire and looting, the call of the hunt and plunder, but he has become even more dangerous in that calling, since he has become more efficient in evil-doing.

Several tens of major world cities have been burned at the hands of educated humanity, but humanity lacking moral tuition, during the wars of the twentieth century, in both West and East—as though it were the wish of all this educated humanity, with its lack of moral tuition, to turn the whole world into a cave, a vast image of fire, flames, and smoke. Jalaluddin Rumi wrote that reason serves humanity that is educated but without moral tuition in just the same way that a candle serves a thief while he is stealing.

* * *

For at least a decade now we have been hearing more and more often on the news about a pupil or pupils who open fire with an automatic weapon in their own school, killing or injuring half the class of their peers. These news items and this phenomenon are being widely analyzed today. However, what many who are attempting to get to the heart of this problem, if not to put an end to it, have failed to observe is that this is news not of a cause but of its consequences. The causes are far deeper, in both West and East, and go back two or more centuries. Mass education and modern schools welcome their pupils with orderly classrooms, effective curricula and textbooks, but modern physics textbooks say nothing about humility. Modern chemistry books say not a word about self-effacement. Modern biology textbooks make no allusion to modesty.

One could go through the names of every contemporary discipline, and always express the categorical judgment that the textbooks make no mention of any form of nurture or moral constant, and still less are they conceived according to those constants. What is more, those voices in the world today that insist on the introduction of moral content into textbooks are held up to ridicule. It is as though, say, man is man only by virtue of his wisdom and not his modesty.

This indicates that these textbooks read nature, including human nature, as though it were a machine, failing to read in its numerous pages the higher purpose that exists beyond the level of the world that we can grasp with our reason. It is not only humility, modesty, the pangs of conscience that have been banished from physics, chemistry, and biology textbooks. Banished from their pages too are themes such as the graciousness, wonder, beauty, the infinity of the world and of nature. Modern education has ceased to marvel at the wondrous nature of water. Water has long since been seen as a mere industrial resource.

All this shows that these textbooks educate, but they do not elevate.

* * *

Moral tuition implies, above all, a recognition of the higher purpose and superior reasons for learning, knowledge, and instruction. Moral tuition is grounded in culture, culture in faith, and faith in the Ultimate Purpose, God. To know the laws of hydraulics, to know how to make water conduits is a matter of education; to clean oneself with water, however, is a matter of upbringing, of culture. To know the formula for soap and to make soap is a matter of science; to use soap when it is necessary is a matter of upbringing. To capture enemy troops in wartime is a matter of military skill and. knowledge; to spare their lives and preserve their dignity is a matter of upbringing.

Modern systems will have to recall, sooner or later, the classic debate on the human spirit and upbringing, and will have to return to the ancient teachings of mankind that defined the spheres of education and moral tuition. Just as education is the exercise of mental powers, so moral tuition is the education of the inner conscience, the enlightenment of the heart itself Thus education and moral tuition are two equal elements of man's spiritual upbringing, just as a bird flies equally with both of its wings. In modern education, however, those two elements are in a state of disequilibrium.

Education without moral tuition seeks to transform itself into a destructive force against nature and against human society. Moral tuition without education, although it leads to moral rectitude, slackens with time and changes into consolation as the only refuge. When once again establishing the balance between the "known" and that which is "worthy and how to do it well," it is important to bear in mind that neither education nor moral tuition are processes that man acquires once and for all, as he acquires his adult teeth after his milk teeth fall. Education and moral tuition are long-term and repetitive processes to which one must constantly and vigilantly return, just as a bird, to remain in the air, must continually beat both its wings.

II.

Education in Traditional Societies

Traditional Native American Education

Charles Eastman (Ohiyesa) & Joe Medicine Crow

The Grandparents Teach the Young Children

It is commonly supposed that there is no systematic education of their children among the aborigines of this country. Nothing could be farther from the truth. All the customs of this primitive people were held to be divinely instituted, and those in connection with the training of children were scrupulously adhered to and transmitted from one generation to another.

Very early, the Indian boy assumed the task of preserving and transmitting the legends of his ancestors and his race. Almost every evening a myth, or a true story of some deed done in the past, was narrated by one of the parents or grandparents, while the boy listened with parted lips and glistening eyes. On the following evening, he was usually required to repeat it. As a rule, the Indian boy is a good listener and has a good memory, so that the stories were tolerably well mastered. The household became his audience, by which he was alternately criticized and applauded.

This sort of teaching at once enlightens the boy's mind and stimulates his ambition. His conception of his own future career becomes a vivid and irresistible force. Whatever there is for him to learn must be learned; whatever qualifications are necessary to a truly great man he must seek at any expense of danger and hardship. Such was the feeling of the imaginative and brave young Indian. It became apparent to him in early life that he must accustom himself to rove alone and not to fear or dislike the impression of solitude.

Indeed, the distinctive work of both grandparents is that of acquainting the youth with the national traditions and beliefs. It is reserved for them to repeat the time-hallowed tales with dignity and authority, so as to lead him into his inheritance in the stored-up wisdom and experience of the race. The old are dedicated to the service of the young, as their teachers and advisers, and the young in turn regard them with love and reverence.

Storytelling

Storytelling was the traditional way of passing on our tribal history and educating the young children—the grandfathers and grandmothers were our teachers. In my youth, the storytellers who educated me were my immediate family members. I remember that my grandfather, my mother's father, whose name was Yellowtail, was my main teacher. I followed him around wherever he went. When he went to go take a sweat bath, I would follow him. While the rocks were heating he told stories. I was fortunate as a boy because so many storytellers were ready to educate the young. Now the television is on all the time and the children no longer follow the elders—they don't take the time to listen to their grandparents. In today's world it is difficult to learn about the olden-day stories, so books that preserve this wisdom have great value.

There are different variations of the same story that are told among the many tribes; even the Crow people have different variations of the legend about creation. The storytellers can go on with their account for hours when they add the many details and variations. The best way to learn about tribal history and culture is to read several different accounts of these stories in order to understand the wisdom of our traditional teachings.

—Joe Medicine Crow, Crow tribal historian and the last traditional Plains Indian war chief

Storytelling among the Pikuni Blackfeet

An Indian Boy's Training

> It seems to be a popular idea that all the characteristic skill of the Indian is instinctive and hereditary. This is a mistake. All the stoicism and patience of the Indian are acquired traits, and continual practice alone makes him master of the art of woodcraft. Physical training and dieting were not neglected. I remember that I was not allowed to have beef soup or any warm drink. The soup was for the old men. General rules for the young were never to take their food very hot, nor to drink much water.
>
> —Charles Eastman

At the age of about eight years, if the child is a boy, his mother turns him over to his father for more Spartan training.

My uncle, who educated me up to the age of fifteen years, was a strict disciplinarian and a good teacher. When I left the teepee in the morning, he would say: "Hakadah, look closely to everything you see"; and at evening, on my return, he used often to catechize me for an hour or so.

"On which side of the trees is the lighter-colored bark? On which side do they have most regular branches?"

It was his custom to let me name all the new birds that I had seen during the day. I would name them according to the color or the shape of the bill or their song or the appearance and locality of the nest—in fact, anything about the bird that impressed me as characteristic. I made many ridiculous errors, I must admit. He then usually informed me of the correct name. Occasionally I made a hit and this he would warmly commend.

He went much deeper into this science when I was a little older, that is, about the age of eight or nine years. He would say, for instance:

"How do you know that there are fish in yonder lake?"

"Because they jump out of the water for flies at mid-day."

He would smile at my prompt but superficial reply.

"What do you think of the little pebbles grouped together under the shallow water? and what made the pretty curved marks in the sandy bottom and the little sand-banks? Where do you find the fish-eating birds? Have the inlet and the outlet of a lake anything to do with the question?"

He did not expect a correct reply at once to all the voluminous questions that he put to me on these occasions, but he meant to make me observant and a good student of nature.

"Hakadah," he would say to me, "you ought to follow the example of the *shunktokecha* (wolf). Even when he is surprised and runs for his life, he will pause to take one more look at you before he enters his final retreat. So you must take a second look at everything you see."

"In hunting," he would resume, "you will be guided by the habits of the animal you seek. Remember that a moose stays in swampy or low land or between high mountains near a spring or lake, for thirty to sixty days at a time. Most large game moves about continually, except the doe in the spring; it is then a very easy matter to find her with the fawn. Conceal yourself in a convenient place as soon as you observe any signs of the presence of either, and then call with your birchen doe-caller.

"When you have any difficulty with a bear or a wild-cat—that is, if the creature shows signs of attacking you—you must make him fully understand that you have seen him and are aware of his intentions. If you are not well equipped for a pitched battle, the only way to make him retreat is to take a long sharp-pointed pole for a spear and rush toward him. No wild beast will face this unless he is cornered and already wounded. These fierce beasts are generally afraid of the common weapon of the larger animals—the horns, and if these are very long and sharp, they dare not risk an open fight."

All boys were expected to endure hardship without complaint. In savage warfare, a young man must, of course, be an athlete and used to undergoing all sorts of privations. He must be able to go without food and water for two or three days without displaying any weakness, or to run for a day and a night without any rest. He must be able to traverse a pathless and wild country without losing his way either in the day or night time. He cannot refuse to do any of these things if he aspires to be a warrior.

Sometimes my uncle would wake me very early in the morning and challenge me to fast with him all day. I had to accept the challenge. We blackened our faces with charcoal, so that every boy in the village would know that I was fasting for the day. Then the little tempters would make my life a misery until the merciful sun hid behind the western hills.

I can scarcely recall the time when my stern teacher began to give sudden war-whoops over my head in the morning while I was sound asleep. He expected me to leap up with perfect presence of mind, always ready to grasp a weapon of some sort and to give a shrill whoop in reply. If I was sleepy or startled and hardly knew what I was about, he would ridicule me and say that I need never expect to sell my scalp dear. Often he would vary these tactics by shooting off his gun just outside of the lodge while I was yet asleep, at the same time giving blood-curdling yells. After a time I became used to this.

When Indians went upon the war-path, it was their custom to try the new warriors thoroughly before coming to an engagement. For instance, when they were near a hostile camp, they would select the novices to go after the water and make them do all sorts of things to prove their courage. In accordance with this idea, my uncle used to send me off after water when we camped after dark in a strange place. Perhaps the country was full of wild beasts, and, for aught I knew, there might be scouts from hostile bands of Indians lurking in that very neighborhood.

Yet I never objected, for that would show cowardice. I picked my way through the woods, dipped my pail in the water and hurried back, always careful to make as little noise as a cat. Being only a boy, my heart would leap at every crackling of a dry twig or distant hooting of an owl, until, at last, I reached our teepee. Then my uncle would perhaps say: "Ah, Hakadah, you are a thorough warrior," empty out the precious contents of the pail, and order me to go a second time.

With all this, our manners and morals were not neglected. I was made to respect the adults and especially the aged. I was not allowed to join in their discussions, nor even to speak in their presence, unless requested to do so. Indian etiquette was very strict, and among the requirements was that of avoiding the direct address. A term of relationship or some title of courtesy was commonly used instead of the personal name by those who wished to show respect. We were taught generosity to the poor and reverence for the "Great Mystery." Religion was the basis of all Indian training.

I recall to the present day some of the kind warnings and reproofs that my good grandmother was wont to give me. "Be strong of heart—be patient!" she used to say. She told me of a young chief who was noted for his uncontrollable temper. While in one of his rages he attempted to kill a woman, for which he was slain by his own band and left unburied as a mark of disgrace—his body was simply covered with green grass. If I ever lost my temper, she would say:

"Hakadah, control yourself, or you will be like that young man I told you of, and lie under a green blanket!"

In the old days, if a youth should seek a wife before he had reached the age of twenty-two or twenty-three, and been recognized as a brave man, he was sneered at and considered an ill-bred Indian. He must also be a skillful hunter. An Indian cannot be a good husband unless he brings home plenty of game.

These precepts were in the line of our training for the wild life.

Indian Etiquette

No one who is at all acquainted with the Indian in his home can deny that we are a polite people. As a rule, the warrior who inspired the greatest terror in the hearts of his enemies was a man of the most exemplary gentleness, and almost feminine refinement, among his family and friends. A soft, low voice was considered an excellent thing in man, as well as in woman! Indeed, the enforced intimacy of tent life would soon become intolerable, were it not for these instinctive reserves and delicacies, this unfailing respect for the established place and possessions of every other member of the family circle, this habitual quiet, order, and decorum.

Our people, though capable of strong and durable feeling, were not demonstrative in their affection at any time, least of all in the presence of guests or strangers. Only to the aged, who have journeyed far, and are in a manner exempt from ordinary rules, are permitted some playful familiarities with children and grandchildren. Grandparents are the only ones allowed to speak harshly in their criticism. Our old age was in some respects the happiest period of life. Advancing years brought with them much freedom, not only from the burden of laborious and dangerous tasks, but from those restrictions of custom and etiquette which were religiously observed by all others.

—Charles Eastman

Games and Sports

The Indian boy was a prince of the wilderness. He had but very little work to do during the period of his boyhood. His principal occupation was the practice of a few simple arts in warfare and the chase. Aside from this, he was master of his time.

Whatever was required of us boys was quickly performed: then the field was clear for our games and plays. There was always keen competition among us. We felt very much as our fathers did in hunting and war —each one strove to excel all the others.

It is true that our savage life was a precarious one, and full of dreadful catastrophes; however, this never prevented us from enjoying our sports to the fullest extent. As we left our teepees in the morning, we were never sure that our scalps would not dangle from a pole in the afternoon!

Our sports were molded by the life and customs of our people; indeed, we practiced only what we expected to do when grown. Our games were feats with the bow and arrow, foot and pony races, wrestling, swimming and imitation of the customs and habits of our fathers. We had sham fights with mud balls and willow wands; we played lacrosse, made war upon bees, shot winter arrows (which were used only in that season), and coasted upon the ribs of animals and buffalo robes.

It was considered out of place to shoot by first sighting the object aimed at. This was usually impracticable in actual life, because the object was almost always in motion, while the hunter himself was often upon the back of a pony at full gallop. Therefore, it was the off-hand shot that the Indian boy sought to master.

Races were an everyday occurrence. At noon the boys were usually gathered by some pleasant sheet of water and as soon as the ponies were watered, they were allowed to graze for an hour or two, while the boys stripped for their noonday sports.

As soon as the foot race was ended, the pony races followed. All the speedy ponies were picked out and riders chosen. If a boy declined to ride, there would be shouts of derision.

Last of all came the swimming. We loved to play in the water. When we had no ponies, we often had swimming matches of our own and sometimes made rafts with which we crossed lakes and rivers. It was a common thing to "duck" a young or timid boy or to carry him into deep water to struggle as best he might.

I remember a perilous ride with a companion on an unmanageable log, when we were both less than seven years old. The older boys had put us on this uncertain bark and pushed us out into the swift current of the river. I cannot speak for my comrade in distress, but I can say now that I would rather ride on a swift bronco any day than try to stay on and steady a short log in a river. I never knew how we managed to prevent a shipwreck on that voyage and to reach the shore.

Wrestling was largely indulged in by us all. It may seem odd, but wrestling was done by a great many boys at once—from ten to any number on a side. It was really a battle, in which each one chose his opponent. The rule was that if a boy sat down, he was let alone, but as long as he remained standing within the field, he was open to an attack. No one struck with the hand, but all manner of tripping with legs and feet and butting with the knees was allowed. Altogether it was an exhausting pastime—fully equal to the American game of football and only the young athlete could really enjoy it.

One of our most curious sports was a war upon the nests of wild bees. We imagined ourselves about to make an attack upon the Ojibways or some tribal foe. We all painted and stole cautiously upon the nest; then, with a rush and war whoop, sprang upon the object of our attack and endeavored to destroy it. But it seemed that the bees were always on the alert and never entirely surprised, for they always raised quite as many scalps as did their bold assailants! After the onslaught upon the nest was ended, we usually followed it by a pretended scalp dance.

We had some quiet plays which we alternated with the more severe and warlike ones. Among them were throwing wands and snow-arrows. In the winter we coasted much. We had no "double-rippers" or toboggans, but six or seven of the long ribs of a buffalo, fastened together at the larger end, answered all practical purposes. Sometimes a strip of basswood bark, four feet long and about six inches wide, was used with considerable skill. We stood on one end and held the other, using the slippery inside of the bark for the outside, and thus coasting down long hills with remarkable speed.

The Boy Hunter

It will be no exaggeration to say that the life of the Indian hunter was a life of fascination. From the moment that he lost sight of his rude home in the midst of the forest, his untutored mind lost itself in the myriad beauties and forces of nature. Yet he never forgot his personal danger from some lurking foe or savage beast, however absorbing was his passion for the chase.

The Indian youth was a born hunter. Every motion, every step expressed an inborn dignity and, at the same time, a depth of native caution. His moccasined foot fell like the velvet paw of a cat—noiselessly; his glittering black eyes scanned every object that appeared within their view. Not a bird, not even a chipmunk, escaped their piercing glance.

I was scarcely over three years old when I stood one morning just outside our buffalo-skin teepee, with my little bow and arrows in my hand, and gazed up among the trees. Suddenly the instinct to chase and hunt seized me powerfully. Just then a bird flew over my head and then another caught my eye, as it balanced itself upon a swaying bough. Everything else was forgotten and in that moment I had taken my first step as a hunter.

Our hunting varied with the season of the year, and the nature of the country which was for the time our home. Our chief weapon was the bow and arrows, and perhaps, if we were lucky, a knife was possessed by someone in the crowd. In the olden times, knives and hatchets were made from bone and sharp stones.

For fire we used a flint with a spongy piece of dry wood and a stone to strike with. Another way of starting fire was for several of the boys to sit down in a circle and rub two pieces of dry, spongy wood together, one after another, until the wood took fire.

We hunted in company a great deal, though it was a common thing for a boy to set out for the woods quite alone, and he usually enjoyed himself fully as much. Our game consisted mainly of small birds, rabbits, squirrels and grouse. Fishing, too, occupied much of our time. We hardly ever passed a creek or a pond without searching for some signs of fish. When fish were present, we always managed to get some. Fish-lines were made of wild hemp, sinew or horse-hair. We either caught fish with lines, snared or speared them, or shot them with bow and arrows. In the fall we charmed them up to the surface by gently tickling them with a stick and quickly threw them out. We have sometimes dammed the brooks and driven the larger fish into a willow basket made for that purpose.

It was part of our hunting to find new and strange things in the woods. We examined the slightest sign of life; and if a bird had scratched the leaves off the ground, or a bear dragged up a root for his morning meal, we stopped to speculate on the time it was done. If we saw a large old tree with some scratches on its bark, we concluded that a bear or some raccoons must be living there. In that case we did not go any nearer than was necessary, but later reported the incident at home. An old deer-track would at once bring on a warm discussion as to whether it was the track of a buck or a doe.

> Whenever, in the course of the daily hunt, the red hunter comes upon a scene that is strikingly beautiful and sublime—a black thunder-cloud with the rainbow's glowing arch above the mountain; a white waterfall in the heart of a green gorge; a vast prairie tinged with the blood-red of sunset—he pauses for an instant in the attitude of worship. He sees no need for setting apart one day in seven as a holy day, since to him all days are God's.
>
> —Charles Eastman

Wilderness Cooking

It became a necessary part of our education to learn to prepare a meal while out hunting. It is a fact that most Indians will eat the liver and some other portions of large animals raw, but they do not eat fish or birds uncooked. Neither will they eat a frog, or an eel. On our boyish hunts, we often went on until we found ourselves a long way from our camp, when we would kindle a fire and roast a part of our game.

Generally we broiled our meat over the coals on a stick. We roasted some of it over the open fire. But the best way to cook fish and birds is in the ashes, under a big fire. We take the fish fresh from the creek or lake, have a good fire on the sand, dig in the sandy ashes and bury it

Sioux man cooking meat by throwing heated stones into a buffalo-stomach container

deep. The same thing is done in case of a bird, only we wet the feathers first. When it is done, the scales or feathers and skin are stripped off whole, and the delicious meat retains all its juices and flavor. We pulled it off as we ate, leaving the bones undisturbed.

Our people had also a method of boiling without pots or kettles. A large piece of tripe was thoroughly washed and the ends tied, then suspended between four stakes driven into the ground and filled with cold water. The meat was then placed in this novel receptacle and boiled by means of the addition of red-hot stones.

An Indian Girl's Training

The Indian mother was the spiritual teacher of the child, as well as its tender nurse, and she brought its developing soul before the "Great Mystery" as soon as she was aware of its coming. At the age of five to eight years, she turned her boy over to his father for manly training, and to the grandparents for traditional instruction, but the girl child remained under her close and thoughtful supervision. She preserved man from soul-killing materialism by herself owning what few possessions they had, and thus branding possession as feminine. The movable home was hers, with all its belongings, and she ruled there unquestioned. She was, in fact, the moral salvation of the race; all virtue was entrusted to her, and her position was recognized by all. It was held in all gentleness and discretion, under the rule that no woman could talk much or loudly until she became a grandmother.

Katie Blue Thunder, Brule Dakota

Crow girl with doll in cradle board

The young maiden has not only the experience of her mother and grandmother, and the accepted rules of her people for a guide, but she humbly seeks to learn a lesson from ants, bees, spiders, beavers, and badgers. She studies the family life of the birds, so exquisite in its emotional intensity and its patient devotion, until she seems to feel the universal mother-heart beating in her own breast. In due time the child takes of his own accord the attitude of prayer, and speaks reverently of the Powers. He thinks that he is a blood brother to all living creatures, and the storm wind is to him a messenger of the "Great Mystery."

Orphans and the aged are invariably cared for, not only by their next of kin, but by the whole clan. It is the loving parent's pride to have his daughters visit the unfortunate and the helpless, carry them food, comb their hair, and mend their garments. A girl who failed in her charitable duties was held to be unworthy of the name.

Piegan play tipi

Oesedah was my beautiful younger cousin. Perhaps none of my early playmates are more vividly remembered than is this little maiden. The name given her by a noted medicine-man was Makah-oesetopah-win. It means The-four-corners-of-the-earth. As she was rather small, the abbreviation was considered more appropriate, hence Oesedah became her common name.

Although she had a very good mother, my grandmother, Uncheedah, was her efficient teacher and chaperon. Such knowledge as my grandmother deemed suitable to a maiden was duly impressed upon her susceptible mind. Oesedah was my companion at home; and when I returned from my play at evening, she would have a hundred questions ready for me to answer. Some of these were questions concerning our everyday life, and others were more difficult problems which had suddenly dawned upon her active mind. Whatever had occurred to interest her during the day was immediately repeated for my benefit.

There were certain questions upon which Oesedah held me to be authority, and asked with the hope of increasing her little store of knowledge. I occasionally referred to little Oesedah in the same manner, and I always accepted her explanation of any matter upon which I had been advised to consult her, because I knew the source of her wisdom. In this simple way we were made to be teachers of one another.

We also had many curious wild pets. There were young foxes, bears, wolves, raccoons, fawns, buffalo calves and birds of all kinds, tamed by various boys. My pets were different at different times.

We were once very short of provisions in the winter time. My uncle, our only means of support, was sick; and besides, we were separated from the rest of the tribe and in a region where there was little game of any kind. Oesedah had a pet squirrel, and as soon as we began to economize our food she gave portions of her allowance to her pet.

The Maiden's Feast

It was a custom of the Plains Indians to hold peaceful meetings in summer, at which times they would vie with one another in friendliness and generosity. Each family would single out a family of another tribe as special guests of honor. Valuable horses and richly adorned garments were freely given at the feasts and dances. During these intertribal reunions the contests between the tribes were recalled and their events rehearsed, the dead heroes on both sides receiving special tributes of honor.

There were many peculiar customs among the Indians of an earlier period, some of which tended to strengthen the character of the people and preserve their purity. Perhaps the most unique of these was the annual "feast of maidens." The casual observer would scarcely understand the full force and meaning of this ceremony.

The last one that I ever witnessed was given at Fort Ellis, Manitoba, about the year 1871. In this spot there was a reunion of all the renegade Sioux on the one hand and of the Assiniboines and Crees, the Canadian tribes, on the other. They were friendly. The matter was not formally arranged, but it was usual for all the tribes to meet here in the month of July.

When circumstances are favorable, the Indians are the happiest people in the world. There were entertainments every single day, which everybody had the fullest opportunity to see and enjoy. If anything, the poorest profited the most by these occasions, because a feature in each case was the giving away of wealth to the needy in honor of the event. At any public affair, involving the pride and honor of a prominent family, there must always be a distribution of valuable presents.

One bright summer morning, while we were still at our meal of jerked buffalo meat, we heard the herald of the *Wahpeton* band upon his calico pony as he rode around our circle.

"White Eagle's daughter, the maiden Red Star, invites all the maidens of all the tribes to come and partake of her feast. All pure maidens are invited. Red Star also invites the young men to be present, to see that no unworthy maiden should join in the feast."

The herald soon completed the rounds of the different camps, and it was not long before the girls began to gather in great numbers. This particular feast was looked upon as a semi-sacred affair. It would be desecration for any to attend who was not perfectly virtuous. Hence it was regarded as an opportune time for the young men to satisfy themselves as to who were the virtuous maids of the tribe.

There were apt to be surprises before the end of the day. Any young man was permitted to challenge any maiden whom he knew to be unworthy. But woe to him who could not prove his case. It meant little short of death to the man who endeavored to disgrace a woman without cause.

The young boys had a similar feast of their own, in which the eligibles were those who had never spoken to a girl in the way of courtship. It was considered ridiculous so to do before attaining some honor as a warrior, and the novices prided themselves greatly upon their self control.

From the various camps the girls came singly or in groups, dressed in bright-colored calicoes or in heavily fringed and beaded buckskin. Their smooth cheeks and the central part of their glossy hair was touched with vermilion.

The maidens' circle was formed about a cone shaped rock which stood upon its base. This was painted red. Beside it two new arrows were lightly stuck into the ground. This is a sort of altar, to which each maiden comes before taking her assigned place in the circle, and lightly touches first the stone and then the arrows. By this oath she declares her purity.

There was never a more gorgeous assembly of the kind than this one. The day was perfect.

The whole population of the region had assembled, and the maidens came shyly into the circle. The simple ceremonies observed prior to the serving of the food were in progress, when among a group of *Wahpeton* young men there was a stir of excitement. All the maidens glanced nervously toward the scene of the disturbance. Soon a tall youth emerged from the throng of spectators and advanced toward the circle. Every one of the chaperons glared at him as if to deter him from his purpose. But with a steady step he passed them by and approached the maidens' circle.

At last he stopped behind a pretty Assiniboine maiden of good family and said:

"I am sorry, but, according to custom, you should not be here."

The girl arose in confusion, but she soon recovered her self-control.

"What do you mean?" she demanded, indignantly. "Three times you have come to court me, but each time I have refused to listen to you. I turned my back upon you. Twice I was with my friend Mashtinna. She can tell the people that this is true. The third time I had gone for water when you intercepted me and begged me to stop and listen. I refused because I did not know you. My chaperon, Makatopawee, knows that I was gone but a few minutes. I never saw you anywhere else."

The young man was unable to answer this unmistakable statement of facts, and it became apparent that he had sought to revenge himself for her repulse.

"Woo! woo! Carry him out!" was the order of the chief of the Indian police, and the audacious youth was hurried away into the nearest ravine to be chastised.

The young woman who had thus established her good name returned to the circle, and the feast was served. The "maidens' song" was sung, and four times they danced in a ring around the altar. Each maid as she departed once more took her oath to remain pure until she should meet her husband.

Traditional Hindu Education

HH the 68th Jagadguru of Kanchipuram

The Vedic Religion: Introductory

If ours is a primeval religion, the question arises as to who established it. [Our greatest sages] state that the Vedas existed before them. If that be the case, are we to point to the *risis*, the seers, who gave us the Vedic *mantras*, as the founders of our religion? But they themselves declare: "We did not create the Vedas." When we chant a *mantra* we touch our head with our hand mentioning the name of one seer or another. But the sages themselves say: "It is true that the *mantras* became manifest to the world through us. That is why we are mentioned as the '*mantra risis*'. But the *mantras* were not composed by us but revealed to us. When we sat meditating with our minds under control, the *mantras* were perceived by us in space. Indeed we *saw* them; we did not compose them."

All sounds originate in space. From them arose creation. According to science, the cosmos was produced from the vibrations in space. By virtue of their austerities the sages had the gift of seeing the *mantras* in space, the *mantras* that liberate men from this creation. The Vedas are *apauruṣēya* (not the work of any human author) and are the very breath of the *Paramātman* (supreme Self) in his form as space. The sages saw them and made a gift of them to the world.

If we know this truth, we have reason to be proud of the fact that we do not know who founded our religion. In fact we must feel happy that we have the great good fortune to be heirs to a religion that is eternal, a religion containing the Vedas which are the very breath of the *Paramātman.*

The Vedas, the Root of All

We find that there is but one scripture as the source common to the different sects and schools of thought in the Hindu religion. This source includes the Upanishads. It emerges that for all the divisions in our religion there is but one scripture—a scripture common to all—and one Godhead which is known by many names. The Vedas are the common scripture and the Godhead common to all is the *Brahman.* Thus we can say with finality, and without any room for doubt, that all of us belong to the same religion.

The Vedas that constitute the scripture common to all and which reveal the Godhead that is common to us also teach us how to lead our life, and—this is important—they do us the ultimate good by showing us in the end the way to become that very Godhead ourselves. They are our refuge both here and in the hereafter and are the source and root of all our different traditions, all our systems of thought. All sects, all schools of our religion, have their origin in them. The root is one but the branches are many.

The Vedas in their Original Form

Some do not seem to attach any special significance to the fact that the Vedas are in Sanskrit. They think that these sacred texts could be known through translations.

Nowadays a number of books are translated from one language into another and in this process the original form or character is changed or distorted. The words spoken by a great man on a particular subject may not be fully understood today. But if they are preserved in the original in the same language, there is the possibility of their meaning being fully grasped at some future date. You use a beautiful word to convey an idea in your language, but its equivalent may not be found in any other tongue. Also, it may become necessary to express the same in a roundabout way.

There is also the possibility that the opinion expressed first, in its original context, may not come through effectively in a translation. We must consider the further disadvantage of the translation being circumscribed by the mental make-up of the translator, the limitations of his knowledge and understanding of the subject dealt with. The translation done by one may not seem right to another. When there are a number of translations of the same work, it would be hard to choose the right one. We shall then be compelled to go back to the original.

This is the reason why I insist that the Vedas must be preserved in their original form. They are the source of the philosophical systems associated with the great *ācāryas* (teachers). These masters evolved their doctrines without making any modifications in the Vedas to suit themselves; nor did they establish any religions of their own outside the Vedic tradition. The source, the root, of their systems of thought is one and the same—the Vedas. It is because this source has remained unchanged in its original character that thinkers and teachers have, from time to time, been able to draw inspiration and strength from it to present new viewpoints. But these viewpoints have not meant the creation of new religions. The reason is that all of them—all these systems—belong to the larger system called the Vedic religion.

Preserving the Vedas: Why it Is a Lifetime Mission?

"The sages transcended the frontiers of human knowledge and became one with the Universal Reality. It is through them that the world received the Vedic *mantras*": this is one of the basic concepts of our religion. If you do not accept that human beings can obtain such atmic power as exemplified by these seers, any further talk on the subject would be futile. One could point out to you great men whom you can see for yourself, great men who have perfected themselves and acquired powers not shared by the common people. But if you think of them to be cheats or fraudulent men, any further talk would again be useless. In our present state of limited understanding, the argument that denies the existence of anything beyond the range of human reason and comprehension itself betrays the height of irrationalism.

Are sounds and vibrations spontaneously produced? No. If vibrations arise on their own they will be erratic and confusing and not related to one another. But what do we see in the cosmos? There is a certain orderliness about it and one thing in it is linked to another. What do we infer from this? That a Great Intelligence has formulated this scheme that we see, that it has created it from its own vibrations.

The Vedas are sounds emanating from the vibrations of this Great Intelligence, the Great Gnosis. That is why we believe that the *mantras* of the Vedas originate from the *Paramātman* himself. We must take special care of such sounds to ensure the good of the world. Yes, the Vedic *mantras* are sequences of sounds that are meant for the good of the world.

Whatever is present in space is also present in the individual being. These elements exist in the human body in a form that is accessible to the senses. The sounds a person makes in his throat have their source in space in a form not audible to us. The radio transforms electrical waves into sound waves. If a man can grasp the sounds in space and make them audible, he will be able to create with them what is needed for the good of the world. Yoga is the science that accomplishes such a task. Through yogic practice (perfection) one can become aware of what is in the macrocosm and draw it into the microcosm. I shall not be able to give you proof of this in a form acceptable to human reason. Yoga transcends our limited reason and understanding.

The purpose of the Vedas is to speak about matters that are beyond the comprehension of the human mind.

When we look at this universe and the complex manner in which it functions, we realize that there must be a Great Wisdom that has created it and sustains it. It is from this Great Wisdom, that is the *Paramātman*, that all that we see are born and it is from It that all the sounds that we hear have emanated. First came the universe of sound and then the universe that we observe. Most of the former still exists in space. All that exists in the outer universe is present in the human body also. The space that exists outside us exists also in our heart.

The *mantras* of the Vedas are remarkable in that they bring blessings to the world in the form of sound—even if their meaning is not understood. Of course, they are pregnant with meaning and represent the lofty principle that it is the One Truth that is manifested as all that we perceive. They also confer blessings on us by taking the form of deities appropriate to the different sounds (of the *mantras*). Sound does not bring any benefits, any fruits, by itself. *Īśvara* (the Lord) alone is the bestower of benefits. However, instead of making the fruits available to us directly, he appoints deities to distribute them in the same manner as the king or president of a country appoints officials to carry out his dictates. The *mantras* represent various deities in the form of sound. If we attain perfection (*siddhi*) by constant chanting and meditation of a *mantra*, it should be possible for us to see the deity invoked in his physical form. The deities also arise if we make offerings into the sacrificial fire reciting specific *mantras*. If a sacrifice is conducted in this manner, the deities give us their special blessings. We do not pay taxes directly to the king or president. In the same way, we pay taxes in the form of sacrifices and Vedic chanting to the aides of the *Paramātman* for the sake of the welfare of the world. The sounds of the *mantras* constitute their form.

The Vedas have won the admiration of Western scholars for their poetic beauty. They bring us face to face with many deities—they bring us also their grace. Above all, through the Upanishads they teach us the great truths relating to the Self. The Vedas are thus known for the profundity of the truths contained in them, but their sound is no less important. Indeed their sound has its own significance and power. All *mantras*, it must be noted, have power, not only Vedic *mantras*.

The Vedic *mantras* do good to all creatures in this world and the hereafter: we must have implicit faith in this belief. It is not proper to ask whether what we ourselves cannot hear with our ears will be heard by the seers. There is such a thing as the divine power of seeing and hearing. Our sight is dependent on the lens in our eyes. Were this lens different what we observe would also be different. Through the intense practice of yoga we can obtain the divine power of seeing and hearing.

Rituals

In our present state of immaturity it is not possible to think of the world being unreal.

Recognizing this, the Vedas provide us the rituals to be performed for happiness in this world. Because of our inadequacies we are unable to devote ourselves to a formless *Paramātman* from whom we are not different. So the Vedas have devised a system in which a number of deities are worshipped. But, in course of time, as we perform the rituals and worship the deities, we must make efforts to advance to the state of wisdom and enlightenment in which the world will be seen to be unreal and the rites will become unnecessary. Instead of worshipping many deities, we must reach the state in which we will recognize that we have no existence other than that of our being dissolved in the *Paramātman*. We must perform Vedic sacraments with the knowledge that they prepare us to go to this high state by making our mind pure and one-pointed.

If we perform rituals with the sole idea of worldly happiness and carry on trade with the celestials by conducting sacrifices (offering them oblations and receiving benefits from them in return), we will never come face to face with the Truth. Even if we go to the world of the celestials, we will not be blessed with Self-realization. Our residence in paradise is commensurate with the merit we earn here and is not permanent. Sooner or later we will have to return to this world and be in the womb of a mother. The ritual worship and other sacraments of the Vedas are to some extent the result of making an adjustment to our present immature state of mind. But their real purpose is to take us forward gradually from this very immature state and illumine us within. It would be wrong to refuse to go beyond the stage of ritual worship.

If one has to qualify for the B.A. degree one has to begin at the beginning—one has to progress from the first standard all the way to the degree course. One cannot naturally join the B.A. class without qualifying for it. At the same time, is it not absurd to remain all the time as a failure in the first standard itself? Graduating to the Upanishads without being prepared for them through the performance of Vedic rites is a greater offence than failure to go along the path of *jnāna* (knowledge) from that of karma (ritual action). After all, one has to go through the primary and secondary stages of education before qualifying for admission to college.

To start with, we must perform the rites prescribed by the Vedas. But in this there must be the realization that they are but steps leading us to the higher state in which we will ultimately find bliss in our Self, a state in which there will be neither rites nor duties to perform. Similarly, to start with, the deities must be worshipped but again with the conviction that such worship serves the ultimate purpose of arriving at the point where we will recognize that the worshipper and the worshipped are one. Thus, to begin with, all differences in functions must be recognized and life lived according to them. Different divisions of people have different duties, and the customs and rites assigned to each are such as to help them in the proper discharge of those duties. But in the very process of maintaining such differences there must be the conviction within that ultimately there are no differences, that all are one.

Distinctive Features of *Sanātana Dharma* (Eternal Code of Conduct)

All religions have their own philosophical and theological systems. Also all of them deal with individual life and conduct and, to a limited extent, with social life. "Look upon your neighbor as your brother." "Regard your adversary as your friend." "Treat others in the same way as you would like to be treated yourself." "Be kind to all creatures." "Speak the truth." "Practice non-violence." These injunctions and rules of conduct relate to social life up to a point—and only up to a point. To religions other than Hinduism social life or the structure of society is not a major concern. Hinduism alone has a sturdy sociological foundation, and its special feature, *varnāśrama dharma*, is an expression of it.

Varna dharma (caste system) is one concept and *āśrama dharma* (four stages of life) is another—together they make up *varnaśrama dharma. Āśrama dharma* deals with the conduct of an individual during different stages of his life. In the first stage, as a *brahmacārin* (student), he devotes himself to studies in a *gurukula* (*āśram*, or home of a guru). In the second stage, as a youth, he takes a wife, settles down in life, and begets children. In the third, as he ages further, he becomes a forest recluse and, without much attachment to worldly life, engages himself in Vedic karma. In the fourth stage, he forsakes even Vedic works, renounces the world utterly to become a *sannyāsin* (ascetic who has renounced the world) and turns his mind towards the

Paramātman. These four stages of life or *āśramas* are called *brahmacarya* (student), *garhasthya* (householder), *vānaprastha* (forest dweller) and *sannyāsa* (ascetic).

Varna dharma (caste) is an "arrangement" governing all society. It is very much a target of attack today and is usually spoken of as the division of society into *jātis* (sub-divisions of the castes). But *varna* and *jāti* are in fact different. There are only four *varnas* but the *jātis* are numerous.

Critics of *varna dharma* brand it as "a blot on our religion" and as "a vicious system which divides people into high and low". But, if you look at it impartially, you will realize that it is a unique instrument to bring about orderly and harmonious social life.

What is Expected of Brahmins

The question that now occurs is why there should be a separate caste [Brahmins] committed to Vedic learning and Vedic practices even if it is conceded that Vedic *mantras* have the power to do good. In answering this question we must first remember that the Vedas are not to be read from the written text. They have to be memorized by constant listening and repeated chanting. The learner then becomes a teacher himself and in this manner the process goes on from generation to generation. Maintaining such a tradition of learning and teaching is a whole-time occupation. Neither the teacher nor the taught may take up any other work.

We must also remember that the Brahmin is expected to master subjects other than the Vedas also, like the arts and crafts and the various sciences. He has in fact to learn the vocations of other *jātis* (sub-divisions of castes)—but he must not take up any for his own livelihood. It is the responsibility of the Brahmin to promote knowledge and culture. He is expected to learn the hereditary skills of all *jātis*, including the art of warfare, and pass on these skills to the respective *jātis* to help them earn their livelihood. The Brahmin's calling is learning and teaching the Vedas. According to the *śāstras* he must live in a modest dwelling, observe strict rules and vows so as to gain mastery of the *mantras.* He must eat only as much as is needed to keep body and soul together. All temptations to make money and enjoy sensual pleasures he must sternly resist. All his actions must be inspired by the spirit of sacrifice and he must pass his days sustaining the Vedic tradition and practices for the good of mankind.

A Wrong Notion about Brahmins

A wrong notion has gained currency that in the *varnaśrama* system the Brahmin enjoys more comforts than others, that he has more income, that he has to exert himself less than others.

In the order created by our *śāstras* the Brahmin has to make as much physical effort as the peasant. Since, at present, there is ignorance about the rites he has to perform, people erroneously believe that he makes others work hard and himself lazes about and enjoys himself. The Brahmin has to wake up at four in the morning and bathe in cold water, rain or shine, warm or cold. Then, without a break, he has to perform one rite after another and one of the twenty-one sacrifices. If you sit before the sacrificial fire for four days you will realize how difficult it is with all the heat and smoke. How many are the vows and fasts that the Brahmin has to keep and how many are the ritual baths.

Other castes do not have to go through such hardships. A Brahmin cannot eat "cold rice" in the morning like a peasant—he has no "right" to it. The *Dharmaśāstras* are not created for his convenience or benefit, nor to ensure that he has a comfortable life. He would not have otherwise imposed on himself the performance of so many rites and a life of such rigorous discipline. When he has his daytime meal it will be 1 or 2. (On the day of certain prescribed rites it will be 3 or 4.) This is the time the peasant will have his rest after his meal under a tree out in the field where he works. And the Brahmin's meal, mind you, is as simple as the peasant's. There is no difference between the humble dwelling of the peasant and that of the Brahmin. Both alike wear cotton. The peasant may save money for the future but not the Brahmin. He has no right either to borrow money or to live in style.

If daytime is divided into eight parts, the Brahmin may have his food only in the fifth or sixth part after performing all his rites. Before that he has neither any breakfast nor any snacks. And what does he eat? Not any rich food, no sweets like almonds crushed in sweetened milk. The Brahmin eats leafy vegetables growing on the banks of rivers, such areas being no one's property. Why is he asked to live by the riverside? It is for his frequent baths and for the leafy vegetables growing free there and for which he does not have to beg. He should not borrow money because if he developed the habit of borrowing he would be tempted to lead a life of luxury. Poverty and non-acquisitiveness (*aparigraha*) are his ideals. A Brahmin ought not to keep even a blade of grass in excess of his needs.

A Brahmin must not leave his birthplace and settle elsewhere. Honor or dishonor, profit or loss, he must live in his birthplace practicing his *dharma*. Nowadays, for the sake of money, people settle in England or America abandoning their motherland and their traditional way of life—and they are proud of it. Such a practice is condemned severely by the *śāstras*.

If all castes worked hard and lived a simple life there would be no ill-will among people and there would then be no cry that caste must be done away with. One reason for the "reformist view" is that today one caste is well to-do and comfortable while another is poor and has to toil. Simplicity and hard work bring satisfaction and inward purity. Such a state of simple and happy life prevailed in our country for a thousand, ten thousand years.

I said that in these days vocations are not chosen on the basis of a man's qualities or natural inclinations. The only considerations are income and comforts. All people are on the lookout for all kinds of jobs and this has resulted in increasing rivalry and jealousy, not to speak of growing unemployment.

In the beginning, when vocations were determined on the basis of birth, everyone developed an aptitude for the work allotted to him as well as the capacity to learn it easily. This is no longer the case now. In the past a man's vocation was like a paternal legacy and he was naturally very proficient. Now there is universal inefficiency and incompetence.

The Fourth *Varna* (*Sūdras*) has its Own Advantages

The *dharma* of the fourth *varna* (*Sūdras*) involves much physical exertion and effort in its practice. Outwardly it may seem that its members do not enjoy the same status and comforts as others do. But we must note that they are comparatively free from the discipline and rituals to which the rest are tied down. In the past, they knew more contentment than the other castes, living as they did by the side of the Lord. Vyāsa himself says: "The age of *Kali* is in no way inferior to the other ages nor are *Śūdras* inferior to the other castes. *Kali* is indeed elevated and *Śūdras* exalted."[1] In other *yugas* or ages Bhagavān is attained to (Self-realization) with difficulty by meditation, austerities, and *pūjā*, but in *Kali* He is reached by the mere singing of His names. The Brahmin, the *Kshatriya,* and the *Vaiśya* are likely to have self-pride, so they cannot earn Ātmic liberation easily. The Brahmin is likely to be vain about his intellectual superiority, the

[1] "*Kalih sādhuh, Śūdrah sādhuh.*"

Kshatriya about his power as a ruler, and the *Vaiśya* about his wealth. So these three *varnas* will tend to stray from the path of *dharma*. A member of the fourth *varna*, on the contrary, is humble.

If a *Śūdra* does not have enough food to fill his belly, if he does not have enough clothing, and if he has no roof over his head to shelter him from rain and sun, the whole community and the government must be held responsible—and both must be held guilty.

I repeat that the Brahmin's means of livelihood was in no way better than the *Sūdra's*, nor did he enjoy more comforts than members of the fourth *varna*.

Why Not All Rites for All?

Various rites are common to all *varnas* (castes). Only Brahmins (priestly caste), *Kshatriyas* (warrior caste), and *Vaiśyas* (merchant caste) have the *upanayana* ceremony. There is nothing discriminatory about this nor need there be any quarrel over the same. People belonging to the fourth *varna* (*Sūdras*) do physical work to serve the world and in the process acquire inner purity. They will gain proficiency in their hereditary vocations only by learning them from their parents or grandparents. They do not require *gurukulavāsa* (study at the home of the guru) over some twelve years nor do they have to learn the Vedas. If they do so their work will suffer.

Upanayana is the first step taken towards *gurukulavāsa*. When a boy learns the Vedas he must have no ego-feeling. At home he has a lot of freedom. His father will not be able to discipline him because his affection will come in the way. That is why the child is to be brought under the care of a guru. Vocations that require physical effort are different from the pursuit of the Vedas. There is no room for intellectual arrogance in them or for the nursing of the ego. So such work may be taught at home by the father or some other elder in the family.

Those who serve by doing manual work do not require to go through *upanayana* or *gurukulavāsa*. Certain special skills or the finer aspects of an art or craft that *cannot* be taught at home may be learned from a Brahmin teacher. The Brahmin is expected to be proficient in all arts, all subjects, but none of these is meant to be a source of his livelihood. His vocation is teaching and the chanting of the Vedas and the performance of Vedic rites.

There is a relationship between the *rites* prescribed for a man and his vocation and mental outlook. So it would be wrong to think poorly of certain *varnas* who do not have to perform certain *rites*. You may think it strange, but it is my view that it is those who have to undergo more *rites* than others that must have been thought of poorly. The idea is that these people need more rites to be rendered pure. Others are not in need of so many to be cleansed within. The larger the dose of medicine taken by a patient the greater must be his affliction.

None excels the sages in impartiality. They do not talk glibly like us of equality but they are truly egalitarian in outlook since they look upon all as one with *Īśvara*. The conduct of the world's affairs is such that it requires people following different vocations, doing different jobs, and with different mental qualities in keeping with them. It is in conformity with these differences and dissimilarities that the sages assigned the *rites* also differently to different people. There is no question of high or low among them.

Upanayana (Leading a Child to the Guru)

The *upanayana* of a boy is performed when he is old enough to understand things and to chant the *mantras*. During this ceremony he is asked to go begging for alms. "Bādham", he replies ("I will do so"). So, before his *upanayana*, the child must know enough Sanskrit to understand the meaning. When he starts learning at the age of five he will have a basic knowledge of Sanskrit by the time he is eight years old, the age fixed for the *upanayana samskāra.*

The world will stand to gain if eight-year old children wear the sacred thread, have sufficient knowledge of Sanskrit, and chant the *Gāyatrī mantra* (a *mantra* regarded as the essence of the Vedas). Today things have so changed that godlessness is thrust into tender minds.

Upa = near; *nayana* = to take or lead (a child). Near whom or what is (the child) taken? Near the guru. That is what *upanayana* means. Who is a guru? One who has mastered the Vedas. There is one guru during the *brahmacaryāśrama* (student-bachelorhood) and another during the last *āśrama* of *sannyāsa.* The first guru is learned in the Vedas, while the second is one who has forsaken all including the Vedas. In the first *āśrama* you acquire *vidyā* (learning); in the last *āśrama* you realize *jnāna* (knowledge).

Upanayana is initiation into the *brahmacaryāśrama* while *samāvartana* is the completion of this stage of life. *Samāvartana* means "return". To repeat, from the *upanayana* to the *samāvartana* is student-bachelorhood or *brahmacaryāśrama. Samāvartana* thus denotes returning home on completing one's study of the Vedic discipline in the *gurukula.*

An entire *āśrama* or stage in life is set apart for the study of the Vedas: this is *brahmacarya.* The minimum period for student-bachelorhood is twelve years which is the time taken to master the Vedas.

Qualities of a *Brahmacārin* (Student-Bachelor)

Brahmacarya implies adherence to a number of rules with regard to food, the performance of rites, and the observance of religious acts of devotion. If a *brahmacārin* makes any mistake in chanting the Vedas, in the matter of tone or renunciation, he must do penance.

At mealtime the student can have his fill. The only restriction is that he must not give free rein to his appetite. He must beg for his food for such a practice makes him humble. The *śāstras* do not require him to fast. The student must be nourished properly during his growing years. But he must, at the same time, learn to develop pure and virtuous qualities and there must be nothing rude or rough about him. It is by serving his guru that these qualities are inculcated in him.

During the twelve years in the *gurukula* the student must learn his recension of the Vedas. On completion of his stay in the *gurukula* he performs the *samāvartana,* returns home and marries.

What About Women?

I said that the twice-born must perform *sandhyāvandana* with the well-being of women and other *jātis* in mind. I also explained why all *rites* are not prescribed for the fourth *varna* (*Sūdras*—manual laborers). Now we must consider the question of women, why they do not have such rituals and *rites.*

Even though we perform the certain ceremonies, including naming ceremonies, for new-born girls and celebrate their first birthday, we do not conduct their *upanayana* nor the other *rites* or vows laid down for *brahmacārins.* Of course, they have the marriage *samskāra.* But in other rites like sacrifices the main part is that of the husband, though she (the wife) has to be by his side. In *aupāsana* (daily rites with the sacrificial fire) alone does a woman have a part in making oblations in the sacred fire.

Why is it so? What reason did I mention for the fourth *varna* not having to perform many of the *rites*? That these were not necessary considering their vocations and the fact that they can work for the welfare of the world without the physical and mental benefits to be derived from the *rites*. If they also spend their time in Vedic learning and in sacrifices, what will happen to their duties? So most of the *rites* are not necessary for them. They reach the desired goal without these rites by carrying out their duties.

Just as society is divided according to occupations and the *rites* are correspondingly different, so too there are differences between men and women in domestic life. Running a household means different types of work, cooking, keeping the house clean, bringing up the children, etc. By nature women can do these chores better than men. If they also take an active part in rituals, what will happen to such work? Each, by serving her husband and by looking after her household, becomes inwardly pure.

In truth there is no disparity between men and women, nor are women discriminated against as present-day reformers allege. Work is divided for the proper maintenance not only of the home but the nation on the whole; and care has been taken not to have any duplication. There is no intention of lowering the status of any section in this division of labor.

The High Status of Our Women

Those who complain that women have no right to perform sacrifices on their own must remember that men too have no right to the same without a wife. If they knew this truth they would not make the allegation that Hindu *śāstras* look down upon women. A man can perform sacrifices only with his wife. He does them for the well-being of all mankind and for his own inner purity. It is for this purpose that, after the *samāvartana* (return) following the completion of his student-bachelorhood, he goes through the *samskāra* called marriage.

Marriage is known as *saha-dharma-cārinīsamprayoga*. It means (roughly) union with a wife together with whom a man practices *dharma*. The clear implication is that carnal pleasure is not its chief purpose, but the pursuit of *dharma*. The *śāstras* do not ask a man to pursue *dharma* all by himself but require him to take a helpmate for it. The wife is called *dharma-patnī* (*dharma* partner), thus underlining her connection with *dharma*, and not with *kāma* or sensual pleasure. Here is proof of the high esteem in which the *śāstras* hold women.

The celibate-student and the ascetic alike follow the *dharma* of their respective *āśramas* (stages of life) not in association with anyone else. The householder has to conduct the karma as well as the *dharma* of domestic life with his wife as a companion, such being the rule laid down in the *śāstras*. The *dharma* of domestic life is their common property. Only a householder with a wife may perform sacrifices, not student-bachelors and ascetics. If the wife were meant only for sensual gratification, would the *Dharmaśāstras* have insisted that a man cannot perform sacrifices after her death? Women's libbers, who note that a woman cannot perform a sacrifice on her own, must also recognize the fact that the husband loses the right for the same without the wife and this is according to the Vedas themselves.[2] A great man lamented thus at the time of his wife's death: "You have taken away all my sacrifices as well as other rituals."

Our *śāstras* have thus given a high place to women in the matter of duties and works.

Aupāsana (Daily Rites with Sacrificial Fire) and Women

I said [in an earlier talk] that members of all castes must perform *aupāsana* (daily rites with sacrificial fire). The husband and wife must do it together. Even when the husband is away the wife must perform it by offering unbroken rice grains in the sacrificial fire. The Vedas

[2] "*Patnīvatasya Agnihotram bhavati.*"

themselves have given women such a right. We hear people talk of "rights". It is my wish to create an awareness among women about their right, the right to *aupāsana.* I should like every home to become bright with the sacred *aupāsana* fire. Women should fight for this right of theirs and impress upon their husbands the importance of performing *aupāsana.* Women must make their husbands perform *aupāsana. Aupāsana* is indeed their one great Vedic "property". Like *aupāsana, agnihotra* (fire sacrifice) must also be performed twice a day and must be performed with both husband and wife.

Marriage is conducted with offerings made in the fire, is it not? *Aupāsana*, which must be performed every day, is commenced in this fire and it must be preserved throughout one's life. [Many rites] must be conducted in the *aupāsana* fire. The son lights his *aupāsana* fire during his marriage from his father's *aupāsana* fire. The son's *aupāsana* fire, like his father's, must be maintained throughout his life. Thus, without any break, the sacred fire is kept burning in the family generation after generation.

The Conflict between Tradition and Modernity

Politicians and intellectuals alike say that *varna* (caste) is part of an uncivilized system. Why? Who is responsible for the disintegration of so worthy an arrangement as *varna dharma*?

These are questions that I raised earlier and I shall try to answer them. The wrong ideas that have developed about *varna dharma* must be ascribed to the Brahmins themselves. They are indeed responsible for the decay of an ages-old system that contributed not only to our Ātmic advancement (progress toward Self-realization) but also to the well-being of the nation as well as of all mankind.

The Brahmin relinquished the duties of his birth—the study of the Vedas and performance of the rites laid down in the Vedic tradition. He left his birthplace, the village, for the town. He cropped his hair and started dressing in European style. Giving up the Vedas, he took to the mundane learning of the West. He fell to the lure of jobs offered by his white master and aped him in dress, manners, and attitudes. He threw to the winds the noble *dharma* he had inherited from the Vedic seers through his forefathers and abandoned all for a mess of pottage. He was drawn to everything Western, science, life-style, entertainment.

The canonical texts have it that the Brahmin must have no love for money, that he must not accumulate wealth. So long as he followed his *dharma*, as prescribed by the *śāstras*, and so long as he chanted the Vedas and performed sacrifices, he brought good to the world, and all other castes respected him and treated him with affection.

Others now observed how the Brahmin had changed, how his life-style had become different with all its glitter and show and how he went about with all the pretence of having risen on the scale of civilization. The Brahmin had been an ideal for them in all that is noble, but now he strayed from the path of *dharma*; and following his example they too gave up their traditional vocations that had brought them happiness and contentment and left their native village to settle in towns. Like the Brahmin they became keen to learn English and secure jobs in the government.

A question that arises in this context is how Vedic studies which had not suffered much even during Muslim rule received a severe setback with the advent of the European. One reason is the impact of the new sciences and the machines that came with the white man. Granted that many a truth was revealed through these sciences—and this was all to the good up to a point. But we must remember that the knowledge of a subject per se is one thing and how we use it in practice is another.

The introduction of steam power and electricity made many types of work easier but it also meant comforts hitherto unthought-of to gratify the senses. If you keep pandering to the senses more and more new desires are engendered. This will mean the production of an increasing number of objects of pleasure. The more we try to obtain sensual pleasure the more we will cause injury to our innermost being. The new pleasures that could be had with scientific development and the introduction of machines were an irresistible lure for the Brahmin as they were to other communities. Another undesirable product of the sciences brought by the white man was rationalism which undermined people's faith in religion and persuaded some to believe that the religious truths that are based on faith and are inwardly experienced are nothing but deception. The man who did not give up his duties even during Muslim rule now abandoned them for the new-found pleasures and comforts. He dressed more smartly than the Englishman, smoked cigarettes, and even learned to dance like his white master. Those who thus became proficient in the arts of the white man were rewarded with jobs.

Now occurred the biggest tragedy. Up till now all members of society had their hereditary jobs to do and they did not have to worry about their livelihood. Now, with the example of the Brahmin before them, members of other castes also gave up their traditional occupations for the jobs made available by the British in the banks, railways, collectorates, etc. With the introduction of machinery our handicrafts fell into decay and many of our artisans had to look for other means of livelihood. In the absence of any demarcation in the matter of work and workers, there arose competition for jobs for the first time in the country. It was a disastrous development and it generated jealousy, ill-will, disputes, and a host of other evils among people who had hitherto lived in harmony.

Ill feelings developed between Brahmins and non-Brahmins also. How? Brahmins formed only a small percentage of the population. But they were able to occupy top positions in the new order owing to their intelligence which was the result of the spiritual efforts of their forefathers. They excelled in all walks of life—in administration, in academics, in law, in medicine, engineering, and so on. The white man made his own calculations about developing animosity between Brahmins and non-Brahmins and realized that by fuelling it he could strengthen his hold on the country. He fabricated the Aryan-Dravidian theory of races and the seeds of differences were sown among children born of the same mother. It was a design that proved effective in a climate already made unhealthy by rivalry for jobs.

The Brahmin spoiled himself and spoiled others. By abandoning his *dharma* he became a bad example to others. Now, after he had divested himself of his *dharma*, there was nothing to give him distinction, to mark him out from others. As a matter of fact, even by strictly adhering to his *dharma* the Brahmin is not entitled to feel superior to others. He must always remain humble in the belief that "everyone performs a function in society; I perform mine". If at all, others respected him in the past and accorded him a high place in society, it was in consideration of his selfless work, his life of austerity, discipline, and purity.

Now he had descended to such depths as to merit their most abrasive criticism. Is it not better then to starve and yet be attached firmly to our *dharma* so long as there is breath in us? Is not such loyalty to our *dharma* a matter of pride? Why should we care about how others see us, whether they honor us or speak ill of us? So long as we do not compete with them for jobs they will have no cause for jealousy or resentment. Let them call us backward or stupid or think that we are not capable of keeping abreast of the times. Are we not now already their butt of ridicule? Let us be true to our *dharma* in the face of the mockery of others, even in the face of death. Is not such a lot preferable to suffering the slings of scorn and criticism earned by forsaking our *dharma* for the sake of filling our belly? People nowadays die for their motherland; they lay down their lives for their mother tongue. Was there any demonstration of faith like this, such willingness to die for a cause or a belief, when the British came here with their life-style? At that time did we protect our *dharma* with courage, in the belief that even death was a small price to pay for it?

The Lord himself has declared in the Gītā that it is better to die abiding by one's *dharma* than prosper through another man's *dharma.* Brahmins who had seen no reason to change their life-style during the long Muslim period of our history changed it during British rule. Why? New sciences and machinery came with the white man. The motor car and electricity had their own impact on life here. Brahmins were drawn to comforts and conveniences not thought of before. This could be a reason for their change of life, but not a justification.

The Brahmin is not to regard his body as a means for the enjoyment of sensual pleasures but as an instrument for the observance of such rites as are necessary to protect the Vedas—and the Vedas have to be protected for the welfare of mankind. The basic *dharma* is that to the body of the Brahmin nothing must be added that incites his sensual appetite. It was a fundamental mistake on the part of the Brahmin to have forgotten the spirit of sacrifice that imbues his *dharma* and become a victim of the pleasures and comforts easily obtained from the new gadgets and instruments. There is pride in adhering to one's *dharma* even when one is faced with adverse circumstances. Brahmins (during British rule) committed a grave mistake by not doing so and we are suffering the consequences. See the ill-will in the country today among children of the same mother. We have created suffering for others also. At first Brahmins were denied admission to colleges and refused jobs. Now things have come to such a pass that other communities also suffer the same fate.

All was well so long as man, using his own innate resources, lived a simple life without the help of machines. With more and more factories and increasing machine power, life itself has become complicated. The situation today is such that everyone is facing difficulties in getting admission to college or in getting a job.

People ask me: "What is the remedy today? Do you expect all Brahmins to leave their new life-style and return to Vedic learning?" Whether or not I expect them to do so and whether or not such a step seems possible, I must ask them to do so (to return to their Vedic *dharma*). Where is the need for a *gurupītha* (*āśram*) or a seat on which an *ācārya* (great teacher) is installed if I am to keep my mouth shut and watch idly as the *dharma* that is the source of everything is being endangered? Even if it seems not possible (Brahmins returning to the *dharma* of their birth) it must be shown to be possible in practice: that is the purpose of the *āśrams.* They must harness all their energies towards the attainment of this goal.

The Least Expected of Brahmins

This is the least Brahmins can do to preserve the Vedic traditions. Arrangements to impart Vedic learning to children must be made in every Brahmin household. I know that there are not enough teachers, a sad reflection on the state of our *dharma.* Considering this and the likely economic condition of parents I would suggest that Veda classes may be conducted for all children together of a locality or neighborhood. Children of poor families may be taught on a cooperative basis.

Step by step in this way the boys will be able to memorize the *mantra* part of the Vedas and also learn how to conduct rites like *upākarma* (first step for a young boy to become a Vedic student). I speak here about *prayoga*, the conduct or procedure of rites, because in the absence of priests in the future everyone should be able to perform Vedic rites himself.

The sound of the Vedas must pervade the world for all time to come. Everyone must sincerely work towards achieving this end. It is your duty to ensure the good not only of the Brahmin community, not only of all the castes of India, but of all the countless creatures of earth. It is a duty imposed on you by *Īśvara*—it is a divine duty.

It is important that we perform this duty we owe to the people of the present. But it is equally important that we perform it so as to be saved from committing a crime against future generations. "As it is nobody cares for the Vedas," you are likely to tell me. "Who is going to care for them in the coming years? What purpose is served by all the efforts we take now to keep up their study?" I do not share this view. When the wheel keeps turning, that part of it which is now down has necessarily to come up. Modern civilization with its frenzied pace is bound to have its fall after attaining its peak. We have been carried away by the supposed comforts made possible by advanced technology. But one day we will realize that they do not give us any feeling of fullness and that we have indeed created only discomforts for ourselves through them.

Divided by Work but Still of One Heart

Any society has to depend on the proper execution of a variety of jobs. It is from this social necessity that the concept of division of labor arose. But who is to decide the number of people for each type of work? Who is to determine the proportions for society to function in a balanced manner? In the West they had no answer to these questions. Everybody there competes with everybody else for comfortable jobs and everywhere you find greed and bitterness resulting from such rivalries. And, as a consequence of all this, there are lapses from discipline and morality.

In our country we based the division of labor on a hereditary system and, while it worked, people had a happy, peaceful, and contented life. Today even a multimillionaire is neither contented nor happy. Then even a cobbler led a life without cares. What sort of progress have we achieved today by inflaming evil desires in all hearts and pushing everyone into the slough of discontent? Not satisfied with such "progress" there is talk everywhere that we must go forward rapidly in this manner.

Greed and covetousness were unknown during the centuries when *varna dharma* flourished. People were bound together in small well-knit groups and they discovered that there was happiness in their being together. Besides they had faith in religion, fear of God and devotion, and a feeling of pride in their own family deities and in the modes of worshipping them. In this way they found fullness in their lives without any need to suffer the hunger and disquiet of seeking external objects. All society experienced a sense of well-being.

One more point must be considered. Even if you concede that the social divisions have caused bitterness among the different sections here, what about the same in other countries? Can the existence of such ill-will in other lands be denied? The differences there, based on wealth and status, cause bitterness and resentment among the underprivileged and poorer sections. In America, it is claimed that all people have enough food, clothing, and housing. They say that even a domestic servant there owns a car. It is reasonable to infer from this that the Americans are a contented people. But what is the reality there? The man who has only one car is envious of another who has two. Similarly, the fact that one person has a bank balance of a hundred million dollars is cause for heart-burning for another with a bank balance of only a million. Those who have sufficient means to live comfortably quarrel with people better off over rights and privileges. Does this not mean that even in a country like the United States there are conflicts between the higher and lower classes of society?

It seems to me that better than the distinctions prevailing in the West—distinctions that give rise to jealousies and social discord—are the differences mistakenly attributed to the hereditary system of vocations. In the old days this arrangement ensured peace in the land with everyone living a contented life. There was neither envy nor hatred and everyone readily accepted his lot.

Divided we have remained united, and nurtured our civilization. Other civilizations have gone under because the people of the countries concerned, though seemingly united, were in fact divided. In our case, though there were differences in the matter of work, there was unity of hearts and that is how our culture and civilization flourished. In other countries the fact that there were no distinctions based on vocations (anyone could do any work) itself gave rise to rivalries and eventually to disunity. They were not able to withstand the onslaught of other civilizations.

It is not practicable to make all people one, nor can everyone occupy the same high position. At the same time it is also unwise to keep people divided into classes that are like water-tight compartments. The *Dharmaśāstras* (scriptures on *dharma*) have shown us a middle way that avoids the pitfalls of the two extremes. I have come as a representative of this way and that is why I speak for it: that there ought to be distinctions among various sections of people in the performance of rites but that there must be unity of hearts. There should be no confusion between the two.

Though we are divided outwardly in the matter of work, with unity of hearts there will be peace. That was the tradition for ages together in this land—there was oneness of hearts. If every member of society does his duty, does his work, unselfishly and with the conviction that he is doing it for the good of all, considerations of high and low will not enter his mind. If people carry out the duties common to them, however adverse the circumstances be, and if every individual performs the duties that are special to him, no one will have cause for suffering at any time.

Religion and Society

If our goal were but a comfortable and happy life in this world, matters concerning social life could be changed now and again. But ours is an exalted goal and it concerns the Self. The rules of worldly life are in keeping with this high purpose and they cannot be changed according to our convenience. The *śāstras* (scriptures) do not regard happiness in this world as of paramount importance. They teach us how we may experience joy in the other world even by suffering many kinds of hardships or discomforts here. So it is not right to seek changes in them to suit our worldly existence.

The views of the reformers must have been shaped by our present system of education and so it is no use blaming them. In other countries no contradiction exists between their religion and their system of education. Unfortunately, the schools established by the British in India had nothing to do with our religion. People were compelled to take to Western education for the sake of their livelihood. Soon a situation arose in which they came to be steeped from childhood itself in an alien system of instruction. They had therefore no way of developing acquaintance with, or faith in, our ancient *śāstras*. And, since they were kept ignorant of their scriptures and their underlying purpose, they persuaded themselves to take the view that the *śāstras* could be changed according to their convenience.

Our youngsters are exposed to criticism of our religion and our sacred texts from a tender age. They are told that the *Purāṇās* (traditional stories) are a tissue of lies, that the *śāstras* help the growth of superstition. How can they have any attachment to our faith, to its rites, and traditions?

Faith in religion and God must be inculcated in people from their childhood. They must get to know about great men who lived and continue to live an exemplary life true to the tenets of our religion. Faith in the works of the seers must be instilled in them, works based on the experience of the seers themselves, experience beyond a life of sensation, and pointing the way to spiritual uplift. They must also be helped to believe that the *risis* (seers) formulated the *śāstras* in such a way as to make worldly happiness and social life subservient to the advancement of the Self. Only then will people recognize that the rules of religion have a far higher purpose than the comforts and conveniences of temporal life.

The Basic Texts of Hinduism: Our Ignorance of Them

Our education follows the Western pattern. We want to speak like the white man, dress like him and ape him n the matter of manners and customs. We remain so even after our having won independence. In fact, though we keep speaking all the time about our culture, about *svadeśī* [Gandhi's philosophy that it is a person's duty to patronize indigenous goods] and so on, we are today more Westernized than before. Religion has been the backbone of our nation's life from time immemorial. If we wish to remain *svadeśī*, both inwardly and outwardly, we must receive religious instruction from childhood itself. The secular state is of no help in this matter because, in the secular set-up, education continues to be imparted to our children on the Western pattern and the children are taught that our *sastras* are all superstition. The result is that most of us do not know what the sacred text is that is common to all Hindus.

Our religious texts must be taught early in life. When a child grows up and goes to college, he believes his studies will perhaps prove useful to him. If he reads for a B.L. or LL.B. degree, it is to become a lawyer. Similarly, if he reads for an L.T. (or B.Ed.) degree or an M.B.B.S., it is to become a teacher or a doctor. If you ask a teenager to study our religious texts, he would retort: "Why should I learn them? How will it help me in my career?" So religious texts should be taught in childhood, that is, before the youngster is old enough to question you about their utility or harbor doubts about the texts. Only then will he develop an interest in our religion and *śāstras.* Do we pay our children for their being interested in sports, music, or cinema? Similarly, they must be made to take an interest in religion also and such interest must be created in the same way as in sports and entertainment. If children take to sports and entertainment which afford only temporary pleasure, they are bound to take to religion which will confer on them everlasting happiness. The present sorry state of affairs is due to our basic education being flawed.

Today we have come to such a state that people ask whether knowledge of religion is of help in their upkeep. This is a matter of shame. The *śāstras* admonish: "Do not ask whether Vedic education will provide you with food. We eat and live but to learn the Vedas." Your approach must be based on this principle. Today, a child born in a faith which has such high ideals is cut off from all opportunities of religious instruction at his very birth. Our concern is imparting worldly knowledge from the very start. Our children must be brought up properly and faith in God inculcated in them early in life.

My Work

It does not matter if you are unable to create conditions in which Brahmins henceforth will make the pursuit of the Vedic *dharma* their lifelong vocation. All I ask you is the minimum you can do: make arrangements to impart to your children the Vedic *mantras*, to teach them the scripture for at least one hour a day from the time they are eight years old until they are eighteen. Teach them also the *prayoga* (the conduct of rites). Do this on a cooperative basis in each locality. If you succeed in this you will have truly honored me with a shower of gold coins.

It gives me joy that more and more *bhajans* (sacred singing ceremonies) are conducted in the towns than before, that work connected with temples is on the increase, and that purānic discourses (discourses on traditional stories) are given more often than before. But we must remember that the Vedas constitute the basis of all these. If our scripture suffers a decline, how long will the activities based on it survive? The Vedas must be handed down from father to son, from one generation to the next. It is because we have forgotten this tradition that our religion itself has become shaky. All the trouble in the world, all the suffering and all the evil must be attributed to the fact that the Brahmin has forsaken his *dharma*, the Vedic *dharma*.

I am not worried about the system of *varnas* being destroyed, but I am worried about the setback to the welfare of mankind. I am also extremely concerned about the fact that, if the Vedic tradition which has been maintained like a chain from generation to generation is broken, it may not be possible to create the tradition all over again.

The good arising in a subtle form from the sound of the Vedas and the performance of sacrifices is not the only benefit that constitutes the welfare of mankind. From *Vedānta* are derived lofty truths that can bring Ātmic uplift to people belonging to all countries.

Education in the Borderlands of Tibet

Marco Pallis

I now turn to the discussion of a practical problem, that of modern education, as it affects the peoples living on the borders of Tibet. We had ample opportunities for considering this question during our stay at Kalimpong and Gangtok,[1] for standing as they do on the frontiers of modernity and of the last traditional civilization left substantially intact in the world, they offer an ideal field for the investigator who wishes to observe the inter-reactions of these two forces. Independent Tibet is the only country where some measure of consistent and conscious opposition continues to be offered in the face of the leveling tendencies of Pan-Occidentalism. In India, where there has also been some resistance, there is so much lost ground to make good that the final outcome is as yet impossible to forecast. There was a day when Japan hoped to remain like a second Tibet; but in her case, though the will was there, the menace of the guns of the squadron under the American Commodore Perry in 1854 forcibly opened her ports. Many people now living would give much to undo that chapter of history and to see their dangerous commercial and political rivals safely back in the refined inoffensiveness of their feudal ages.

Tibet has been favored by the remoteness of her geographical position and by the possession of a mountain barrier so impenetrable, that she has found it possible to persevere in a policy denied to her larger and more powerful neighbors. Physical obstacles alone, however, would hardly have been sufficient to protect Tibet's isolation—nowadays engineers, given money and adequate time, might even force a way to the top of Everest—but Heaven, in its mercy, was pleased to make a great part of Tibet stony, sterile, and unattractive to lovers of comfort. A heart-straining altitude and the biting winds of the plateau have proved to be gifts more enviable than the fertility and kinder weather of temperate climes.

This central area of Tibet acts therefore as a preserving-ground for a society constituted on traditional lines, in the middle of a world which has thought that it could dispense with the traditional safeguards and which, when not actively hostile towards the ancient institutions, regards them with contemptuous indifference, dubbing them picturesque anachronisms. This epithet fits, if it is to be taken as merely meaning a minority carrying on in the old ways, when the majority of men, for reasons valid or unsound, have discarded them: but the word normally carries with it some additional notion of censure leveled at the discarded institutions, and an implication that those things which have been abandoned by the majority as useless, have been rightly so abandoned and that the minority, in striving to row against the tide, is simply showing a retrograde tendency.

The late eighteenth and nineteenth centuries invested the word "Progress" with sentimental attributes, picturing it as a continuous straight track along which humanity, with occasional unfortunate deviations, was fated to move steadily forward towards Utopia. The spectacular victory of the Evolutionary hypothesis invested the new theory, in the eyes of the populace, with the same categorical authority that had previously been accorded to the old beliefs which it superseded. In its later developments, especially in the theory of Natural Selection, which Darwin had presented as no more than a blind force that was helping to mold the living world, Evolution began to acquire moral, or rather moralistic, attributes. It was supposed that whatever

[1] Editor's Note: the author made these travels in 1936.

was exterminated by something else, showed, by its very weakness, that it was inferior to its destroyer and that its disappearance was required by the service of the new juggernaut of Progress. It might just as well have been argued, when some epidemic carried off men in their prime, including eminent doctors engaged in fighting the plague, that the bacilli must enjoy a "higher" civilization than the scientists and athletes who fell victims to their attack, and that the germs deserved their victory in a moral sense.

Lest my readers should think that this suggestion is too far-fetched I quote a writer who in the year 1935 declared that: "An attack by poisonous gas is another form of the effect of environment to secure the survival of the fittest and the elimination of decadent and unworthy persons and races."

It is at least comforting to be assured that the gas will know how to select its victims and will pass over the brave, the gifted and the healthy, even as the Angel of the Lord passed over the houses of the Israelites in the land of Egypt—this is Selection indeed![2]

It can readily be seen how convenient such theories must have proved, when they first came into vogue, in furnishing excuses for every brutal act of brigandage, political or commercial. They seemed to set the seal of Nature's approval on the sordid tale of grab and exploitation. The victims were beaten, therefore their defeat was a just defeat, their loss a public gain. These dogmas—for theories soon harden into convictions—form the darker side of nineteenth-century liberalism; at the time of their general acceptance, they were acclaimed as the most epoch-making discoveries, the scientific Charter, legalizing the subjection of the weak and lowly to Nature's own strong men. More tender consciences consoled themselves with the pious thought that the Almighty had given them a commission to govern all "inferior" or "native" peoples for their own good; they even went so far as to dress up this duty in the garb of self-sacrifice, as expressed in the famous phrase "The White Man's Burden," surely the most smug and hypocritical that has ever passed human lips. Humane evolutionists, such as Kropotkin, protested against this travesty of biological theories, but to small purpose: the new formula was far too convenient in providing the desired theoretical basis for the working alliance between the two dominant forces of Puritanism and predatory commercialism. The former contributed moral self-confidence and the latter boundless material ambition and drive. In the firm of Messrs. Mammon & God Unlimited, the lawless, trader's vanity was flattered by the fancy that in pushing his conquests he was acting under Providence as the agent of Progress, while the busybody guardians of everyone else's virtue found the material rewards that accrued in the shape of social prestige and all that it brought with it, very much to their taste. Cecil Rhodes, whose outlook was much affected by semi-digested Darwinism, put the idea very neatly when he said that a guiding principle of British imperialist policy should be "philanthropy + 5 per cent."

Brawny Gospellers and empire-building adventurers, as well as the new captains of industry, stood singularly close to one another in their outlook.

The same mixture of moralizing and cupidity enters into the actions of many comparatively respectable pioneers of the period of European expansion. In England this tendency has only begun to play itself out in our lifetime. I can remember the time when the old Jingoism was still considered a respectable creed; but since then, there have been some welcome changes

[2] In fairness to the author of the above quotation it must be explained that he is not condoning the use of poison gas: his aim is to goad slack citizens into taking adequate defensive measures. My quarrel is with those who accept the popularized view of Natural Selection, and invest that hypothesis with a moral purpose.

in public and official opinion: Imperialism is forced to look round for disguises. But the world is by no means rid of the old arrogance yet: certain nations seem only too eager to inherit our discredited theories of racial superiority.

Nineteenth-century cooperation between religiosity of the "fundamentalist" type, always peculiarly untroubled by doubts, and the new commercial enterprise, flushed with the first-won victories of mechanization, brought about a concentration of forces acting in one direction such as had never been known in all previously recorded history. The Anglo-Saxon race led the vanguard of the movement and succeeded in cornering most of the places in the sun before other nations could follow suit, an initiative for which we are now paying in bitter jealousies. But most of the races of European blood, even those who did not participate directly in the colonial expansion, shared the extrovert mentality of the Empire builders. Drawn by this new focus of attention, all Western nations devoted their energies increasingly to large-scale exploitation, and in proportion as they did so, tended to approximate nearer and nearer to one model, and this in spite of the most violent national antagonisms. To the civilization which was thus produced I give the name of "Occidental," so as not to confound it with genuine European culture; though nowadays some of its most frenzied exponents are of Oriental blood. This civilization seems totally unlike any of the others of which we possess records, whether in written form or inferred from archaeological remains. One can almost go so far as to say that there is more in common between any two traditional civilizations picked at random—say Celtic and Inca, than between any one of them and that of modern times. Taking a bird's-eye view of history, would it be altogether far-fetched to speak of modern Occidental civilization as the one and only anachronism, the anachronism *par excellence*?

Among the ancients, nevertheless, there is one partial exception. The Romans seem to have tended, in some measure, towards a similar system. Among them we see the same preoccupation with the purely practical, the same harping upon ethical applications to the disregard of the intellectual side, resulting, in logical consequence, in a deification of human society in the State. It is perhaps only the fact that Post-Renaissance Europe was able, through the rapid development of Natural Science, to harness material forces on an unprecedented scale, that has caused us to leave the Romans so far behind; but their ideals, if one can give them such a name, were in many respects akin to ours and it is doubtless no accident that the so-called Renaissance, the time of the final rupture with the regular Occidental Tradition, was characterized by an uncritical enthusiasm for everything Greco-Roman and by hatred and contempt for everything non-classical. The men who saw in gothic cathedrals nothing but barbarous excrescences and who scoffed at the speculations of the Schoolmen, were the spiritual ancestors of those who affect to despise everything Oriental.

Post-war Europe has lost the comfortable sense of security of the nineteenth century; but it has not yet been able to shake off its habits; nor are there yet signs of any general abandonment of the notion of continuous Progress. If anything, the general trend is still all towards the elimination of lingering traces of tradition. Those who aspire to play the part of reformers usually look for their panacea, not in a rebirth of the genuine traditional spirit, but in a further development of the forces which liberalism brought into being, in more elaborate organization and in the division of labor carried to greater and greater extremes. The ideal proclaimed is that of a world reduced to one vast termites' nest: to this dream is attached the grandiloquent euphemism of "a pooling of the resources of humanity." But the pool has been carefully pre-engineered, so that the trickle that represents the united contribution of all the other civilizations cannot help being swamped by the drainage from the Euro-American quarter.

In Tibet and Bhutan, the only wholehearted non-cooperators in this scheme, the authority of Tradition remains unquestioned, and the more intellectually conscious classes usually profess the will to preserve it. "We feel that our institutions suit us best. Possibly your civilization suits you, though some of us think it has gone astray; but that is your affair"—this verdict sums up their attitude. But these countries are surrounded by a ring of small states, and racially allied districts which, though they still look to Lhasa for their cultural leadership, are living on the edge of two worlds, and therefore cannot escape having to face a difficult problem of adaptation, one that does not confront dwellers in the center of Tibet. Residents on the border, whether they are engaged in business or in making social contacts with those, both Indian and European, who are partly or wholly imbued with Occidentalism, find themselves called upon to handle things which would not enter into their normal environment at home—to cite a few of them: cars, newspapers, the persuasive technique of advertising, modern medicine, speed, bureaucratic organization, democracy and its catchwords; some things good, others evil, and others again neutral, able to make useful servants but bad masters.

To pick a way through this labyrinth, certain knowledge is needed, mainly in the material field. Parents realizing that their children, if they are to go on living on the borderland, must solve these problems or go under, have to decide how their minds are to be equipped for the ordeal. They find that their own education, however uplifting in a cultural sense, requires supplementing in certain branches that lie outside its normal scope. Therefore the question of education is paramount and on the method of its solution depends, to a large extent, the survival or the rapid disintegration of the culture of the frontier nations. If they also become Westernized, then the invading host, having pierced the outer ring of defenses, will batter on the gates of the inner keep of Tibet proper. Even now, the Lhasa-Kalimpong trade route, opened up by the treaty of 1904, offers one avenue by which a tentacle of the octopus can probe right into the heart of the land. Though foreigners are restricted from entering, their goods, less obviously suspect than their persons, do penetrate and serve to disseminate foreign taste. Also, Tibetans and Bhutanese who come south to trade are liable to become infected with Western influences.

Effective decisions are only possible for members of the cultured classes, those whose example is bound to be a model for the less educated, and who alone are capable of taking a long view of the situation and of influencing more simple souls, whether by precept or in a practical way, by organizing educational facilities for them on safe lines. In studying this whole problem, the first step is to analyze the early reactions of these people to Occidental contacts; nowhere can this research be carried out more conveniently than at Kalimpong and in Sikkim.

The Tibetans, like all the yellow races, are imbued with an avid passion for learning and a natural predisposition in favor of education and schools and teachers, in contrast to that half-antagonism which the Englishman often shows and which, one must admit, has sometimes saved him from falling such an easy prey to regimentation as his more obedient continental neighbors. Reverence for the teacher is a great asset provided the education offered be the right one; otherwise it is better to be a lazy and insubordinate pupil.

It cannot for a moment be maintained that the Tibetan race is devoid of education. In spite of the presence of many illiterates, the culture of the country is vigorous and consistent. The clergy, natural custodians of learning, whose adequate leisure for study is effectively provided for by the social system in vogue, includes many lettered persons, whose marvelous memories enable them to repeat whole books by heart. Even among the poor, I was surprised to find how many possessed a smattering of literacy. Higher education is almost entirely doctrinal and literary: metaphysical treatises, chronicles of saints, legends, and sacred poetry form the bulk of the reading of the laity as well as the lamas. Apart from these studies, writing a fine hand and the rudiments of reckoning complete the list. Officials, in addition, must acquire a mastery of the correct styles of address, which are often rather too flowery; if to these be added the rules of grammar and logic, the result is an education comparable to that of the Scholastics in medieval Europe.

When foreign educators came and settled in places like Kalimpong and Darjeeling, it was natural that the well-to-do should hasten to place their children in the new schools, as being the best locally available, without stopping to peer with an overcritical eye into the drawbacks, as well as the advantages, of the tuition offered, and without feeling apprehensive of any possible evil results in the distant future. These institutions are of two sorts, either missionary schools of various denominations, or secular schools, endowed by Government, or, as in Sikkim, by the native State in imitation of the schools of British India. Thus the children of parents who had themselves been brought up on strictly traditional lines, with sacred studies coming first, the art of courtesy holding second place, and secular knowledge counting third, came to be placed trustingly under the care of exponents of alien systems, actuated by motives which were either frankly hostile to the existing culture, as in the case of missions, or simply indifferent to it, as in the case of lay schools. In both, the curriculum allots a preponderant share to the knowledge of material things, which is the specialty of the West and which serves as the bait to entice pupils.

In mission schools there may or may not be direct imparting of Christian teaching; but in either case, the moral code and all sorts of undefined implications and tendencies derive from what is now commonly accepted in so-called Christian Europe. The teaching is there, even if the word "religion" is not so much as named. A person who makes no secret of his hope for the eventual substitution of Christianity for Hindu or Buddhist belief, can hardly be blamed if he shows, at least, indifference to the interests of the native culture of his pupils, inextricably interwoven as it is with the threads of metaphysical thought. In appraising the legitimate methods of implanting ideas into the minds of their young charges, some doubtless try to be nicely scrupulous, while others stretch a point here and there. In the case of a missionary teacher the more zealous he is, the further he is likely to allow himself to go in the matter of deliberately undermining the foundation laid by the parents—or not laid, as is too often the case; for in a traditionally regulated society, where everything hangs together, the environment is sufficiently strong to relieve the private individual of some of his responsibility in this matter, and to lull him into a complacent mood that does not befit the present times of crisis.

Whereas the missionary is, by his profession, inclined to regard the native beliefs as so much superstition, to the secular-minded modern teacher they appear rather in the light of primitive folklore, which education will force a person to outgrow. The man with the religious axe to grind will rush to implant his own official version of the Christian code, which is not always that of the Gospel. The secular schoolmaster will probably expound a stoical system of ethics, possibly with a faint Christian tinge. He may also blend with it a sentimental belief in the magic benefits of "the public-school spirit," which regards competition as a virtue and sees in physical activity, as expressed in organized games, an automatic power to uplift; while gentleness is slightly suspect as a sign of weakness.

There are striking differences between the things that the pupil, in the traditional scheme, would have been taught and those that he is likely to acquire in an average Westernized school, even a good one. The sacredness of life, other than human, will certainly not be overstressed, even if it is mentioned at all. The whole emphasis will be on Man and his interests, everything else will be shown as ministering to these; a very different story from the Hindu or Buddhist duty of solicitude for all suffering creatures. A good many of the teachers in high-class secular schools, specially designed for the rich and aristocratic, are keen on shooting. Therefore it cannot be expected that they will go to any special trouble to discredit that pastime in the eyes of their charges and the latter are likely to grow up to tolerate the idea. I turned up a few Hindu, and even Buddhist, names at random in the pages of *Who's Who*, and found that they nearly all had put down "Shooting" under the heading "Recreation"!

Secondly, the contemplative ideal placed before the true Oriental as the highest possible calling for a man, is dismissed by most Occidentals as equivalent to laziness. For them the great ideal is work, that is to say, visible work with measurable results. The difference of point of view is so fundamental that two educators, respective adherents of these opposing philosophies, ought not to share the same professional designation.

Thirdly, the great aim of our education at its best is the development of individuality to its utmost, just as at its worst, by the cultivation of blind *esprit de corps*, it encourages the instincts of the herd, to the submerging of personal independence of thought. Both these aims are out of keeping with Buddhist doctrine, the first because it derives all its justification from the belief in a real "Ego," which Buddhism denies, and the second because it favors an over-sensitiveness to public opinion and evokes an easy response to emotional stimulation from outside which is incompatible with that deliberate, detached judgment which the true Buddhist must ever be at pains to exercise.

Then, there is the question of language. Since Macaulay in his educational policy set out to turn the Indians into "colored Englishmen," in the sincere belief that this was the highest boon conferrable on any member of the human race, irrespective of temperament, geography, or history, English has been regarded as the chief vehicle of education throughout Indian territory, and proficiency in English has come to be the hallmark of education above all others. In higher-class schools, a great part of the tuition is given in the English language and so it comes about that a child of native parentage develops all its early thought through the medium of a foreign idiom, rather than through the tongue learnt at its mother's knee.

A language is the faithful mirror of the thought and character of a people and becomes nicely adapted to the expression of its particular genius; no foreign tongue can be substituted without making it difficult for the thoughts themselves to take shape. If the means for voicing thought are perfect, thoughts rise to the surface freely in a continuous flow; this state of affairs favors, through constant practice, the coming into being of fresh thoughts. But let the pumping-machine be gritty and ill-adapted, then the flow will become irregular, and there will be a tendency for the well itself to dry up from disuse. As language is our principal vehicle for conveying our thoughts to our neighbors and as we act as a whetstone for each other's minds, faulty, slipshod, or inexact expression, and the consequent interference with communication, will also bring about a drop in the general level of intelligence. Wherever any unnatural tongue has been adopted as the common vehicle of education, whether a foreign language has been chosen or even some insincere, pedantic version of the native language, the result has always been lamentable.

Traveling homeward, we happened to have as fellow passengers on the boat, a number of Indian students on their way to join English Universities. We noticed that a good many of them tried to talk English among themselves, especially in the public saloons. At first we thought that they must have come from provinces lying far apart, where different dialects were spoken; but we found out that in some cases they were neighbors and that this was simply an attempt to show off their education. And what an English they spoke! It would take a Kipling to reproduce its ungrammatical and pompous verbiage. Such a practice argues a serious degree of demoralization.

I once came across two students from Burma, both of whom spoke English, the one rather well and the other passably. I happened to ask the latter what was the name of his friend. "Smith," he answered. "But surely he is not a half-caste?" I said. "He does not look like one anyway."

"Oh, no, he's a full-blooded Burman; only he went to an English school."

"How do you mean? A school run by English masters?"

He explained that there was in his country a special school to which the epithet "English" was attached, in which tuition was exclusively carried on in English, the national language being ignored. The pupils were encouraged to be as English as possible. They might not wear their native dress and, to complete the illusion, they were advised to assume English names.

The story seemed incredible: yet I could picture the assemblage of young Smiths and Browns, olive-skinned Joneses and Thomases, almond-eyed McGregors and O'Learys—Lord Macaulay's dream of "colored Englishmen" come true. They are growing rusty in the tongue which their mothers spoke—Mr. Smith had become so himself, so his friend told me. They feel awkward when called upon to eat with their fingers, the smell of garlic nauseates them, and they laugh at the fairy-tales believed in by their grandfathers and grandmothers, and at the symbols to which they bow down. They have learned to worship the god of Soccer and the god of Rugger, the goddess of Good Form and the Spirit of the Corps. Our friend assured us that there was such a premium set on mastery of English that a number of parents, at the price of their self-respect, were willing to allow their children to submit to these insulting regulations. If that is the case, those parents are more to be blamed than the inventors of this obnoxious system.

In an education based on English, the pupil not only reads the literature of a remote country before that of his own, but he is also brought up on history as viewed through foreign eyes. Also the excessive importance attached to games is such as to alter a boy's outlook permanently; for in many English schools games are looked on as something more than a means for recreation or health. In the question of games, Mr. Smith had come to out-English the English and showed a quite pathetic anxiety as to whether he would find adequate facilities for football in the British college for which he was bound! There is also a danger of the children acquiring some of that gaucherie and shyness which we associate with the "awkward age." When traveling in the Himalaya, I noticed that all the children were free from this self-consciousness; it made me ask myself whether its regular incidence among us was not due to some preventable maladjustment in the school system. It is not a fault to be ignored. The only Tibetan pupils whom I ever found to be suffering from this ailment were boarders in a European school, and they had been badly affected.

And lastly, I must again mention the question of dress. In nearly all schools run by Europeans in the border districts, I saw a large proportion of the pupils wearing European clothes. In certain mission schools of a high class, this change had been imposed under the specious plea of a school uniform. That foreigners should come to a country and demand on any grounds whatsoever that their pupils should abandon their own dress in favor of that of their teachers, is outrageous, for it contains the plain implication that the native dress is the badge of an inferior culture. Were this not the case, it would be just as simple to design a uniform modeled on the local costume. Could one imagine an alien headmaster founding a school in England and requiring his scholars to adopt any style of un-English costume, let us say German or Russian school uniform? Would a single parent entrust his children to such a person, however tempting the educational facilities offered?

The intangible influences must not be forgotten either, the imperceptible effect of surroundings upon habits and taste. Furniture will be different and will be used differently. The floor will be replaced by the desk—a considerable physical change for growing children and an even greater social one, liable, later on, to make them feel uncomfortable among their own people. As soon as an Oriental begins to require chairs and tables, his domestic outlook has already undergone a tremendous revolution. There are also pictures on the walls, in which the symbolical and decorative treatment of traditional art will have yielded to the conventions of photographic naturalism, a dangerous experience for the innocent eye of a child, which may well mean that the child's own art will eventually become a closed book to it. It would be easy to multiply these examples, but enough has been said to indicate the main lines of criticism.

But surely there are the holidays, it will be argued; that is an opportunity for parents to provide a counter-influence. Firstly, it should be observed that under a fully traditional education, both parents and teachers are exerting their authority along parallel lines. There is never a question of pulling different ways. Once the two influences part company, the result is bound to be a compromise, with the scales becoming weighted more and more against tradition, and in favor of innovation, as each generation passes. In an aristocratic home, the force of example and convention, and social pressure in general, is greater; but in the case of an uneducated family, which lives from hand to mouth, the parents are not likely to trouble much. To counteract a dangerous influence deliberately needs foresight, and one cannot yet expect that from the average man.

If the foreign educators, whether secular-minded or religious, were to use their schools openly for the proselytism of the pupils, parents might be roused to action at once and would withdraw their children. But there is no need to go as far as that: indeed, no one but a fool would thus invite trouble. The insidiousness of the poison lies in the fact that children, being at a plastic age, unsuspicious, naturally docile and keen to learn, are only too ready to assimilate an unseen influence administered in small doses. The Jesuits are credited with having said: "Give me the child before it is eight; after that you can do as you like with it." They knew, from age-long experience, that early impressions, gained before the critical faculty has been awakened, count heavily in after-life and that if only a doubt can be sown early or the embryo of an idea implanted, it may continue to work like a ferment capable of destroying the most ancient loyalties. In the case of the Jesuits, of course, the end in view is not to undermine, but to preserve a certain tradition against the temptations of unbelief.

Once the sense of reverence towards ancient customs and ideas has been weakened, the power of the doctrine which permeates them is itself on the wane. If the child who has been exposed to the new schooling does not lose his hold on the Doctrine in the first generation, his own children in the next will be well on the way to deserting it; for they will start, not with a clean sheet, but from the point where their father and mother ceased their own education. Whatever traditional ideas may survive to the third generation will be mere remnants—superstitions in the true etymological sense of the word. It is at this point that the chance of proselytizing to another religion is at its greatest; though in the modern world it is still more likely that atheism or agnosticism or mere indifference, will follow.

It is almost inconceivable that Oriental children who pass through a modern schooling of the ordinary type, whether good or bad—the more efficient the school, especially if it is a boarding-school, the graver the danger—will retain a real sense of reverence. The feeling may survive for a time in an impaired form in good homes; in slack homes it will die, or only show itself in a few lingering external customs. The children will become moral and intellectual half-castes and in the following generation all will be lost. The old people will eventually realize the puzzling fact that they, who tried, as they thought, to give their children "the best available chances of education" are now regarded by them as:

Credulous old fogies: back numbers
Half savages

The children will also think that:

Their parents' doctrines are nothing but fairy-tales
Their art is to be put in glass cases as antiques
Their clothes are out-of-date and ridiculous

Are the teachers then to be accused of having acted dishonestly? Doubtless there exist flagrant cases of unscrupulousness; but in general, one cannot expect them to teach principles that they do not believe themselves. If they are conscientious, they do the best they can for the pupils according to their lights. If parents are willing to send their children to the foreign schools, the decision is their disaster, or rather the children's and that of the whole nation. For the parents, it is a great temptation to make use of educational advantages which happen to lie so close at hand, and which call for no effort on their own part. For the sake of the lesser, but immediate, advantage, they turn a blind eye to the cost—the loss of things which they should think most precious.

From the opposite point of view of the teacher, who feels that he is the bringer of inestimable benefits to a "backward" people, the methods followed all seem justifiable and even meritorious. To influence the children has proved to be the effective way, not only in Asia, but also in every part of Europe; that is why the new absolutist states have concentrated their biggest effort on the immature, rather than on the adult, mind, with the certainty of reaping the harvest in due course. In the case of religious schools, the type of man who feels the call to the mission field, is not usually a philosopher who wishes to see both sides—philosophers do not take kindly to a life of propaganda, with its inevitable hurry and superficiality; the qualifications needed are the single eye and the sense of superiority that comes from the flattering conviction that one possesses and can dispense the message, the true message, and nothing but the message. The men who take up these tasks—but there are of course exceptions—must hold the native culture to be worthless, or at least, unimportant. It is difficult for them, even when they intend to act honestly, to judge the meaning of the word "scruple"; for in their eyes the result overshadows every other consideration. The attitude of the secular-minded school-teacher is less positive; but he also cannot be expected to go to the trouble of bolstering up a lot of "medieval nonsense," to the prejudice of the "real, practical things" that he sets out to teach.

The fact is, that in regard to the fundamental things of life, impartiality is not easy in practice, even if the wish be present. Admittedly, there is such a thing as unscrupulous and dishonest abuse of the sacred calling to educate the young; but even apart from this, every person disseminates ideas by the mere fact of being himself. It is only one who himself participates in a living Tradition, who can be said not to be opposed to Tradition, at least unconsciously. It is not a question only of how many hours are to be spent in imparting set religions or moral teachings: it is the imponderable influences and the general atmosphere that surrounds the pupil which count even more than dogmatic instruction. The various totalitarian opponents of the Christian Church have been vehement in their determination to wrest the control of growing children out of the hands of the Church and, to a great extent, of parents. They are banking on the effects of early school environment becoming permanent. Let this be an object-lesson. To those Asiatic parents who have proved so unsuspicious in entrusting their own children to alien cares, one would like to put the following questions: If the Communists were to found a school in England equipped with every modern appliance, would non-Communists be likely to send their children there? Or if a non-Catholic school, giving the most up-to-date education superior to what is available locally, were to be opened in the West of Ireland, do you think that it would get many pupils?

It is not a question of approving narrow-mindedness, much less personal hostility, towards the purveyors of unacceptable creeds. Grown-up people ought to be able to look after themselves in these matters; but children are in no such position, and to expose them to outside pressure of that sort at a tender age is not a sign of open-mindedness, but of sheer foolhardiness. It is astonishing the risks that many Oriental parents are willing to take. In this we see the trustfulness and passivity of the Oriental character pushed to a vice. A little of the Occidental promptness to react, might be borrowed with advantage. Some time ago, the papers reported a speech by a missionary leader in a Buddhist country, who was speaking optimistically of the prospects of his mission, consequent upon the breakdown of the old traditions under the impact of modernity. He used the phrase "The Wall of Buddha has been smashed." This coarse expression, which should never have crossed the lips of a professed Christian, can leave no doubt as to the attitude to be expected of its author in educational matters: yet in all probability, in the schools under his control, many children would still be found belonging to Buddhist parents who had been too inert to be aware of the menace. Again it must be said that no one wishes the Orientals to depart from their excellent tradition of tolerance and courtesy towards foreign religions; but if they withdrew their children from the schools, it would be an act, not of fanaticism, but of common prudence.

If their national traditions mean anything to the parents, even were there no alternative choice, would not total illiteracy be better than the present risks? Which do they really think more important for their children:

Buddha or Baths?
Milarepa or Mathematics?
The Four Truths or Football?

Now is a critical hour; to drift is to court disaster. If there is a remedy, it lies in the parents' hands. The same applies to Tibetans, Indians, and all races similarly placed. But though a man with his back against the wall, should be ready in an extreme case, to abandon education altogether, rather than to agree to the cultural debauching of his children, he need not give up hope of finding an alternative way till he has exhausted every means at his disposal. There *does* exist an alternative, and that is to plan a system of education *consciously founded on Tradition*, but which may be made to include any modern knowledge that local circumstances render necessary; ever remembering that as between the various branches of knowledge, the traditional hierarchy must be uncompromisingly maintained. Even so, many difficult decisions will have to be taken; the best chance of deciding rightly will fall to the man who remains with his feet firmly planted on the rock of his own culture and who takes the trouble to study its principles even more diligently than ever before. Deliberate choice is the sign of the free spirit; those who talk of political or economic freedom, without intellectual freedom, are babblers.

If, through their earlier easy-going attitude towards the pressing educational problem, the leaders of Oriental society find themselves setting out late in the day to solve it, they must accept the fact and be patient and start again from the beginning, without hoping to find a short cut. To have been caught unawares is no sin; but to persist in ostrich-like self-delusion will lead inevitably and deservedly to an utter breakdown.

To build up from the beginning in difficult circumstances needs vision, enthusiasm, and also diligent attention to detail. In this, a leaf could be taken out of the book of some European races who have had comparable difficulties, often with the addition of a degree of physical oppression, which in the present case is fortunately absent. Faced with a threat either to their religious or national teaching, what Hungarian or Irishman would tamely accept the situation, consoling himself with a few regrets?

The starting-point must be a firm adherence to Tradition, not mere pig-headed conservatism or patriotism, but reverence founded on the unbroken experience of the ages handed down through master and pupil in the intellectual élite or true spiritual aristocracy. In case of an inescapable choice between two courses of action one should always lean towards continuing the established usage; change should only be tolerated if, after due weighing up of the question, the existing practice is found to be hopelessly inconsistent with one's principles. In the same way the general trend should be against the importation of foreign usages; but that does not mean that there are not a few cases where these would be found to be definitely advantageous and could be accepted and digested into the traditional scheme, exactly like a foreign word that is assimilated into a language and takes on its character.

Let us now consider the possibility of creating new schools in the borderland of Tibet, and the practical details of their organization. They should be conducted in a manner consonant with Tradition, but they must also impart certain selected branches of knowledge borrowed, under careful control, from the West, to meet the special needs of those who are forced to dwell on the frontiers of two incompatible theories of life. It is assumed that, having experienced a revulsion of feeling against the present state of affairs, the minds of the leaders of the border peoples are cleared of all hankering after a compromise and that they are firmly determined that, unless they can act in accordance with the spirit of traditional doctrine as applied in action, they would prefer to have no education at all. A mere copy of the Occidental system, accepting all its standards, except for the substitution of say Buddhist or Hindu scriptural teaching in place of Christian, is no solution; a school run on these lines would be nothing but a masked Occidental school and its founders would betray their doubt in the power of Tradition to provide all they wanted. Ultimately it would be a sign that they valued the new material knowledge above the Tradition, but wished to pay lip-service to the latter. Mere modified copies of existing schools will not do. A clean sweep must be made without impatience; and whoever embarks on such a task must for a time rest content with small-scale beginnings.

He must be prepared to make mistakes, before he can work out his program to be both sound doctrinally and efficient practically. Quality must, as far as possible, take precedence over rapid results on a large scale.

What elements, in the traditional civilization, exist to provide the basis for such an enterprise? What is the fundamental principle of the existing education? We must not forget that it is fortunately not a question of starting education in an educationless society, but of applying the existing experience to certain immediate problems, almost entirely confined to the material field. The training of the mind for the greatest and most essential of its functions, namely the discovery of metaphysical reality, is an art so highly developed among the intellectual élite of India, Tibet, and China that it would be an impertinence to offer any suggestions in that direction. The keystone of education can continue to be the selfsame agency that keeps Tradition itself perpetually functioning, namely, the reverence of the pupil for the teacher. The fact that in the Hindu and Buddhist Traditions it has been possible to combine such devotion to the teacher on the part of the taught, with the most unrestricted exercise of the right of free examination and inquiry, constitutes one of the greatest of human achievements.

Accepting, therefore, that we shall build upon the teacher-pupil relationship from the start, it is important that all those external customs which nourish that relationship should be preserved exactly as they would be in Tibet itself. All outward ceremonies, courtesies, and other customs are a language which symbolizes the inner relationship. They are in the nature of sacramentals, acting as "supports" for the doctrine. For instance, a pupil in Tibet, desiring to learn the alphabet, presents himself before his master and having done obeisance, asks for knowledge of the alphabet. Similarly his master, after having ceremonially repeated the alphabet and authorized the study, proceeds to the practical job of actually imparting the letters; thus this apparently simple and ordinary business of the alphabet becomes something more—it also affirms the master-pupil kinship, which carries the pupil through the entire chain of earthly teachers and heavenly Lamas back to the recognition of the principle of Knowledge itself.

As regards the curriculum, teaching should, in the main, be carried out in the language of the pupils. If they need to learn English or Urdu or any other foreign tongue, they can do so, provided it is taught as a useful addition, and is not turned into the main vehicle of education. Good literature, not only from the varied knowledge which it incidentally provides, but even more for its example of accurate speech and good style, must always take a high place: so should history by rights if only it could be taught honestly and without nationalistic bias. "Modern" subjects must be fitted in circumspectly: they ought to be comparatively harmless if the foundation has been well laid in the first place. Doctrinal teaching should be carried out by the old methods, which can hardly be improved upon. It is too individual a matter to be taught through the medium of a class and each pupil cannot do better than have recourse to "his own Lama." If doctrine is allowed to take its place in a school on terms of mere equality with arithmetic or any other subject, its preeminence in the hierarchy ceases to be apparent. The Monday morning scripture lesson must have done much to discredit Christianity in our own schools. As the Doctrine comprises and transcends all other knowledge, it seems unsuitable for a school subject; but that does not mean that its presence will not be felt. Far from it: in the general traditional atmosphere it will always be there, as the sufficient cause for all the rest.

Both educators and pupils working on these lines should be at pains to preserve friendly relations with local Europeans. There should be no question either of flattering them or of keeping them at arm's length. They must be treated with all the courtesy due to them as guests in a foreign land; and in the case of officials, with the respect due to their rank, as enjoined by the traditional laws of hospitality.

Certain details are specially important: the traditional surroundings should be preserved in the school buildings and their interior fittings. Everyone should wear his own national dress, which he can be encouraged to make as pleasing as possible. The practice of doing lessons sitting on the floor should be invariably followed, unless there be a particular lesson which necessitates some other posture. Not only does this habit make for grace of pose and economize needless furniture, but it is a great safeguard against becoming Occidentalized. I believe that dress and the way of sitting are among the most decisive factors at the present moment.

There is no need to introduce a competitive system. The ideal of acquiring knowledge is the prize and privilege aimed at. To know which pupil has attained it the quickest, is no help to anyone; and in so far as it strengthens the "Ego-forming" tendencies, it is anti-Buddhistic. A gentle bearing should be encouraged and the conventions of politeness as between pupils should not be relaxed. A proper relationship with animals should be inculcated at all times, both by example and by the exposition of the correct doctrine. As regards games, national games, such as archery, should, if anything, be preferred to imported ones; but there is no reason to restrict oneself very narrowly in this matter, provided games do not become exalted into a sort of religion; the ideal of games as a light recreation seems worth adopting.

If at any time it should be necessary to employ foreign teachers, as might well be the case for special subjects, they should be carefully selected out of the ranks of those few who are willing, for the time being at any rate, to participate, as a privilege, in the traditions of the country. If possible, not less than five years of preparation should be demanded of the teacher, during which time he should not only master the words of the language, but also its spirit; and he should spend enough time among the people for whom he is engaged to work, to get used to their way of living and to cease to feel and act like a stranger. It is his duty and his privilege to make himself acquainted with their way of thinking and to let the spirit of their culture sink into his heart. If he will adopt their clothes and habits, all the better: for then the influence which he is bound to gain over his pupils, will not be associated in their minds with something exotic.

At first there will be obvious difficulty in finding the necessary teachers, especially for certain subjects. If they cannot be found they must be trained. Parents in educated families should be ready to take a hand themselves if no one else is available. If they want to impart something which they do not know, let them first learn it themselves and then pass it on: in so doing they will acquire much merit. It is always through the leaders of society that corruption or improvement must come. If those who enjoy traditional rights become slothful about the duties that naturally devolve on them, they can act as destroyers of the culture of their country. Where the aristocrat goes, there the rest will follow. He cannot divest himself of his responsibility as national ruler or mis-ruler.

In dealing with the education of children, charity must always begin at home. If so-called traditional schools were to be organized for the children of the poor, while the aristocratic children still continued to be sent to the Occidental schools of Simla or Darjeeling, no one would be deceived, least of all the children themselves. The newly-founded schools would then probably become nationalistic instead of national, anti-Christian instead of Buddhistic. The full participation of the aristocratic element is demanded in any community governed on traditional lines. Besides it is idle for a parent to profess devotion for his Tradition unless he shows that he regards it as the highest good for his own children also. That is always the acid test, which shows what a man thinks in his heart of hearts.

For the sake of anyone who may feel faint-hearted at the prospect of attempting to shut the sluice gates in the face of the flood, I should like to relate a true story about a poor woman who, with no private resources, was able to start an educational enterprise which is now both flourishing and widespread. Lest any misunderstanding should arise, it must be mentioned that her educational movement has nothing to do with the question of tradition; the example is given simply to show what can be done by conviction, even against great physical and social odds.

She was born of slave parents in South Carolina, U.S.A., and her name was Emma J. Wilson. From an early age she showed a strong desire to be educated; but in those days only white children went to school. Eventually some ladies became interested in her and helped her to enter Scotia Seminary, where, after winning a scholarship, she completed a three years' course. She hoped to take up missionary work in Africa; but on her return to South Carolina she saw that her work lay elsewhere—to use her own words she "found her Africa at her own door." She began a school in a disused shed: friends gave her a few books and the children paid for their tuition in eggs, chickens, and vegetables, which her mother cooked and sold for the benefit of the work.

The school soon outgrew its shed and the need for proper premises became urgent; but there was no money and the Negro community was too poor to raise funds. Undaunted, Emma Wilson decided to start for the north where she hoped to find sympathizers. Her minister gave her the proceeds of the Sunday evening after-collection—just fifty cents! It seemed so little that she carried it home in tears; but her mother said: "Don't cry, child, God ain't dead yet." So she started off, begging her way or doing odd jobs of work till she reached Philadelphia. A Quaker, true to the wonderful charity of his Society, was the first to listen to her story. After all sorts of rebuffs and trials, she won through, and out of these small beginnings has grown the magnificently organized Mayesville Industrial Institute, with a hundred and twenty-two acres of farm-land and five hundred pupils. It is undenominational—as Miss Wilson said: "It is the Lord's work and belongs to all."

Once when her main building was gutted by fire, someone said to her: "You must not be discouraged, for you have done such wonders." She replied: "The Lord told me long ago He had no use for discouraged folks." That is the message which a great saint, Emma Wilson, sends across the sea to the borderlands of India and Tibet. If she, a poor colored girl, daughter of slaves and member of an abjectly poor community, could conceive and bring to success this wonderful educational enterprise, how much more ought it to be possible for wealthy nobles and merchants, heirs to an unbroken tradition of rule, and members of one of the most civilized and talented of races.

But someone may ask: "What is to be done at this actual moment by leaders of society, to prepare their children, on whom the task of continuing their work will eventually devolve; for a certain amount of time is bound to elapse before anything new is adopted? If the children are not to continue in their present schools, how is their education to be carried on?" In the case of those who enjoy a certain amount of wealth the problem is really not so difficult, for they have the resources to engage private tutors, who can impart to the children whatever knowledge may be desired. It is not even certain that for those fated to rule, this time-honored system is not, on the whole, the best. One remembers the great tutors of fifteenth-century Europe and their accomplished pupils. Even if some of the tutors engaged were not found to be perfectly satisfactory at the start, one must not forget that they will be working under the eyes of the parents, who will thus be able to exercise a much stricter control over their doings. In the case of children of the great Lhasa families I believe that private tuition would expose them to far less danger than being sent to questionable schools. The selection of a private tutor is difficult; it is not sufficient for him to have won a good degree. The conditions that I suggested some paragraphs back in connection with the appointment of foreign schoolteachers, should apply to private tutors with double force. A man who is willing or, better still, eager, to conform to the traditional conventions, and who possesses the right personality, can mold himself into a tutor capable of discharging his high service. For purely native subjects, doctrinal and literary, the best lamas should be sought out, for their presence will set the tone to the whole educational environment. In that way too the supremacy of the spiritual Order will be acknowledged.

If the present practice of supporting Occidental schools goes on unchecked, not only will the dangers already mentioned grow, but they will breed fresh ones, and so accelerate the process of denaturing the children. Clever pupils will eventually be encouraged, as in India, to "complete their education"—that is to say to attend foreign universities, whence they will return, a prey to a chaos of undigested impressions. Later, some parents will be persuaded, instead of placing their children in schools in their own country, to give them a "pukka" public-school education and send them over to Eton or Harrow. The results are likely to be equally lamentable. A child who has been brought up in a home still partially run on the old lines, if suddenly plunged into a whirl of complexities all new to his experience and asked to deal with them at the dangerous moment of adolescence, when all his ideas are still fluid, will be exposed to such pressure, that even an exceptional character may well be swept away by the tide of materialism.

The suggestions contained in this chapter for dealing with the school problem have not been put forward with the idea that a solution on the lines indicated will necessarily save the day. Subversive forces may be too strong, and resistance may prove a forlorn hope. To expect to discover a panacea for deep-seated intellectual poisons in this change of system or in that measure of reorganization is a common delusion that dies hard. If the thought, of which Tradition is the vehicle, has been affected in a vital part, nothing can resuscitate the corpse. Nor can any multiplying or reorientating of Activities replace Knowledge as the first and last remedy against Ignorance. I believe myself, that the Tibetan civilization still retains the vital spark. All that can be said on the subject of improved schools is that in the absence of some such radical changes, the end is a foregone conclusion, for the present easy-going policy is nothing short of suicidal.

Decisive action in this matter of education lies especially in the hands of the leaders of the border districts. Their children are far more exposed to temptation than those who are brought up within Tibet itself, and they are called upon to face the problems of adaptation, due to contact with Western things, in a far more acute form. However, a few sons of great families are also being sent from Tibet to the schools of the borderland. Were schools available, organized on a sound traditional basis, those pupils, officials of the future, would surely be diverted to them instead of being placed in the charge of those who care nothing for Tradition. The border peoples are stationed in the post of honor: may they not shrink feebly from the great task of confronting them. Every broad-minded European can wish them success, for we too have suffered from the degradation of our own rich culture, due to the selfsame forces that have corrupted that of Asia. A turn in the tide, wherever it may occur, should be welcomed by men of good-will everywhere, irrespective of their religion or race.

Learning in the Confucian Tradition

Sachiko Murata

In Chinese the word "teaching" (*jiao* 教) is commonly used to designate a body of knowledge, a school of thought, or a religious tradition, as in the expression, "the three teachings," meaning Confucianism, Daoism, and Buddhism. Confucianism itself is commonly called *rujiao* 儒 教, meaning "the teaching of the *ru*." *Ru* means learned or scholar. Mathews' *Chinese-English Dictionary* offers a traditional definition of a *ru*: "one who is conversant with heaven, earth, and humans." These are the three domains of human knowledge, outside of which there is nothing to be known.

The goal of the Confucian tradition is to become worthy of the title *ru*. One does so by "learning" (*xue* 學), which is the process of assimilating the teachings passed down by the *ru*. Learning is not simply a mental process, for it aims at a transformation of character. The greatest of the *ru* were the sages, specifically Confucius and various more ancient figures. It is they who thoroughly penetrated the meaning of heaven, earth, and humans. Those who follow their teachings can hope to become sage-like, or "great men," also translated "profound persons" (*junzi* 君子).

Confucius spoke of "one thread" going through all of his teachings, and this is typically identified as *ren* 仁, a word that has been translated with expressions such as humanity, human-heartedness, benevolence, perfect virtue, love, benevolent love, goodness, altruism, co-humanity, and true manhood. Traditional Chinese definitions of the term include *airen* 愛人, "love for people" and *zhongshu* 忠恕, "magnanimous." The nineteenth-century translator of the Chinese Classics, James Legge, explained that *chungshu* means staying true to the principles of our nature and exercising these principles toward others in a benevolent way. This notion is often associated with the Confucian "golden rule" set down in the Analects: "Do not do to others what you do not want done to yourself."

In a famous passage, Mencius, the second great teacher of the Confucian tradition, explains the concept of *ren* in terms of qualities of the human heart. The word "heart" (*xin* 心) has typically been translated as "mind," but it designates something far deeper, the inmost center of the human reality, the root of all consciousness and awareness. Mencius says that the human heart has four essential qualities, and anyone who does not have these qualities is not in fact human. The first he calls "the heart of commiseration," the heart that cannot bear the suffering of others. Second is the heart of shame and dislike, third the heart of modesty and yielding, and fourth the heart that discerns between right and wrong. Mencius goes on to say that these four qualities are the germs of four essential human characteristics. The heart of commiseration is the germ of *ren*, the heart of shame and dislike the germ of righteousness (*yi* 義), the heart of modesty and yielding the germ of propriety (*li* 禮), and the heart of discerning right and wrong the germ of wisdom (*zhi* 智). These germs are just as basic to our human nature as are the four limbs to the body. Everyone has all four, and failure to develop and actualize them is to fail in the task of becoming human.

For Confucius *ren* is a single quality that brings together all the essential qualities of human nature. If a person does not have *ren*, his observance of propriety is insincere, for he observes it only for his own personal benefit. The goal of learning, he says, is *keji fuli* 克己復禮, "overcoming oneself and returning to propriety" (Analects 12.1). A man of *ren*, having overcome his own likes and dislikes, loves people impartially and hates people impartially. If a man's will is to achieve *ren*, there is no worry that he will do evil. In this way of looking at things, there are only two roads before us: that of *ren* and that of negating *ren*.

In a well-known passage, Mencius laments that most people show no concern for realizeing their own human nature:

> *Ren* is the human heart, and righteousness is the human path. People leave aside the path and do not rely upon it. They let go of their own hearts and do not know to seek them. When their fowls and dogs get lost, they know to go out and seek them. When their own hearts get lost, they do not know to go seek them.

In brief, the human task is to learn how to be human, and the path of learning entails searching for one's lost heart. That lost heart is *ren*, and it embraces righteousness, propriety, wisdom, and all other positive human qualities. The whole of the Confucian tradition is founded on the notion of recovering one's lost humanity, and "the sages and worthies" are held up as the examples of those who have paved the way. The identification of *ren* with the human heart, and the understanding that a fully developed human heart is a consciousness that embraces heaven, earth, and the ten thousand things, has resulted in a constant stress on learning as the way to perfection, true humanity, compassion, right speaking, right acting, and appropriate behavior in all circumstances.

Confucian practice, then, aims at cultivating the heart. This helps explain why, from the time of the famous scholar Zhu Xi (1130-1200), a one-page treatise ascribed to Confucius came to be considered one of the four great classics of the tradition, along with the Analects, Mencius, and *The Doctrine of the Mean*. This is *The Great Learning*. The core of its message is presented at the beginning:

> The ancients who wished to clarify their clear virtue under heaven would first govern their countries. Those who wished to govern their countries would first regulate their families. Those who wished to regulate their families would first cultivate their personal lives. Those who wished to cultivate their personal lives would first make their hearts true. Those who wished to make their hearts true would first make their intentions sincere. Those who wished to make their intentions sincere would first extend their knowledge. . . . From the Son of Heaven down to the common people, all must regard cultivation of the personal life as the root or foundation. There is never a case when the root is in disorder but the branches are in order.

Notice that in this passage, "extending knowledge" (*gezhi* 格知) is taken as the foundation of human perfection. Clearly, one extends one's knowledge by learning, by studying the classics and by conforming oneself to their teachings. This conformity is called *ren*, and the process of actualizing *ren* is precisely the path that leads to the recovery of one's lost heart.

The Goal of Islamic Education

William C. Chittick

Notions of "education" are embedded in the values and goals of modern society. Human individuals are understood in terms of their social roles, and human goals are defined in terms of ideology. By "ideology," I mean schemes of improving the human situation based on the presuppositions of modern thought as developed during the eighteenth century, that is, the historical period known as the Enlightenment.

The new style of thinking that appeared during the Enlightenment rejected all traditional notions of truth, authority, hierarchy, and human nature. It laid the groundwork for the various systems that have been enacted in modern times in the attempt to shape human society to humanistic ideals—systems such as democracy, socialism, and Marxism, with all their varieties and offshoots. Among the more prominent of these offshoots today are the modern Islamist movements, which are the same as other ideological systems in the attempt to impose an abstract, human-devised system on society.

All ideology begins with certain assumptions about human nature that are not shared by pre-modern thought. Human beings are understood in terms of the findings of modern science, which excludes de facto, if not de jure, any possibility of transcendence, any notion of prophecy and revelation, any serious consideration of everlasting life. Reading the Enlightenment in Islamic terms, we can say that it is a new style of thinking based on the rejection of the three fundamental principles of Islamic thought. These are *tawḥīd* or divine unity, prophecy (*nubuwwa*), and the Return to God (*maʿād*). In other words, modern notions of human nature are founded on the rejection of the truths that have always formed the core understanding of Muslims.

I do not mean to imply that these basic Islamic truths are simply Islamic—they are shared by every pre-modern civilization, not least the Christian. In other words, the worldviews of pre-modern civilizations acknowledged *tawḥīd*, the unity of the Ultimate Reality. They also held that human perfection could not be achieved without the initiative of that Reality, that is, without the help of figures known as prophets, avataras, buddhas, or sages. These pre-modern worldviews also maintained that our mode of existence in this life is simply one stage of human becoming and that each individual human being is responsible, to some degree, for the manner of his or her existence after death.

In short, any discussion of "education" in the context of Islamic teachings has to begin with the fact that notions of education in modern times are based on concepts of human nature grounded in the Enlightenment. These concepts are profoundly incompatible with Islamic notions of human nature. It follows that modern education, which serves the needs of the ideologies of modern states, is profoundly incompatible with Islamic education, which serves the needs of the human soul in its quest to return to God in the best possible manner.

* * *

What makes something "Islamic" is that it be based on the teachings of the Koran and the prophet Muhammad. No Arabic word in the early sources corresponds exactly with our modern notion of education. Certainly, the Koran and the hadith literature are full of exhortations to seek knowledge and to improve oneself by conforming to the norms provided by God and His Prophet. But knowledge and improvement are always understood in terms of a specific goal, and that goal is to become fully human in this world and to achieve everlasting happiness in the next world. In and of itself, knowledge is not valuable. Otherwise the Prophet would not have prayed, "O God, I seek refuge from a knowledge that has no benefit."

The word "educate" derives from a Latin root that means to lead forth, to pull out. One can argue that the Koran does indeed provide a somewhat parallel notion, a notion that lies at the heart of Muslim prayer. The Fatiha, recited several times a day by every practicing Muslim, revolves around the sentence, "Guide us on the Straight Path." The Straight Path is the path that leads to human happiness and wholeness. In other words, the path that leads to "success." Success, however, is defined not in terms of this world, but rather in terms of another much more real and lasting world.

The Fatiha is traditionally said to encapsulate the message of the whole Koran. It points clearly to the three principles that are the foundation of the Islamic worldview. Let me suggest how these three notions are embedded.

Generally, *tawhīd* is said to be expressed most succinctly in the Koranic formula, "(There is) no god but God." This formula has always been understood to mean that all of existence comes from God, that all of reality is constantly sustained by God, and that all things eventually return to God. Every positive quality experienced in the world and in ourselves can only be a pale reflection of God's qualities. God alone is truly good, God alone is truly beautiful, God alone is truly powerful, God alone is truly independent, and so on down the list of the divine names. In short, *tawhīd* means that there is nothing truly real but God.

The Fatiha begins with the statement, "Praise belongs to God," which is simply a statement of *tawhīd*: It means that that there is none praiseworthy but God, for there is nothing truly good but God. In the same way, *tawhīd* is also expressed in the statement, "You alone we serve, and from You alone we ask for help." There is no other god but God, so there is no one worthy of service and no one who can provide real help other than God. Notice that this sentence is commonly regarded as setting down an ideal: Muslims *should* serve God alone and ask assistance only from Him. However, if we look carefully, we can see that it is also a statement of fact. The Unity of Reality demands that everyone, Muslim or not, serves God and asks help from Him in the actual course of living out their lives. Given that there is only one true Reality, all things act in keeping with that Reality—all things are the servants of that Reality by definition. When people seek help, they are in fact seeking help from that One Reality, whether or not they are aware of this fact.

This brings us to the second principle of Islamic thought, which the Fatiha mentions most explicitly by using the verb "guide." *Tawhīd* teaches, "There is no guide but God." As the Koran puts it, addressing the Prophet, "You do not guide whom you like, but God guides whomsoever He wants" (28:56). Nonetheless, the Koran also says to the Prophet, "You guide to a Straight Path" (42:52). This is to say that God guides by sending the prophets, and their function in the universe is precisely to guide people on the Straight Path, which leads to everlasting happiness.

The third principle of Islamic thought is the Return to God. It is implied by the very notion of Straight Path, *al-sirāt al-mustaqīm*. Why is this path important? Because it leads to happiness after death. Its significance is indicated among other things by the fact that the so-called "bridge over hell" on the Day of Resurrection is also called *al-sirāt*. Those who are able to cross the Bridge without falling into the Fire are those who received guidance on the Straight Path in this life. Those who fail to cross the Bridge are those who did not follow the Straight Path—instead, as the Fatiha says, they were among those who went astray, or those against whom God was angry.

* * *

As I said earlier, the word "educate" means to lead out. In Latin, *ducere* means to lead and to guide. When Muslims pray to be guided on the Straight Path, they are asking God to lead them out of ignorance, hatred, spite, and all the vicious traits of character that prevent the flowering of wholesomeness and virtue. These negative character traits are deeply rooted in the human soul. The reason for this is simply that people are not God, and God alone is good and true. As the Koran says, "Man was created weak" (4:28). Adam fell from paradise because of his weakness, which the Koran calls "forgetfulness" (*nisyān*) and "heedlessness" (*ghafla*). Forgetfulness is woven into human existence. To escape from forgetfulness, people must be *led out* from it—one needs to be "educated." No one can achieve the fullness of human possibility, no one can reach true knowledge, wisdom, virtue, and goodness, by his or her own efforts. Everyone needs an educator, someone who can show the path to knowledge and salvation. The educator is precisely the "guide" (*hādī*).

In traditional Islamic society, guidance was provided by the ulama. According to a commonly quoted saying (often attributed to the Prophet), "The ulama are the inheritors of the prophets." The ulama are literally "those who have knowledge," and there are different sorts of ulama depending on the sort of knowledge that they have inherited from the prophets. There are three basic realms of knowledge, all of which are encompassed by the Koran and embodied in the Prophet. The ideal inheritor of the Prophet will have actualized all three sorts of knowledge, but most ulama are in fact rather limited in their learning. Certainly, none of the ulama can be as complete a guide as the Prophet himself.

The three basic sorts of Islamic knowledge that should ideally be embodied by the ulama are knowledge of right activity, knowledge of the True Reality, and knowledge of spiritual perfection. "Knowledge of right activity" is the domain of the Shariah and jurisprudence. "Knowledge of the True Reality" is the realm of those ulama who study Kalam, theoretical Sufism, and/or philosophy. These scholars explain Koranic teachings related to the reality of God, the nature of the cosmos, and the becoming of the human soul. In other words, this second group of ulama studies metaphysics, theology, cosmology, and spiritual psychology. The third realm, "knowledge of spiritual perfection," deals with the manner of inner transformation and conformity with the norms of God, not only in activity and thought, but also in the inner being of the soul. This realm is the specialty of the Sufi teachers.

* * *

I said that modern education is incompatible with traditional Islamic education. By traditional Islamic education I mean "guidance on the Straight Path," the path that leads to right activity, right understanding, and right transformation of the soul. As soon as we see that traditional Islamic education focused on achieving human perfection in terms of the norms of God—not the humanistic norms of the Enlightenment—we can easily understand why modern education destroys the bases on which an Islamic education must be built. Let me suggest a few places where the conflict between Islamic and modern education appear, specifically as relating to the fundamental principle of Islamic thought, *tawhīd*.

Modern education claims to be based on "science," and it gains its authority by being "scientific." Scientific thinking is characterized by its focus on multiplicity, on the empirical study of the realm that is manifest to the senses, whether the senses gain access to this realm directly or by means of instruments. Scientific thinking rejects, implicitly or explicitly, any kind of knowledge that cannot be verified empirically. This sort of approach is useful for gaining control over the environment and people, as is all too obvious in the way that it is used by governments, the military, and industry. Once, however, people claim that scientific knowledge is the only valid and legitimate knowledge, then we are no longer dealing with science, but with "scientism," which is the belief that science alone allows access to truth. Good scientists are usually too sophisticated to believe in scientism, because they understand that scientism is an ideological position that cannot be demonstrated empirically.

Nonetheless, scientism is a powerful component of the modern worldview. Most people believe in the truth claims of science more than they believe in the truth claims of religion. They believe that science deals with knowledge and objective reality, and they think that religion deals simply with the subjective realm of opinions and feelings.

This belief in science is profoundly incompatible with the approach of Islamic learning. In Islamic terms, the only real knowledge, the only absolutely reliable and true knowledge, is *tawhīd*, the fact that there is nothing real but the Reality. This has always been recognized as being a truth, a fact, not a belief. It is a "belief" only for simple people who accept it on the basis of authority but do not understand what it means. For any person of sound intelligence (*'aql salīm*), it is the foundational truth in terms of which all other truths must be understood and all knowledge must be built. Any form of knowledge that ignores *tawhīd* is ignorant of the one truth upon which all truth depends.

Everyone knows that Muslim civilization developed a number of scientific disciplines in extremely sophisticated ways—disciplines like mathematics, astronomy, and medicine. These disciplines, however, were always part of a greater vision, and that vision was *tawhīd*. The Islamic worldview began by asserting the reality of God, the unity of the ultimately Real, the rootedness of all things in God. This meant that true understanding of things depended upon understanding them in terms of God—the Ultimate Reality. Any knowledge of the world that does not situate the world in terms of its Transcendent Source is in fact ignorance, because it prevents people from seeing things as they truly are.

It is fairly obvious that an intuition of unity drives modern-day scientists in their search for overarching theories of nature and the universe. But there can also be little doubt that the actual theories that rule over contemporary scientific and academic disciplines are manifestations of a principle that we can call *takthīr*. *Tawhīd* is derived from the word *wahda*, oneness, and it means to assert the oneness of God, to declare the unity of the Ultimate Reality. *Takthīr* derives from the word *kathra*, manyness, and it means to assert the manyness of reality. A worldview of *takthīr* implicitly or explicitly denies *tawhīd*. In place of One Reality, it posits many realities. The net result is the dispersion of human knowledge, the proliferation of scientific and academic disciplines, the multiplicity of human goals, and never-ending disagreement, dissension, disintegration, conflict, and corruption.

Takthīr is not necessarily a bad thing. Muslim philosophers sometimes employed the word to designate the very act by which the One God creates a world of multiplicity. But, the human task is to escape from *takthīr*, to see beyond the multiplicity and dissension that rule over the visible realm. Human beings are called upon to establish *tawhīd*, which means to bring about unity, harmony, balance, equilibrium, and peace. They are called to do this, however, in their own lives. No one can bring about harmony, balance, and peace in the world if that person is not already at peace with God.

That *tawhīd* must begin with the individual points to one of the basic differences between traditional thought and modern ideological systems. Islam has always taught that every individual is responsible before God. Without fulfilling one's own responsibilities, one cannot live by God's norms. In contrast, modern thought holds that a harmonious society can be build by fiat, by imposing a system on society. When everyone conforms to the imposed system—a system invented by ideologues and enforced by bureaucrats—society will be harmonious. In other words, traditional thought says, "Begin with yourself." Modern thought says, "Reform others."

Tawhīd, in short, is a vision that needs to be achieved by every human being. It is the task of individuals. The way to achieve it is called the Straight Path. Those who lead people on the Straight Path are first God, then the prophets, then the inheritors of the prophets. Nonetheless, one cannot simply follow one's teachers. What your teacher understands does not help you unless you understand it as well. It is the responsibility of each Muslim to seek his own knowledge and his own understanding. "The search for knowledge is incumbent on every Muslim, male or female," said the Prophet. And that search lasts "from the cradle to the grave," as he also said. Without the search to understand, people will remain ignorant and forgetful, no matter how much they may have mastered science and engineering, philosophy and sociology, or any other discipline rooted in *takthīr*.

* * *

Traditional Islamic education attempted to provide the means whereby people could achieve a vision of *tawhīd* for themselves. Following the Straight Path was looked upon as an individual endeavor that demanded working out the implications of *tawhīd* for one's own soul. Only then could one come to the aid of others. According to many Muslim scholars, especially those with a philosophical bent, the goal of following the Straight Path is *tahqīq*, which means realization and verification.

The word *tahqīq* derives from the word *haqq*, a Koranic name of God that means true, real, right, appropriate, worthy. The implication of this divine name is that God alone is truth, reality, rightness, and appropriateness. But, the Koran tells us that God created everything with *haqq*, that is, with truth, rightness, and appropriateness. The Prophet said that everything has its own *haqq*, and that people must give to each possessor of a *haqq* its *haqq*. This is to say that everything has a truth and a rightness. It is also to say that the human "responsibility" (*haqq ʿalaynā*, "the right against us") is to act toward everything in keeping with its truth and its rightness.

According to a famous hadith, God has a *haqq*—a right—against human beings, and that right is for them to declare his unity, to assert *tawhīd*. In other words, *tawhīd* is the first human *responsibility*. The hadith goes on to say that if people live up to that responsibility, it is their right against God to be given everlasting happiness. In other words, it is God's *responsibility* to deliver them from hell and to place them in paradise.

I said that the goal of Islamic education is *tahqīq*. *Tahqīq* means to recognize the *haqq* of things and to act accordingly. The first *haqq* that must be recognized is that of God, for there is no real *haqq* but the absolute and true *Haqq*—there is nothing truly right, real, and appropriate but God. Simultaneously, *tahqīq* means to live in accordance with God's *haqq*. The fruit of doing so will be salvation. The manner of achieving *tahqīq* is laid down by the prophets, specifically in the Straight Path. God's right against us—that we assert His Unity—establishes the foundation for all the rights of mankind and creation, because God has given everything its own *haqq* and provided guidance as to how to observe these *haqqs*. This is to say that God's right against us is the foundation for all our human responsibilities.

If there is one basic insight of the Muslim tradition after *tawhīd*, it is that no one can follow the Straight Path for you. Each individual is called upon to engage in the Straight Path by himself or herself, and each person will be held responsible for his or her own efforts. The Koran stresses this by saying in five different verses, "No one carries the burden of someone else" (6:164, 17:15, 35:18, 39:7, 53:38). The ulama have the responsibility of offering whatever knowledge they may have to others, but people have the responsibility of searching for that knowledge. No one can be forced to search for truth, and no one can be forced to understand it. The Koran says, *lā ikrāha fi'l-dīn*, there is no compulsion, no coercion, in the religion. This again is not a moral command, it is a statement of fact. "The religion" is the Straight Path, and it is impossible to force anyone to follow it. All modern Islamist movements ignore this basic truth. They turn religion into an ideological system, and then they try to impose it on society. This helps explain the authoritarian nature of the regimes that they do manage to establish. This is one of many places where modern notions of education conflict with traditional notions. Nowadays people believe in "compulsory education," which is really compulsory indoctrination, or rather, brainwashing. In former times, people were much more aware that understanding cannot be taught, it can only be discovered within oneself.

* * *

In discussing *tahqīq* as the goal of the Straight Path, Muslim scholars are careful to distinguish it from *taqlīd*. *Taqlīd* means imitation, and it is considered appropriate only in matters of practice. In order to be a good Muslim, one needs to follow the Sunnah and imitate the practices of the Prophet, and one needs to take such knowledge from the jurists, the experts in the Shariah.

Taqlīd, however, is not appropriate in *tawhīd*. One cannot say, "I believe in God's oneness because my teacher said I should." Or rather, one can say it, but that would simply prove that one has no understanding and that one's profession of God's unity is based on ignorance. It has not yet entered one's mind and heart.

Notice that the Koran speaks of *tawhīd* as the universal message of all the prophets. Every one of them received the message, "There is no god but I, so serve Me" (20:114). Most scholars maintain that *tawhīd* pertains to human nature, to what is called the *fitra*, the very way in which people were created. The prophets came with guidance, and the guidance begins with "reminder" (*dhikr*, *tadhkira*). To "remind" people means to mention to them what they already know so that they will bring it to mind. The prophets came to awaken the human *fitra*, to remove the forgetfulness that has obscured people's understanding of *tawhīd*. This knowledge is innate to every sound intelligence, every human being. But, to understand what it implies, people need prophetic guidance—that is, they need "education."

Any education deserving the name "Islamic" must lead to the understanding of *tawhīd* and to putting it into practice. Otherwise, it is not guidance, but rather misguidance (*idlāl*, the Koranic attribute of Satan). Knowledge of *tawhīd* gained by *taqlīd* is simply rote learning. No doubt, memorizing the Koran is a great feat and has its reward, but memorization is not understanding. *Tahqīq* or realization is precisely understanding for oneself. It is to recognize the truth and the right of something, and to act in keeping with the truth and the right.

* * *

It is characteristic of modern times that any discussion of "education" revolves around the needs of states and societies. These needs are defined in terms of the multiple gods that rule over the worldview of *takthīr*. These gods are well known to everyone, because they determine the orientation of modern societies and are constantly discussed by politicians and ideologues. People assume that these gods are good gods, and that if they worship the gods by devoting effort to achieving what they promise, they will be happy. Worship of these gods is part of the modern ethos and is taken for granted, just as *tawhīd* was part of the pre-modern ethos and was taken for granted.

In many contexts today it is dangerous to speak against the gods of *takthīr*, because the worshipers of these gods are fanatics who possess a great deal of social and political power. Nonetheless, we should be realistic and acknowledge the names of the ruling gods of our times. No list could be exhaustive, because there are so many gods. But these names are representative: freedom, democracy, science, medicine, technology, progress, development, equality, education.

The worship of the god "education" is held in the highest esteem. All the other gods encourage us to attend at the temples of this god, for education trains people to reject the ancient gods and to abandon the principles of traditional thought—that is, *tawhīd*, prophecy, and the Return. Education in this sense is everywhere a primary concern of politicians and states. States must provide education, they must train people in the worldview of *takthīr* and accustom them to worship at the temples of the many gods. The least responsibility of Muslims in this situation should be to acknowledge that modern education is destructive of the goals of *tawhīd*. Without acknowledging the dead ends of ideology and the worthless promises of paradise made by politicians, there will be no hope for people to follow the Straight Path.

* * *

To conclude my brief remarks, let me quote from one of the greatest "educators" of Islamic history, Mawlānā Jalāl al-Dīn Rūmī. In one his prose works he explains the goal of education in terms of the human obligation to carry the Trust bestowed by God. This Trust, mentioned in the Koranic verse that he quotes, cannot be carried without following the Straight Path.

> There is one thing in the world that you must never forget. If you forget everything else, but not this one thing, then you will have no fear. But if you carry out, remember, and do not forget all things, but you forget this one thing, then you will have done nothing at all.
>
> Suppose a king sends you to a village for an appointed task. You go, and you perform a hundred other tasks. However, you do not perform the task for which you went. So, it is just as if you did nothing.
>
> Human beings have come into this world for a task, and that is their goal. If they do not perform it, they will have done nothing. "We offered the Trust to the heavens and the earth and the mountains, but they refused to carry it and were afraid of it; and the human being carried it. Surely he is a wrongdoer, ignorant" [Koran 33:72].
>
> "We offered the Trust to the heavens, but they did not accept.". . . The heavens, earth, and mountains do all these things, but there is one task that they do not do. This one task is done by man alone. . . . When they do that task, "wrongdoing" and "ignorance" will be negated from them.

If you say, "Even though I don't do that task, I do so many other tasks!"—you were not created for those other tasks.

It is just as if you took a priceless sword of Indian steel, like those found in the treasuries of kings, and you made it into a cleaver for rotten meat. You say, "I don't let this sword stand idle. I carry out so many useful deeds with it!" Or, you take a golden bowl and cook turnips in it. Yet, for a single grain of that gold you could buy a hundred pots. Or, you make a jewel-encrusted dagger into a nail for a broken gourd. You say, "I am making good use of it. I hang a gourd on it. I am not letting this blade stand idle." What intelligence is there in using a dagger worth a hundred dinars in this way?

God has given you tremendous worth. He says, "Surely God has bought from the believers their souls and their property so that they may have paradise" [9:111]. . . . Don't sell yourself cheaply—you have a very high price.[1]

1 *Fīhi mā fīhi* (Furūzānfar edition), pp. 14-15.

Education in Sub-Saharan Africa

Anne Fitzgerald-Lo

The foundation of Islamic education in Africa south of the Sahara is based on the home-school system of medieval Timbuktu. By the 1330s Timbuktu which was a Carrefour for travelers and traders from the Middle East and Africa was renowned as an important cultural center. There were seminars and study sessions on the theology of Islam conducted in private homes in the evenings.

The University of Sankore was built by the Sultan Mansa Musa in the 1330s on the outskirts of Timbuktu. He brought an architect from the Middle East and the university was completed by 1337. There was a curriculum of Islamic studies, law, literature, medicine, surgery, dentistry, astronomy, math, physics and chemistry, and history. The school of medicine was so advanced that eye surgery was taught. At that time in Timbuktu there were many private libraries, some of which contained as many as 700 handwritten volumes.

In the houses of the *alim* (Muslim teacher) the young people studied Quran in the courtyards. The students did not pay and the community sustained the schools where the students passed the entire day. Before the age of 14, a student was expected to memorize the entire Quran of 114 chapters of varying lengths. There were at least 150 of these schools in the environs of Timbuktu, which was estimated to have a population of approximately 25,000 people at that time.

Timbuktu was one of the greatest intellectual centers of Africa and its home-school system of Islamic study has become an integral system of Muslim learning throughout the continent up until contemporary times.

A book which offers an excellent portrait of a Malian *alim* and his school in the early twentieth century in Bandiagara near Timbuktu is *Vie et Enseignment de Tierno Bokar, Le Sage de Bandiagara*[1] by the renowned historian and author Amadou Hampaté Bâ.

Africa's Unique Contribution to Islamic Civilization

The special contribution of Africa to Islamic civilization is family education along with home schooling. Usuman dan Fodio (1754-1817)[2] consolidated Islam in the Northern Territory of Nigeria. Usuman Dan Fodio, descended from the Torodbe Muslim clerics of the Podor region of Futa Toro, Senegal, made an outstanding contribution to the development of Islamic civilization by advocating that all clerics should teach their wives and daughters as well as their sons the *maarif* (knowledge) of Islam. He wrote that any cleric who maintains his wives and daughters only to perform domestic chores is ignorant. His daughter, Nana Asmau dan Fodio (1793-1864), became a respected *alima* and author whose manuscripts in Arabic are available on microfilm at Yale University.[3] She wrote in several languages on the theology of Islam and was a

[1] Paris: Editions de Seuil, 1980. See the recent English translation, *A Spirit of Tolerance: The Inspiring Life of Tierno Bokar*, translated by Jane Casewit (Bloomington, IN: World Wisdom, 2008).

[2] See Mervyn Hiskett, *The Sword of Truth: The Life and Times of Shehu Usuman Dan Fodio* (Oxford: Oxford University Press, 1973).

[3] See Beverly B. Mack and Jean Boyd, *One Woman's Jihad: Nana Asma'u, Scholar and Scribe* (Bloomington, IN: Indiana University Press, 2000) and Jean Boyd, *The Caliph's Sister: Nana Asma'u, Teacher, Poet, and Islamic Lea-*

poet. Nana Asmau was the girl in a set of twins, but her brother Hassan is not well known. She acted as a councilor in the government of her brother Mohamed Bello and this in the nineteenth century. It was unheard of for any woman to exercise political power in the Muslim world in this era. Mohamed Bello, her brother, was the Head of State in this large territory of Nigeria which at that period was independent.

Contemporary Islamic Home Schooling

I have been privileged to observe a Quran school for ten years in the home of Thierno Mountaga Tall (1914-2007) when I resided in Senegal. Thierno Mountaga Tall was the khalif of the Tall family until his death and is a direct descendant of Sheikh Oumar bin Said Tall (1794-1864) who established the Tijani path in the Sahelian region of Africa and controlled an area as large as the ancient Songhai until it was dismantled by the French.[4] The students, who were all Tukulor, came from as far away as Mali and were lodged in the house. They were mainly of the Torodbe clerical class, a group whose only occupation is to learn and teach Quran. Studies were in their language of Halpulaar (Peuhl) and Arabic. Many students left this house to go on to higher studies in Egypt, Morocco, or Saudi Arabia.

The amazing thing about this schooling was the discipline internalized by the students. Students as young as twelve years of age sat outside sometimes in extremely hot weather and there were never problems of discipline. I never heard the teacher raise his voice and the only issues were correct pronunciation of the Arabic. The students had to pay careful attention to how they pronounced the Arabic when reciting Quran.

The Curriculum

Students were to have memorized the entire Quran by the age of 14 years. As western education began to penetrate into these Muslim areas of Africa, parents insisted that the child memorized Quran before they went to European schools. The Senegalese author and former Minister Sheikh Hamidou Kane has written a novel, *The Ambiguous Adventure*, which treats this issue.[5]

After the memorization of the Quran, the students who plan to become clerics often leave their first school to go to another *alim*'s compound to pursue higher education in Islam. In the next stage the student will continue with *tafsir* or interpretation of the holy Quran and exegesis. They will study the biography of the Prophet and review a book written by a thirteenth century Moroccan poet, Al-Fazzazzi, entitled *Ishriniyyat* or the Twenties, which treats the life of the Prophet. The student will also study *fiqh* or Islamic legal theory, which encompasses criminal law and laws of personal status. In the course of these studies the student will continue to refine his knowledge of Arabic grammar and pronunciation. Arithmetic, algebra, jurisprudence, and theology are also incorporated into this curriculum.

After completion of these studies a student receives a type of certificate written by the *alim*, which is the equivalent of a diploma. Many then receive scholarships to continue with their studies in Egypt, Morocco, or Saudi Arabia.

der (London: Frank Cass & Co., 1989).

4 For further information about Sheikh Oumar bin Said Tall, the nineteenth century figure who brought the Tijani Sufi path to the West African Sahel, see John Ralph Willis, *In the Path of Allah: The Passion of Al-Hajj Umar* (London: Frank Cass & Co., 1989).

5 Oxford, UK: Heinemann, 1972.

Islam and its culture are a fundamental component of countries such as Senegal, Mali, Guinea, Gambia, and Mauretania. It is a unifying force and its people have families across the borders as well as ethnic ties. It is therefore a fundamental unifying force and could be a basis for regional integration which would have significant implications for development in areas of communications, transportation, industry and trade, as well as ecology. Hopefully government leaders will have the vision to seize this opportunity for regional development, which could bolster development at all levels.

III.

Dilemmas of Modern Education

Education at the Eleventh Hour

Martin Lings

Let us consider, with special reference to religion and in particular to Christianity, the part played by education in the modern Western world. Generally speaking, and always allowing for exceptions, it would be true to say that in most of their lessons, partly through what they are taught and partly owing to the general outlook that all too clearly prevails among the teachers, the pupils are indoctrinated with the modern pseudo-religion; and in the hour or two a week set aside for the study of the Bible they are given a glimpse of an opposite perspective, though the contradictions are presented as "tactfully" as possible, always at the expense of religion. In some cases the first chapters of Genesis are omitted; in others they are taught without comment; in others they are taught as "myths" in the modern ignoble misuse of that noble word. The pupils' attention is for the most part unlikely to be drawn to the fact that Christianity has some of its deepest roots in these very chapters, to the point that if they are false, then so is it. But a little reflection will bring this out; nor does religion, lukewarmly, fragmentarily, apologetically presented as it is, stand much chance when the pupils are faced with a serious choice between it and modernism. The result is that those who cling to their already precarious faith instinctively block their own channels of spiritual thought, and by a kind of self-imposed mental paralysis, scarcely daring to think about their religion, they sacrifice a vital aspect of sincerity as defined by Christ in his first commandment: "Thou shalt love the Lord thy God . . . with all thy mind"; and it is precisely this part of the commandment that depends most on our human initiative, the part that we should be best able, by our own efforts, to fulfill, though the question of grace can never be absent.

An eminent prisoner within this framework of mental paralysis is Teilhard de Chardin, who also blocks the main and obvious channels of thought in his desperate attempts to combine religion with evolutionism. His appeal lies in his providing certain ingeniously devised side channels which relieve the paralytic by keeping up an illusion of normal mental activity. In other words, with an extraordinary capacity for turning a blind eye and a deaf ear to this and that, he creates a kind of mental hubbub in order to drown the voice of reason, refusing altogether to put himself the following questions which, for anyone who has received a modern Western education, loudly cry out to be asked:

If God exists, as we are taught to believe, and if evolution is a scientific fact, as we are forbidden doubt, what sort of being can God be? Why did He choose to turn mankind back towards the past in longing for a lost Paradise, and to leave them so turned, in all parts of the world, for thousands of years, if He knew that the truth lay in just the opposite direction? Why could He not have taught them about evolution to begin with? Or at least brought them gradually to it, instead of allowing religion after religion to repeat and confirm the same old way of thinking? And why did He allow this to culminate, at any rate for the Western world, in a religion that perhaps more inextricably than any other is bound up with the doctrine of the Fall of man?[1] And why, having prevented all His prophets from divulging evolution, did He allow a mere layman to stumble upon it and to propagate it in defiance of all spiritual authorities of the

[1] Islam is just as explicit about the Fall as Christianity is, but unlike Christianity it is not centered on any historical redeeming sacrifice in view of the Fall.

day, thereby causing millions of people to lose their faith in religion and in Him?

"God moves in a mysterious way," some will argue, in a frantic attempt to retain both God and evolutionism. But you cannot sew up a gaping chasm with such a needle and thread. Seek to retain these two incompatibilities, and you will be left with a deity who is not the Lord of All Mystery but a subhuman monster of incompetence, which is precisely what Teilhardism implies of God.[2] But outside the very special climate of this pseudo-mystical fantasy, one only needs to be able to put two and two together to see that either evolutionism or God must go; and modern education begins to tip the scale in favor of evolutionism at an increasingly early age.

"First of all Copernicus, and the discovery that the earth moves round the sun; then Darwin, and the discovery that men have evolved from apes." Such is the train of thought which is encouraged to prevail. It is never pointed out that the implicit logic is false, that there is no comparison between the two men in question, and that their respective theories did not even result from the same process of thought, inasmuch as Darwin's theory is pure hypothesis. This last fact is in any case unknown to most of the teachers, who in their own youth were misled as they now mislead. So the seemingly unanswerable and conclusive argument of the two discoveries is left unquestioned,[3] to seep into the souls of the young and to eliminate there all respect for tradition, while "proving" the validity of modern skepticism. It is therefore not surprising that many Westerners, even before they have left school, have already opted, if not for atheism, at least for an agnostic reserve of judgment that they, like their parents, will probably never see fit to unreserve. But a normally functioning mind, which is just what they are systematically deprived of—that is, a mind neither warped by rationalism nor spellbound by materialist scientism—would have no difficulty, when faced by the above questions, in finding the right answer and in razing the "card house" of modern ideology to the ground.

"What then," it may be asked, "should we teach?" The answer is: as far as possible the whole truth, which would mean teaching many truths which were not taught in better times, for the needs of the eleventh hour are not the same as those of the sixth or seventh. By way of example, let the young be taught, towards the end of their schooling, that many scientists have conjectured—but in no sense proved—that mankind has evolved from a lower species. This conjecture is an incident in the history of our day. But let them be taught at the same time that the theory in question, which has only crossed the mind of man in relatively recent years, is the exact opposite not merely of what the Bible teaches us but also of the unanimous opinion of the whole pre-Biblical world in all parts of the globe. In particular, the tradition of the four ages of the temporal cycle, Golden, Silver, Bronze, and Iron, which dominated the perspective of classical antiquity, going back into the shadows of prehistory, has also been prevalent from

[2] This escapes the notice of the Teilhardists because they are not really interested in God. Neither was Teilhard de Chardin himself, as he makes clear in the following confession: "If in consequence of some inner subversion, I should lose successively my faith in Christ, my faith in a personal god, my faith in the Spirit, it seems to me that I would continue to believe in the world. The world—the value, the infallibility, and the goodness of the world—this is, in the last analysis, the first and only thing in which I believe." See Kurt Almquist, "Aspects of Teilhardian Idolatry," in *Studies in Comparative Religion*, Summer-Autumn, 1978. See also Wolfgang Smith, *Teilhardism and the New Religion*, and my review of it in *Sophia*, Summer 1997.

[3] If questioned at all, the argument dissolves into nothing, for the one discovery worthy of the name, that of Copernicus, was more in the nature of a rediscovery, since there is reason to suppose that the fact in question was known to some of the ancients. None the less, it is also a cosmological fact that the sun appears to go round the earth, and the human race will no doubt continue to speak of sunrise and sunset for as long as the world exists.

equally ancient times among the Hindus and the American Indians.[4] Or to take one aspect of the evolutionary conjecture, namely that human language evolved from the inarticulate sounds of animals, let it be pointed out that although the origin of language is beyond investigation, linguistic science can none the less take us back to a very remote past, and it teaches us that the oldest languages are the most complex and majestic, while being also the richest in variety of consonantal sounds. All languages in use today have devolved from more elaborate languages which they have simplified and in general mutilated and corrupted. Devolution, not evolution, is also the fate of many word meanings. All students should be made to study the already mentioned degradation of the word "intellect."[5] It is a scientific fact that throughout the ancient world the concept of man's faculties was more exalted and of wider scope that it is today.

Let the traditional and the modern concepts of the universe—or, if one prefers it, of reality—be placed side by side. According to typically modern thought, "reality" is supposed to have originally consisted of the material world alone. It is said that life must have been "sparked off," in some as yet unexplained way, from matter, and that living organisms developed psychic faculties, first of all the senses, then sentiment and memory, and then, as man himself gradually evolved, imagination and reason. According to the traditional explanation, on the other hand it is not the higher which proceeds from the lower but the lower from the higher; nor is existence limited to the psychic and the corporeal. The Supreme Origin—and End—of all things is Absolute Truth, which alone has Reality in the full sense, and which manifests or creates, at lesser degrees of reality, the whole of existence.[6] The traditional theory of existence, common to all religions, is summed up in the Islamic holy[7] tradition: "I was a Hidden Treasure, and I loved to be known, and so I created the world." The psychic and the corporeal, soul and body, are the two lowest levels of reality, and together they constitute what we call "this world." Above them is the domain of the Spirit, known as "the next world" from the standpoint of life on earth, but first in order of creation, for it is no less than the primal "overflow" of the Divine Reality Itself. From that immediate reflection of the Hidden Treasure, the psychic domain is a projected image which in its turn projects the bodily domain.

The language of symbolism, which is part of man's primordial heritage, is based on this hierarchy of the different degrees of the universe. A symbol is not something arbitrarily chosen by man to illustrate a higher reality; it does so precisely because it is rooted in that reality, which has projected it, like a shadow or a reflection, onto the plane of earth. Every terrestrial object is the outcome of a series of projections, from Divine to spiritual, from spiritual to psychic, from psychic to corporeal. But on this lowest plane which is the remotest of all from the Divine Archetypes, and which, being deployed in time and in space, undergoes an extremity of

4 Joseph E. Brown, *The Sacred Pipe*, p. 9.

5 In the "Dark Ages" students were taught that the faculties are ranged in hierarchy, of which the summit is the Intellect, inasmuch as it is connected with transcendent realities, whereas reason, which ranks as a subordinate second to it, is limited to this world. Since the "Enlightenment" however the Intellect in its original sense has been withdrawn from the attention of students; but the word itself, brought down from the supernatural level, has been retained in virtue of its high-sounding effect. In particular, its much used adjective has now taken on the sense of "mentally active"; and since much of the activity is concerned with questioning the existence of the transcendent, many of the so-called "intellectuals" are at the opposite pole from true intellectuality.

6 The etymological sense of this word, from *ex* + *sistere*, "to stand out from" is relevant to our context, for which existence is distinct from Being. God Alone is; from His Being existence proceeds and is ultimately reintegrated into It.

7 So called because in it the Divinity speaks in the first person on the tongue of the Prophet.

differentiation and fragmentation, it is necessary to distinguish between peripheral objects that are no more than faint and fragmentary reflections and the more central objects of each domain, that is, of each subdivision of the animal, vegetable, and mineral kingdoms. The term symbol is reserved for those most direct manifestations which reflect their archetypes with the greatest clarity and which thus have the power to bring about a "remembrance," in the Platonic sense, of the transcendent truth that is symbolized.

In every domain there are orders of precedence which are still felt but no longer, for the most part, understood. The criterion of an object's rank is its symbolic value. By way of example, gold takes precedence over other metals, just as amongst stones the diamond, the ruby, the sapphire, and the emerald rank highest, and all these are powerfully symbolic. In a different domain, the same can be said of such insects as the bee, the butterfly, and the spider. In particular the symbolism of the spider is very relevant to our context, for it would be incapable of weaving its web from its own substance if creation were not woven out of the substance of the Creator. Nor could the web take the form of concentric circles in ever receding distance from the center if the Divine Creative Act did not project the planes of existence in a hierarchy of degrees, each subsequent plane being more remote from its Divine Origin. Nor again could the spider have its centrality and almost at the same time the agile omnipresence which gives it a comprehensive authority over the web if the Infinite and Eternal Truth were not mysteriously both Center and Encompasser of all creation. In this connection we may refer back to the already mentioned rediscovery made by Copernicus, for the metaphysical reconciliation between geocentrism and heliocentrism is closely related to the two Divine Aspects we have just spoken of. On the plane of this world, both man and the sun are outstanding as manifestations or reflections of the Divinity, who is represented as Center by the factual centrality of the sun and as Encompasser by the sun's phenomenal orbit round the earth. Inversely, in the case of man, the Divine Center is symbolized by his phenomenal centrality, whereas the factual orbit of man's earth round the sun is an image of the Divine Encompassing. Considered in this way, both the ignorance of the geocentrists and the enlightenment of the heliocentrists appear to be less absolute than they are often made out to be.

Without the knowledge of the basic traditional concepts which are the theme of these last paragraphs it is impossible to understand ancient thought and therefore, amongst other things, sacred art, which speaks the language of symbolism. Moreover it may be noticed that without the doctrine of the different degrees of universal existence, a whole section of words—not only intellect—becomes unusable, at any rate according to the meanings which alone justify their existence. Specifically modern thought, which refuses to believe that there is anything above the psychic level, thereby denies itself the right to such words as "metaphysical" and "transcendent." Even the word "wisdom" is in jeopardy—or would be if it were not possible to qualify it with the epithet "worldly"—for without the sense of hierarchy and a knowledge of metaphysical truths there could not even be the first glimmerings of what our remote ancestors understood by "wisdom."

Once the exact relationship between science and evolutionism has been established, and once the traditional doctrine of creation has been explained in a way that does justice[8] to it, that

[8] It has to be admitted that the religious fundamentalists, with their altogether literal interpretation of sacred texts have done much to undermine the traditional outlook in the eyes of many of those who are potentially intelligent but spiritually uninformed. Few things do more to further the acceptance of evolutionism than the fundamentalist assertion that the world was created in 4004 B.C.

is, a way which is universal enough to escape from the limitations of one particular perspective, and to open the door to a symbolic interpretation of whatever imagery may be used, then the Darwinist hypothesis is in danger, to say the least, of losing its hold. At the same time, in the light of the science of symbols, a new significance is seen in many features of sacred texts which are often dismissed as childish by the so-called higher criticism. The whole doctrine of the degrees of existence is implicit in what is said on the first page of the Old Testament about "the dividing of the waters"[9] which is itself in fact the main division in the hierarchy of created things, the separation of the domain of the soul and the body from the domain of the Spirit.[10] Or let us take another example, the creation of man "on the sixth day," which is highly significant, in the literal sense of the adverb here used. According to the symbolism of numbers, four denotes the terrestrial state, whence the quaternaries characteristic of it such as elements, seasons, and points of the compass. Five denotes man's place at the center of this state, his quintessentiality, whereas six, being 5 + 1, completes the full status of man by adding the transcendent dimension in virtue of which he is mediator[11] between Heaven and earth.

"The human form marks not only the summit of earthly creatures, but also—and for that very reason—the exit from their condition, or from the *samsāra* as the Buddhists would say. To see man is to see not only the image of God but also a door open towards *Bodhi*, liberating Illumination; or let us say towards a blessed establishment in the divine Nearness. . . . The animal, which can manifest perfections but not the Absolute, is like a closed door, as it were enclosed in its own perfection; whereas man is like an open door that allows him to escape his limits, which are those of the world rather than his own. . . . The splendor of the stag excludes that of the lion, the eagle cannot be a swan, nor the water-lily the rose . . . only man is the image-synthesis of the Creator, by his possession of the intellect—thus also of reason and language—and by his manifestation of it through his very form."[12]

For the evolutionist the whole issue is obscured by the absence from his perspective of any notion of normality. For him the human norm, which in its corporeal aspect is the theme of this last quotation, is a matter of fluctuating opinion. His beliefs oblige him, despite himself, to maintain that what might have seemed a norm for one age will be rejected by subsequent ages as "primitive." We say "despite himself" because notwithstanding the widespread degeneration of the human race that shows itself above all in faces, almost everyone alive today has seen at least one or two examples of human beauty which bear the imprint of the Absolute and which, as his instinct must tell him, are therefore un-outdatable norms.

A book that is particularly relevant to our present context is *From the Divine to the Human*, from which we have just quoted. Its title proclaims in advance its timeliness for a world which, during the last hundred years or more, has been largely dominated by a supposition that might be expressed: "from the subhuman to the human." Schuon draws our attention to the significance of certain basic characteristics which all men have in common and which, if duly weighed, make it impossible to believe in the primacy of matter. There is not one of us who is

[9] For a parallel in Hinduism see René Guénon, *Man and his Becoming According to the Vedanta*, chapter V (closing paragraphs).

[10] That is, in its created aspect, for the Spirit has also and above all a Divine Aspect.

[11] It may be noted in this connection that in Arabic the letter *wāw* and in Hebrew the letter *vāv* both have the numerical value of six, and each constitutes, in its respective language, the linguistic mediator namely the word "and."

[12] Frithjof Schuon, *From the Divine to the Human*, p. 87.

not aware of powers within which are at an incomparably higher level than anything outward and visible. They could be summed up as our subjectivity and our objectivity, our subjective consciousness of being "I," which is inextricably bound up with the mystery of life, and our objective intelligence, which is capable of grasping truths that infinitely transcend our empirical experience.

An argument of great importance which has been neglected by the official representatives of religion is that "the ideas of the 'Great Spirit' and the primacy of the Invisible are natural to man, a fact which does not need to be demonstrated," and that, "what is natural to human consciousness proves *ipso facto* its essential truth inasmuch as the intelligence exists for no other reason than to be adequate to reality." Analogously we could say that the existence of the ear proves the existence of sound; or as Schuon remarks: "We have heard it said that the wings of birds prove the existence of air, and that in the same way the religious phenomenon, common *a priori* to all peoples, proves the existence of its content, namely God and the afterlife: which is to the point if one takes the trouble to examine the argument in depth."[13] The symbolism here is in itself illuminating, for religion gives man "wings" and the air in question is the domain of the Transcendent for which those wings are made and the reality of which they "prove." It is true that such proofs are "inaccessible to certain minds"; but Schuon also gives arguments of common sense, such as might convince some of those who are not—or not yet—open to demonstrations on a higher plane.

"Those who uphold the evolutionist argument of an intellectual progress like to explain religious and metaphysical ideas by inferior psychological factors, such as fear of the unknown, childish hope of perpetual happiness, attachment to an imagery that has become dear, escape into dreams, and the desire to oppress others at small expense *et cetera*; how can one fail to see that such suspicions, presented shamelessly as demonstrated facts, comprise psychological inconsequences and impossibilities which cannot escape any impartial observer? If humanity was stupid for thousands of years, one cannot explain how it could have ceased being so, especially since this is supposed to have happened in a relatively very short space of time; and one can explain it still less when one observes with what intelligence and heroism it was stupid for so long and with what philosophic shortsightedness and moral decadence it has finally become 'lucid' and 'adult.'"[14]

[13] *From the Divine to the Human*, p. 6.

[14] Ibid. p. 12.

Modern Education:

Its History, Theories, and Philosophies

Seyyed Hossein Nasr

For the great majority of young Muslims who come to the West the Western institution most often encountered and the one with which they have the most intimate experience is the educational one. This is also true to some extent of young Muslims who are studying in the modernized educational institutions within the Islamic world itself, institutions which are modeled upon Western ones and have been created since the thirteenth/nineteenth[1] century in different countries of the Islamic world with the express aim of introducing modern learning to Muslims. It is, therefore, important to have a deeper understanding of the role and meaning of education and educational institutions in the modern West and also the historical roots of Western education.

As in the Islamic world, so also in the West before the period of secularization and modernization during the Renaissance and the eleventh/seventeenth century, education was related to religion and the educational institutions were either directly or indirectly controlled by the Church. There were furthermore separate educational institutions for the Jewish minority in Europe wherever there was a sufficiently large number of Jews. Schools in pre-modern Europe sought, therefore, to educate the young in the theological, philosophical, legal, and ethical teachings of the Church or in the case of the Jews the Jewish religion and on the higher levels to prepare Christian students for priesthood and important ecclesiastical positions and Jewish students to become rabbis. This situation is very reminiscent of the *Quranic* schools, *madrasahs* and other religious institutions in the Islamic world attended by students from an early age. However, education was more widespread in the Islamic world than in the pre-modern West.

In the early Middle Ages Islamic educational institutions themselves began to have an influence, especially in the domain of higher learning, upon their Western counterparts through Spain, Sicily and France as well as Italy. In fact, the whole college system which gave rise to the modern Western universities had a close relationship to the Islamic *madrasah* system which survives to this day in the Islamic world. Such terms as the "chair" used in Western universities is, of course, the direct translation of the Arabic word *kursi* and there are many educational practices which have survived to this day in the older institutions of higher learning of medieval origin in the West such as Salamanca, Paris, Bologna, Oxford, and Cambridge which bear deep resemblance to practices in the classical Islamic educational system. It is also important to remember that the Western educational institutions, especially the university, are not part and parcel of the modern world and that in their origin they, like the Church, belong to the pre-modern history of the West.

Very early in the development of modernism, however, educational institutions were for the most part, although not completely, captured by the forces of modernism and modern education became the most important means for furthering the value system of the modern world, for the spread of secularization and for the criticism of the religious worldview. Through

[1] Editor's Note: the author lists the Islamic and Western dates, according to their respective calendars.

educational institutions, not only the sciences but also ideas concerning the amassing of wealth, furthering economic ends, and creating greater social mobility within society were disseminated, this being especially true in America and only more recently in Europe.

The process of secularization of education in the West took several centuries and it is far from being complete. As more and more institutions of learning which had originally been founded by various churches were secularized, new institutions were often created by the state which sought to preserve a separation between religious institutions and those created by the state or other secular bodies. In some countries such as the United States and France this separation between religious and secular education in state sponsored institutions has been rigorously maintained and the government seeks to make certain that schools funded by public money do not have any religious coloring to them. In other countries such as Great Britain and Germany such is not the case and governments do support religious education.

In any case, through the universalization of education in modern times, that is, the establishment of elementary and secondary schools to educate nearly all children as well as through the spread of university education to a larger number of students, secular education has extended its influence. At the same time, however, the religious bodies, whether Catholic or Protestant, have also succeeded in preserving their own educational system from the kindergarten and elementary schools through the university. Furthermore, in both America and Europe there continue to exist to this day traditional Jewish schools called Yeshivas which resemble in many ways the Islamic *madrasahs*. Therefore, if one looks upon the general picture of education in the West, one will see that while there has been a continuous secularization of the older institutions which were originally founded by churches of various kinds and the establishment of numerous secular institutions, one can also observe the continuation of religious education on both sides of the Atlantic despite the great differences of educational philosophy between these two types of educational institutions, namely, the religious and the secular.

As far as the goals achieved by the educational system established by various European states and later on in America are concerned, these have consisted of the propagation of national ideals and philosophies such as the new secularism, nationalism, utilitarianism, public welfare and have included, of course, economic goals spurned by the idea of material progress which in the thirteenth/nineteenth century became almost a religion of its own. The concept of education in the classical sense of training the mind and the soul has not disappeared, especially in older educational institutions and church sponsored schools, and wherever liberal arts education flourishes, but it has been seriously challenged by the new educational philosophy. Consequently, the universities especially, and through their influence secondary and primary schools, have become on the one hand a kind of "secular church" for the spread of secular ideas and the professors and teachers have come to occupy to some extent the role of the earlier priesthood wielding definite authority in their fields especially in the field of the sciences. Almost all of the important secular ideas which have shaken the foundations of religion in the modern world such as evolutionism, the idea of progress, doctrinaire socialism, psychoanalysis, etc. have had their origin in or been spread by modern educational institutions and have spread from there to other parts of society. On the other hand, however, precisely because the university attracts unto itself usually the most perceptive and intelligent members of society and the institution itself predates the rise of modernism, universities have continued to serve even in the modern world as a critic of that world. In fact, the most profound criticism of the very idols of modern thought such as progress and the like have also come from university circles so that the university has been at once a bulwark for the preservation and the spread of modern secular ideas and at the same time a critic of many of the ideas which are now tearing modern society apart.

It is necessary to emphasize the important role of educational institutions in the West, especially since the thirteenth/nineteenth century, in the indoctrination of the general population with various ideologies from nationalism to Marxism, from Communism to Western capitalism and democracy or other ideologies which have been dominant in the modern West. Here, precisely because of the survival of the earlier religious foundation of education and the survival of many educational institutions with a religious orientation, especially in America, there has been and continues to be a constant conflict and tension between secularist ideologies and religious ideas.

It is difficult for a Muslim student brought up even in the semi-traditional Islamic educational system, not to speak of the classical *madrasah*, to realize how the teaching of various branches of knowledge has become separated from religious values in modern education. There has come into being in fact a compartmentalization not only of the branches of knowledge separated one from the other with no cohesive unity in contrast to what one observes in the traditional image of the various branches of the tree of knowledge related to the trunk of the tree, but also a nearly total separation between knowledge and spiritual values. This is to be detected in almost all Western universities except those which are directly sponsored by Catholic, Protestant, and also Jewish religious organizations in which the values of those particular religions are openly taught to the students. For the majority of students going to so-called state sponsored or secular institutions, in fact, the refusal to teach spiritual values has been considered as being essential for the separation of religion from the educational enterprise. By default, therefore, knowledge has become separated from both spirituality and morality.

As far as morality itself is concerned, precisely because of the gradual separation of the educational system from its religious background, the question has now arisen as to what kind of morality to teach if one consider morality at all. The ethical dimension of life has become relativized and sometimes even put aside precisely because the teachers, the state, and the various institutions responsible have not been able to agree as to what ethical norms should be taught to the students. This has resulted in a grave crisis which is now beginning to manifest itself especially among the younger generation in the West as the older ethical norms which even the modern secular West inherited from Christianity gradually begin to wane and disappear.

Western education is therefore caught to a large extent in the throes of the tension between religion and secular humanism. The battle lines have been drawn in many domains and subjects ranging from evolutionism versus creationism, various theories of society, Eurocentrism versus multiculturalism, the question of the meaning of life, the problem of the relationship between the various fields of knowledge and ethics and many other subjects fundamental to the philosophy and theory of education. There exists also tension between what certain people claim should be "objectivism" in educational upbringing and the presentation of a particular point of view and an already determined philosophy within which educational practice should take place. These tensions and conflicts have resulted in the gradual disappearance from the philosophies and theories of education of the concept of truth itself. Today, in most modern Western institutions of learning one speaks seriously about the truth only in the natural and mathematical sciences, whereas in the humanities the social sciences and the like one rarely hears a teacher speak about truth and most subjects are presented in a completely relativistic manner as if there were no such thing as the truth. As stated earlier in this book, many modern philosophers even deny the meaning or significance of the term "truth."

The compartmentalization of knowledge, which is one of the characteristics of the mental and intellectual scene of the modern world, is not only reflected in modern education but is also caused by it. A number of important Western thinkers have sought to overcome this excessive compartmentalization but they have not succeeded in doing so because there is no longer a worldview which would unite various disciplines. There is already the division between the natural and mathematical sciences on the one side and the social sciences and finally the humanities on the other, each with different perspectives and methods while in the case of many practitioners of these latter disciplines there is the attempt to emulate the natural sciences.

Something still remains of the earlier pre-modern idea of the liberal arts, the *artes liberales* of the medieval period, which shares a great deal in common with the classification of knowledge and the curriculum described by certain classical Muslim thinkers and authors. The liberal arts education, which is to be found in America and England, preserves something of the unity of perspective which characterized medieval European learning when European civilization was a religious and integrated civilization in many ways similar to the Islamic, especially in the educational field, but even this hallowed educational philosophy has now become to a large extent compromised by the great emphasis upon the natural sciences and the creation of what are called the social sciences which try to emulate as much as possible the methods of the quantitative sciences and apply them to society as such. The social sciences, moreover, seek to engulf the humanities. As a result, the humanities themselves are struggling hard to survive as humanities.

It is interesting to note here, as far as the young Muslim student is concerned, that most Muslims who come to study in Western institutions rarely take up the subject of the humanities seriously. Most of them study either the sciences, medicine, or engineering and, therefore, the humanities seem somewhat irrelevant to them. In the Islamic world itself also there is a great crisis in the modern established universities precisely because the systems from the West have been transplanted into that world without a close integration between the humanities, which should be drawn totally from Islamic sources, the religious disciplines and the sciences which have been imported from the West.

In any case, whether in the West or elsewhere, modern educational institutions, which are the main repositories of knowledge and which consider themselves to be the main guardians of modern Western civilization, contain within themselves the seeds of profound conflicts as far as the philosophies and theories of education are concerned, these conflicts reflecting and emanating from the separation created at the dawn of the modern period between the domain of knowledge and the domain of the sacred as contained in religion. Many Western educational institutions still preserve something of their medieval past but there are also many innovations based on views of man as the purely earthly and non-religious being defined by twelfth/eighteenth and thirteenth/nineteenth century philosophers or as a single cog in the social machine as envisaged by positivist and Marxist theoreticians since the thirteenth/nineteenth century. These educational institutions, therefore, remain in a state of constant tension with religious institutions and even with the earlier humanism which sought to view human beings as a whole in need of the development of both their mental and spiritual aspects.

There is no doubt that modern Western education has exercised a profound impact upon the Islamic world. This impact has come through the very large number of Muslim students who are sent to the West and who are sometimes bewildered to see the conflicts between what they are taught in class and services held on Sundays, between certain students who are very religious and others who are totally opposed to religion, all of these being representative of the divorce between religious values and science in Western education. But the impact of Western education on the Islamic world is also felt through the presence of modern educational institutions within the Islamic world itself where today there is a great crisis resulting from their conflict with the traditional institutions of learning which have their own philosophy based upon the unity of knowledge, the servitude of man to God, the centrality of the Divine Revelation and all the other principles which characterize the Islamic worldview. This conflict is to be seen to a large extent also in secondary and primary schools in many of the larger cities in most Islamic countries where Western models have been copied in one form or another usually depending upon the accidents of history. A country colonized by Great Britain copied British models as is the case of Pakistan and Muslim India or Nigeria; if it had been colonized by France then French models were copied as we see in North Africa and if colonized by the Dutch then the Dutch model as can be seen in Indonesia. Moreover, American educational models have also been incorporated in many Muslim lands in the past few decades often superimposed upon the earlier European models.

Today, the understanding of modern Western education in both its history and theories is absolutely essential for the Muslim student not only in order to protect himself or herself when that person studies in the West, but also in order to understand the conflict within the Islamic world of two educational institutions and philosophies which produce graduates who belong to the same countries and speak the same language but have two very different worldviews. These worldviews are, furthermore, reflected on every level from the role of the teacher who in Islam is considered to have a very high position in society to the extent that there is a saying attributed to ʿAli that, "He who has taught me a single word, I will become his slave," to the role of the student within that institution, to the relationship between knowledge and ethics, between science and religion, the content of the curricula, the meaning and goal of education and all of the other fundamental elements which constitute education. In the Islamic world as in the West education has always been central because it is through education that the younger generation is trained to carry out and carry forward the ideals, norms, and principles of a particular society.

Today, Western education is in a great crisis even in seeking successfully to achieve the distorted goals of the secularization of knowledge, material domination, cultivation of individualism and all of the other elements which the Islamic worldview rejects. This system is doubly dangerous for Muslims both because it is in a state of crisis within itself and also because even if it were not to be in conflict within itself, it would be in discord with the Islamic perspective and the values which Islam cherishes most dearly. It is therefore, very critical at a time when Muslims must learn various Western disciplines, including not only science and technology but other disciplines as well, in order to be able to provide their own answers and master their own destinies in a world in which they are faced with vast challenges, that they become fully cognizant of the meaning, role, and function of education and educational institutions, including especially the philosophies which underlie them. In this way, they may become able to learn to the extent possible what they wish to learn of Western disciplines without becoming excessively contaminated in an unconscious way by forces which could distort their religious perspective, uproot them spiritually and intellectually, alienate them from their own traditional background and simply add another potent element contributing to disorder and chaos within Islamic society itself.

Intellectual Freedom

Lord Northbourne

The meaning currently attached to the words "intellectual freedom" is very clearly exemplified in the demand that state schools and state aided schools should be neutral in their approach to religion, that religious education should be restricted to the giving of factual information about religion, and that no regular school assembly should be religious in character or content. It is argued that no "prejudice" in favor of religion as such, or of any particular religion, should be instilled into children, who must be free to decide for themselves as individuals whether to accept the truth and the authority of religion or not, or, more generally, free to decide what source of truth and what authority, if any, they should accept. This represents the extension to children of an individualistic "freedom of thought" which has long been widely commended as a sign of intellectual maturity in their elders, and scarcely less widely accepted by them and put into practice in the form of "permissiveness" in behavior.

It is not uncommon today to argue for "intellectual honesty". People who adopt any particular point of view may not like being told that they are enslaved by prejudice, but they resent even more deeply an accusation of dishonesty. Dishonesty is deliberate; it implies deceit practiced for one's own advantage, even though that deceit be only self-deceit. A factor of morality as well as of intelligence is thereby introduced; animosity is aroused and any discussion drops to a lower level.

It is of course a fact that any two people can be as honest to God and to themselves as it is possible for fallible humanity to be, and can still fail to arrive at the same conclusions. That is what people who use the phrase "intellectual honesty" do not seem to accept. If one were to adopt their attitude one would say "do not choose to accept", thereby labeling them as hypocrites, as they so often label people who do not see eye to eye with themselves.

The idea of "intellectual honesty" is the same however it may be expressed. It is derived from the principles of scientific research, with their insistence that no conclusion is fully valid until it has been shown to be in conformity with everything that observation can disclose. That, precisely, is what constitutes and characterizes the scientific approach.

The great changes resulting from the applications of science to industry have led to the growth of the idea that no approach to truth other than the scientific is valid, and therefore that no conception can be said to represent the truth until it has been checked by observation and deduction from observation. This in turn has led to the calling in question of every assumption, every system, every tradition, and every belief that has ever constituted the background of a civilization, and their submission to an investigation which claims to be scientific (whether it be really so or not).

When the arrival of that better world which the progress of science was to have made possible is disappointingly delayed, the relative stability of the ancient traditions leads to their being regarded as obstacles to progress, and being blamed for the delay. Their elimination or supersession can then be claimed as a liberation of the human spirit.

The assumptions, systems, and traditions of the past were based on religion. It constituted their background even when they were not specifically religious in character. Religion, when it is true to itself, postulates that there are truths—and those the most important truths of all—which are neither discoverable nor provable by the faculties of observation and deduction alone, but are accessible only to something that can be called vision or intuition or faith.

To judge the content of religious faith, which is by definition unquestioning, by purely secular preconceptions and prejudices on the grounds that it is unscientific is therefore to deny the very foundations of religion. The opponents of religion lose no opportunity to do just this, and to class religious faith as servile and unworthy of the newly won independence of mankind. They apply similar derogatory epithets to the more or less unquestioning personal loyalties which have until recently been the basis of the unity of all social groupings, from the family upwards, in every civilization. Those loyalties are derived from the hierarchical aspects of religion and its accompanying traditions; any picture of the situation that takes no account of them is therefore incomplete.

Thus the idea has grown up that the scientific approach can alone properly be said to be intellectual, whereas the approach of religion cannot, and that therefore the tendency of religion is to impede intellectuality. This is not to be wondered at in people for whom the word "intellectuality" implies no more than conformity to the scientific approach. The goal of intellectuality is a better understanding of the origin, nature, and end of man and of the universe. It is just such an understanding that religion claims to offer. Insofar as that claim is justified, religion, very far from impeding intellectuality, is an essential part of it. That is the crux of the whole question, yet how seldom do those who seek to defend religion put the question in that form! One can hardly expect its opponents to do so.

Nevertheless, despite all the propaganda for so-called intellectual freedom, the collectivity, the mass of the people, will always have faith in something, and will always follow someone. What philosopher, they ask, what scientist, what President, what demagogue, what quack, what mushroom Messiah will bring them the comfort and the freedom they seek? This is no new phenomenon. The Psalmist says, "There be many that say: who will show us any good?" (Ps. 4:6). Now, in the virtual absence of an established source of authority, the phenomenon has entered into a new dimension, and the cry "who will show us any good?" has become almost universal.

The average mentality, in its search for an authority it need not question, seems instinctively to know itself better than many who seek to guide it seem to know it. The average mentality is by definition mediocre. That is not to its discredit. Mental capacity is, and always will be variable, and while that is so the average mentality will be in the middle range of capacity. It is also a mathematical certainty that it will always be represented by a large majority. It is not reasonable to expect it to be able to formulate the great critical decisions on which everything depends, least of all when those decisions involve a discernment between truth and error, as, for instance, when the issue is between religion and anti-religion in all its many forms and disguises.

Most really critical decisions are of that order; they demand a wisdom that is profound and not commonplace and is therefore rare. Most people are in fact more or less conscious of their limitations and of their dependence on guidance "from above", whatever the sense in which the word "above" may be understood, so that, although they have been told that authority is now in their hands and that they can and must exercise it through the medium of their votes, they will still look for an authority which they can accept without having to think everything out for themselves.

That such an authority existed when it was vested in religion is undeniable. People then looked for guidance, at least in matters of principle, to the religious hierarchy which was guardian and expositor of the spirit and of the teaching of the founder of their religion. Even kings did so, kings whose temporal power was exercised by divine right; but that right conferred on them their temporal functions only which, in principle if not always in practice, did not impinge on the functions of the spiritual authority; it was indeed the main duty of kings to support and defend that authority. This system did not always work perfectly; no system, however admirable, is proof against the imperfections inherent in human individuals and societies. These imperfections are variable in kind and are seldom seen for what they are by those who manifest them at any particular time. Every age seems to have its own characteristic failings and to be much less aware of them than of the failings of its predecessors. The obvious imperfections which marred the operation of the hierarchical system make it easy to attribute them to the people's acceptance of the authority of religion, and to make insufficient allowances for the variety and extent of human perversity and weakness. This is especially true if one is encouraged to do so by an unquestioning faith in the conception of progressive evolution of the human race, with its corollary of the superiority of the present age in every domain, spiritual as well as material.

However that may be, it is apparent that current problems are too complex, too remote, too specialized, too subtle, or too profound to be within the competence of the average mentality, with its enormous numerical preponderance. The best opinions can only be those of an intellectual elite composed of people who can see the human situation most penetratingly, most synthetically, most realistically, and most dispassionately, and such people are necessarily few. Whoever they may be, they alone can put things in their proper place and can escape from being confused or overwhelmed by the weight of the indefinite multiplicity of facts, and of the opinions derived from them, under which our scientific civilization is laboring. It is obvious that such people's opinions ought to prevail; and perhaps they would, if other people's opinions as to who they are did not differ so widely and change so frequently as they do.

These things are seen, clearly or dimly, by most people; but today the necessity of rule by majority vote is an article of faith. The only solution seems to be that the constituent members of society should be educated up to their responsibilities, so that they may vote intelligently. It would seem however that people must on no account be taught what to think; that would be to deny them intellectual freedom and would open the way to a tendentious advocacy in the field of religion; they must therefore presumably only be made familiar with as many facts as possible, and then if possible be taught how to think; how to assess the relevance of facts, how to relate one to another, and then how to discriminate between the indefinity of ideas and opinions that can be based on them. The practicality of this conception is, to say the least, questionable. All that need be said here is that it ignores two facts: one is that though the average of intelligence be raised, it is still an average and not an optimum; the other is that the opinions of the most highly educated people differ at least as widely as do the opinions of those less favored. One suspects that what the advocates of education as a panacea are really thinking in most cases, though they may not realize it, is that other people, if they were properly educated, would then think as they themselves do, and then all would be well. This is very natural, we probably all do it to some extent, but it is too simple to be true.

To expect the impossible of the average adult mentality is foolish; it merely leads to the replacement of intelligence by prejudices that are often largely emotional in origin, and thence to the passing of authority into the hands of any individual or group that is able to seize it. To expect the impossible of children is even more foolish, and it is at the same time cruel. Children are not yet equipped to decide what is best for them even in the simple affairs of daily life; how much less so when fundamental assumptions are in question! Let them be encouraged to think by all means, but only on the simplest issues; they can only be happy when the really adult issues do not arise at all for them, but are covered by an established and unquestioned code of behavior. Moreover it is nothing less than the truth that most adults are in a comparable position. Everyone, child or man, needs a framework, an "establishment", to limit the range of his responsibilities to matters that are within his competence. Children need it even more than do their elders, and it is the first duty of their elders to provide it for them—first their parents, then their teachers. The rigidity of such a framework can be, and perhaps often has been, carried to excess; but that error is probably less damaging in the end than its opposite. Rigidity or otherwise is a question of degree; much more crucial is the question of the foundation on which the framework is built up. For there will always be a framework, there will always be authority, there will always be an "establishment", good or bad, simply because people cannot get on without it and are always seeking it, whatever the theoretical anarchists may say.

In the past the foundation of the social framework was religion. The authority of religion, firstly in matters of fundamental truth concerning the origin and destiny of man and the direction in which the ultimate good is to be sought, and secondly and consequentially in the field of morality and ethics, used to be regarded as final because it was regarded as of divine origin.

If indeed an eternal and all-wise God has revealed Himself to man, it is anything but intelligent to accept as final any authority other than that of this revelation, embodied, as it necessarily is if it is to be handed down from generation to generation, in forms doctrinal, ritual, and moral; and the guardianship of these forms is no less necessarily the function of a specially trained and qualified hierarchy. It certainly seems that this conception must either be substantially true or not true at all. If it is true, the fear of the Lord is in truth "the beginning of wisdom" (Ps. 111:10); it is a first condition without which there can be no real wisdom, and so no well-founded authority, no stable framework within which the inherently limited abilities of humanity can each find its proper place.

Science offers no alternative framework. The best it can offer is material wealth in a wide sense of the term, that is to say, the satisfaction of a wide variety of desires. It does not conceive of any means of achieving that escape from desires we call "contentment" otherwise than through the satisfaction of those desires. It has not yet learnt that there is no limit to the multiplication of desires, nor that, since different people's desires are often mutually incompatible, an indefinite multiplication of desires increases conflict as well as discontent.

The scientific outlook on the origin, nature, and destiny of man, varied though it be within certain limits, leads only to two alternative attitudes. The first, which is the more scientific, is one of an ultimate despair arising from the inevitability of terrestrial, solar, and cosmic cataclysms. The second appears to take no account of the first, and is less scientific both for that reason and because it is based on nothing more than a rather vague hypothesis; it is a utopianism based on the notion of progressive evolution of the human race. The latter has so strong an emotional appeal that it has in practice attained the status of a dogma, unexamined and unquestioned. The first attitude is an ultimate hopelessness, the second is a consolation eagerly grasped at in the prevailing intellectual and social confusion.

The point at issue here is one of truth and not of consolation. The consolations of religion are often spoken of, as if its purpose were to make this life easy. The only real consolation religion offers, and it is no small one, is that of making sense of the world, even when the world seems to be unbearable. Promises of celestial bliss are always conditional, and they are balanced by promises of hell (to reduce a situation covering a very wide range of possibilities to very simple but nevertheless adequate terms). The notion of a life of pleasure ending in total annihilation can be more "consolatory" than the truth, the rigorous aspects of which are so commonly glossed over.

How then, it will be asked, has it come about that the authority of religion has become so weakened? There are two possible answers. The first is that it is because the principles of religion, which are founded on the conception of divinity and revelation, and on the precedence of the eternal over the temporal, are in themselves false or inadequate. If this answer is right, the matter ends there.

The second possible answer is that it is because human failings have allowed the principles of religion to become overlaid and obscured by conceptions or preoccupations which are confined to the universe of phenomena and thereby tend to exclude the divine and the eternal. If the second answer is right, the decline of the authority of religion must be attributed to a substitution of mutable opinion for immutable principles, or of hypothesis for faith, as the foundation of authority. The substitution has been gradual, but by it the conception and the content of revealed religion has by imperceptible degrees been changed, so that eventually religion has ceased to be a foundation and becomes more and more an optional extra, more and more subjected to the uncertainties of opinion, less and less the accepted background and collective of opinion. At the heart of this change lies an enfeeblement of the conception of Divinity, whereby Divinity loses the quality of absoluteness from which the uniqueness of the authority of religion is derived, and becomes relativized.

The form of the questions that often arise concerning the nature of Divinity is revealing in this connection. It is usually something like "is there a God?" or "does God exist?" or "is God a reality?" or "what is God like?". In any such form they are really "leading questions", since they imply that God can properly be considered as one factor in our situation among others; that God "as He is in Himself"—to use an admittedly but inevitably equivocal phrase—can be objectivized distinctively, like the objects of our perceptions and imaginations; that He is not even as real as those objects unless He can be brought into comparison with them; in short, that God is a relativity like everything else we can perceive or know.

It is true that God as Creator can be considered as "relativizing Himself" in His creation, insofar as His creation is a manifestation of His qualities and attributes; but that manifestation is not God "as He is in Himself". To suppose that it is so is the error of pantheism.

It is no less true that every relativity is a Divine manifestation; the conception of God as "Creator" of all things implies nothing less than that. But God is not *a* reality; He does not "exist" distinctively as do His manifestations; as Creator He is the origin of all existence and of all distinctive realities. As such He alone is absolute reality, He is Reality Itself. The reality of all things, from the universe in its entirety to the most evanescent of dreams, is relative and more or less fugitive and illusory; God is the one and only absolute reality and absolute certitude; He alone is That which "cannot not be". By Him alone the universe is sustained; from Him all things come and to Him all things must return. Woe betide those beings who have any choice in the matter if they fail to prepare themselves for that return. Allowing for the inadequacy of words in this connection, such is the foundation of religion, and nothing less will serve. It is not compatible with compromise of any kind.

Of this order, though not necessarily in this form, is the vision that has inspired and guided mankind since the dawn of time. It is a vision and not a deduction; like physical vision it is direct, immediate, "concrete" and convincing; it is "supra-rational" in the sense that, as with physical vision, it is not preceded but followed by reasoning.

In comparison, how dismally trivial are the basic conceptions of humanism, scientism, and secularism, and how unworthy are they of a humanity to which, alone of all creatures, the possibility of a celestial vision has been granted! Uncountable millions have seen things in the light of this celestial vision, always more or less imperfectly because the full blaze of the truth is too strong for the creature, always from within the framework of their religion, guided by the symbol, the spoken word, and the radiance of the saints, and in endless different ways, each according to the light that is in him, whether it be bright or dim, white or colored. It is written: "and if that light be darkness, how great is that darkness!" (Matt. 6:23).

If every relativity is a Divine manifestation, anything can in principle be seen as a "symbol" of Divinity, since it is as it were a reflection on the terrestrial plane of some aspect of the Divine nature. Not least among those symbols is man, "made in God's image and likeness". It is this that justifies, and even necessitates, the use of anthropomorphic symbolisms, whether in the form of sculptures or pictures or fables or parables, for the communication of religious truths that are in their essence ineffable. The spiritual potentiality of the symbol may however always become obscured or lost when the outward or literal or "human" significance of the symbol is taken to be its principal or its only significance. The symbol then becomes an "idol". Thus, in the case of anthropomorphic symbols, the conception of Divinity can come to be increasingly assimilated to the outward form of the symbol. In other words, man may tend increasingly to make God in his own image, to "measure" God by his own capacities and characteristics, so that God becomes, not God, but a more or less magnified and particularized image of man. This is an "idolization", not of a graven image, but of the image that man himself is; and it is the ultimate idolatry.

Since however this idolatry is not recognized as such by its perpetrators, they will tend to attribute an idolatrous intention to anyone who uses symbols, anthropomorphic or otherwise, with a right intention, especially if the symbols in question are those of a religious nature which they have been taught to hold in contempt or to dismiss as "primitive". The conception of Divinity—or the celestial vision—would not however be what it is if only one particular symbolical formulation could be used to suggest it. When the Absolute is in question, the creature tied to relativity must be content with whatever point of view is his by nature or by upbringing; what is important is, firstly, that this point of view should be compatible with the truth, and secondly, that it should not be taken to be more that it is.

At the heart of the decadence of religion lies this kind of relativization of the conception of Divinity, inevitably accompanied by a loss of the celestial vision. The repercussions of this vision, where it exists and whatever form it may assume, are limitless, they cannot but reach into every department of life; its consequences may take a lot of working out, and much may be gained or lost in the process, but the vision itself is of a total simplicity and directness. That is why it is often more accessible to those whose minds are simple and direct than to those whose minds are complex and analytical, and that is why it is accessible to children, and to those who are able to receive it "as a child". It is precisely the opportunity of a glimpse of this vision that so many people are seeking to deny to our children by limiting their contact with religion to mere information concerning the forms it assumes. The final decision however does not rest with man, it rests with God, since vision is a grace, and is therefore neither procurable nor disposable at will. Those who would seek to impede its operation do themselves more harm even than they do to the children.

From the point of view of the militant atheist or agnostic it is good policy to deny participation in religion to children, since, as they know well, religion can only be communicated by participation (always excepting the possibility of a special grace). Information alone, especially if treated as purely historical and conveyed by an agnostic, can be a very good medium for anti-religious propaganda; for no teacher—or parent—can help communicating his own point of view to those he is teaching, whatever the subject of the lesson.

Humanism, through at least some of its avowed representatives, has adopted other tactics, and is now claiming equality of status with revealed religion, and has been admitted in that guise by representatives of the ancient religions to some of their discussions. Apparently those representatives cannot see that the ideals of humanism are fundamentally the same as those of atheism, secularism, and agnosticism in all their forms, insofar as they idolize man by putting him in the place of God as the first object of all service and all devotion. Alas! how many people who profess to be religious do just that, although to do so is to deny—or to distort beyond recognition—the very vision on which their religion is founded. Religion is infinitely more than a mere system of ideas, philosophical, ethical, or otherwise, and its primary function is not one of making this life more agreeable, but of the salvation of souls; its concern with the intemporal takes precedence of, and alone justifies, any concern it may show for the temporal.

What we are in fact witnessing is a dissolution of the sacred traditions. They can properly be called "sacred" because they are derived from revealed religion and are its normal support. It is they that hold a civilization together and give it its distinctive quality. There has never been a stable and coherent civilization constituted on any other foundation—remembering that coherence and stability are necessarily always relative—and there never will be, for the simple reason that humanity is not independent of God, to whom it is linked by revelation and tradition. Without them there is no framework within which freedom, intellectual or otherwise (and itself also necessarily always relative) can be realized without its turning into license and leading to chaos. Tradition however is by no means merely a negative or protective force. In its more important positive and constructive aspect it canalizes thought and activity into ways that are truly profitable, because they lead away from attachment to the world and the ego and towards attachment to a spiritual center.

The sacred traditions in all their diversity manifest the unity of the Absolute; they do so most evidently in what may be called their common celestial orientation; the message is always essentially the same though the symbolical "language" that conveys it be diverse. It is the diversity of that language that strikes most forcibly the modern literalistic mentality, thereby clouding or even discrediting the universal message. If however there is that which transcends and comprehends all human experience, that message can evidently not be reduced to any single formulation, although paradoxically the diverse traditional formulations can each suggest it adequately, provided only that those who live within their influence are so attuned to them that they can recognize them as reflecting on the terrestrial plane realities subsisting on a higher plane. Any such recognition is truly intellectual, since it implies a grasp of fundamental truths at least in some degree; and that is precisely what the human intellect is for.

Everything that had a beginning must have an end, and the sacred traditions are no exception. This applies, however, exclusively to their outward forms, their content being universal and imperishable; it is therefore only from a temporal point of view that they must seem to die. As they split up and dissolve there is less and less to hold society together; in the end nothing remains but secular ideologies, pseudo-traditions of purely human invention, looking earthwards and not heavenwards, having no principle of unity more stable than collective opinion, and therefore always in opposition one to another as well as to sacred tradition itself.

Is all this mere prejudice? If it is true, no; if it is untrue, yes. Prejudice implies the assertion of an opinion based on an unsure foundation, and the only sure foundation for opinion is truth—the whole truth, and not a partial truth. Supporters of the doctrine of intellectual freedom would limit the conception of truth to truth that can be supported by evidence, and it is an article of faith with them that the only valid evidence in the last analysis is the evidence of the senses. The evidence of the senses, however highly developed it may be, reveals the characteristics of the visible universe and nothing more, and so, unless the visible universe contains its own cause within itself—that is to say, unless it "created itself"—scientific investigation can never elucidate the ultimate reason for anything whatever, and least of all for existence as such.

Is it not prejudice or presumption or both to deny that any man can see, or ever has seen, more than the human eye can see, or heard more than the human ear can hear, or known more than can be categorically stated in words; in short, that no man's understanding can be more penetrating or profound than one's own? Or to claim that the scientific approach is the only valid approach to truth, despite the fact that the conclusions of science may be true while still representing no more than a partial truth? Admittedly no dialectical proof of the validity of the religious approach is possible; it seems to be forgotten however that this is equally true of the scientific approach. The only "proof" in either case resides in the quality of the vision on which the approach is founded, that is to say, on the "light that is in you", whether that light be bright or dim or even darkness itself.

Even apart from all this, is it practical or realistic or scientific or even common-sensical to suppose that, provided that the average mentality is "intellectually free" in the sense of having no preconceptions—and thus operating as it were *in vacuo*—it will absorb from its environment whatever is good for it and reject whatever is bad, or even that a sufficient majority will do so? This indeed would postulate a faith in human nature that is not supported by the available evidence. The advocates of intellectual freedom are too intelligent to have any such faith; what they really want is that the average intelligence should be "free" to absorb what may be called the "scientific prejudice" that now predominates in their environment.

Must we then admit something that most of our contemporaries are reluctant or unable to admit, namely, that in the past, and insofar as religion was the final authority, a vision more penetrating than ours provided the foundation for authority? If so, it will be said, the people of those times ought to have behaved more wisely than we do, and ought therefore to have been more harmonious and more contented. The common assumption is, not only that they knew less than we do, but also that they endured so much discomfort and hardship that they cannot possibly have been more contented than we are. Contentment is a difficult thing to prove or disprove at a distance; but one who has passed the Psalmist's three-score years and ten can at least assert that people, even poor people, were in general more contented before the 1914-18 war than they are now, although not nearly so well provided with comforts and luxuries. Incidentally they were also more often people of strong individuality, "characters" or "personalities" as we might say; not of course always either virtuous or agreeable, but qualitatively distinctive, not mere drops in an ocean of mediocrity. And they were more content with their lot than we are. What then is the true criterion of contentment? Can it be anything but the acceptance of one's lot, whatever it may be? Or in other words, knowing one's place and fulfilling faithfully whatever function may be associated with it, with a pride in the quality of the product as the principal incentive rather than any tangible reward; knowing, perhaps, that not to want is better than to have; and above all being intelligent enough not to place one's best hopes in nothing but the satisfactions which a short sojourn in this world can bring. All these things are criteria of contentment, and at the same time they are universal ethical constituents of every religion and tradition.

There are those who think that such criteria of contentment represent something despicable, that they imply a servile submission, a sterile social and intellectual slavery, unworthy of the representatives of an advanced civilization. Let them then propose something better able to bring contentment to a world that is necessarily imperfect because it is other than God, who alone is Perfection; and let it be something more practical than an intellectual vacuum masquerading as freedom.

The more remote from God the world becomes, the more imperfect it becomes. If the confusion, fear, and discontent of our times seem to be reaching towards an extreme, despite a technological development bringing a wealth and a luxury unparalleled in history, why is an exactly coincident decay of religion scarcely ever suggested as a causal factor? To attribute any part of this increase of discontent to an allegedly servile and unintelligent clinging to religion by a diminishing sector of society is a *non sequitur* of which any normal school-child would be rightly ashamed.

No: anyone who clings to religion is clinging, not to an arbitrary framework of man's devising, but to the only framework that can serve as a starting-point for the realization of an inward freedom that is independent of terrestrial contingencies. Moreover this inward freedom is a truly intellectual freedom insofar as it is founded on an integral vision of truth, on a vision which is unified at its source because it comes from within and is not derived exclusively from the observation of the dispersed and fugitive relativities of this world. An outlook which limits itself in principle or in practice to the things of this world is nothing less than an intellectual bondage, since it denies to men the possibility of an inward freedom which is not only the only real freedom, but is also, whether they know it or not, the very freedom they are always seeking.

Let the Psalmist have the last word. He says, "The Lord is King, be the people never so impatient: He sitteth between the Cherubim, be the earth never so unquiet"[1] (Ps. 99:1).

[1] Editor's Note: from the Book of Common Prayer translation.

Schools Adrift

Ghislain Chetan

The Theory of Evolution

Before defining some of the new prejudices that poison academic circles, one must point out a more fundamental and older prejudice, which determines in a particularly perverse manner the mode of Western thought. This is Darwin's theory of evolution, which is unfortunately far from having manifested all of its effects. According to this never-proven premise, which moreover is sometimes even doubted in scientific circles where it was developed—not to mention its incompatibility with all the great Traditions and Wisdoms of humankind, both Western and Eastern—man, having descended from apes, is in constant progression towards the better at all levels. Besides the impossibility of man's descending from apes (in the sense that the latter is evolving), and producing the miracle of human intelligence starting from an animal consciousness—the lesser being unable to give rise to the greater—it would be rather difficult, except under the impulse of passion, to discover among our contemporaries more intelligence and virtues than among the countless generations who came before. Nature, moreover, does not offer and has never offered any example of a spontaneous "jump" from one existential level to another.[1]

Let us specify however, at risk of reiterating the obvious, that Darwin is obviously not the only one responsible for the present situation of our schools. It is in no way by chance that his theory has acquired such fame. It has served its purpose well for all those who exploit it to the fullest, and who are interested in acting in such a way as to attempt a veritable reversal of values, which has finally led to the divinizing of man and ultimately liberating him from his Creator, after having turned him into an evolved ape.

[1] On this subject see the works of F. Schuon, which deal with this subject in a masterly fashion and from which the preceding considerations have been drawn, especially *From the Divine to the Human* (Bloomington: World Wisdom Inc., 1982) as well as Martin Lings' *The Eleventh Hour: The Spiritual Crisis of the Modern World in the Light of Tradition and Prophecy* (Cambridge, UK: Quinta Essentia, 1987). The author quotes Evan Shute's *Flaws in the Theory of Evolution*, and says the following, among other things (p. 21-2): "The realm of conjecture is always the realm of disagreement. Moreover, some evolutionists are more scientific than others, and when their sense of science has been outraged beyond measure, they have not always been able to resist pouring scorn on some of the more fantastic ideas of their fellow evolutionists. As a rule such sallies are isolated and have little effect, if indeed they do not pass unnoticed; but when gathered together, as they are in *Flaws in the Theory of Evolution*, their weight is considerable; and by quoting from the evolutionists themselves, Shute has been able to show that the theory of mega-evolution is no more than a shell inside which its champions have demolished each other's conjectures until there is nothing left.

To sum up his thesis: the more science delves into the amazing intricacies of nature, the more overwhelming the evidence is that piles up against evolutionism. As he himself puts it: 'Mega-evolution is really from the days of biological ignorance; it was a philosophical synthesis built up in a biological kindergarten.'"

As other sources on the denounciation of the phenomenon of evolution, let us also mention those in French: Paul Lemoine, *Encyclopédie française*, Vol. 5, et Louis Bounoure in *Le Monde et la vie* de novembre 1963, whom the author mentions in *Ancient Beliefs and Modern Superstitions*, pp. 11-13 and 99-104. And more recently: Wolfgang Smith, *Evolution: the Facts and the Fantasy*; Stephen Jay Gould, *Life is Beautiful*; Pierre Thuillier, *Darwin & Co* and *Was Darwin a Darwinist?* (These references are taken from the footnote of the book quoted by Martin Lings.)

Let us also mention *Evolution: A Theory in Crisis* by Michael Denton, 1988.

Of course, a fabulous evolution on the technological and material level cannot be denied, and herein lies the strength of the evolutionist illusion. But, it is merely a question of a hypertrophy, undoubtedly spectacular, but which only concerns the least elevated part of man, who is composed of a body, a soul, and a spirit (*corpus-anima-spiritus*).

One can easily imagine the enormous damage that such a system of thought can cause to education, by deliberately substituting the part for the whole. We have taken the trouble to mention this capital prejudice because, as we shall see, all other present prejudices which underlie pedagogical reflection are more or less derived directly from this theory.

Before mentioning them, it will not be superfluous to point out the fundamental viewpoint that Western society has adopted since the Renaissance. In fact, until the period of the Renaissance, archaic societies and Western civilization were characterized by the almost absolute importance they gave to the "objective" and the relativity of the "subjective." This means that man in general—his attitude, his faith, his meditation, and his reflection were determined above all by the Object, the Absolute, God. He was naturally inclined to accord the least importance possible to his individual subjectivity, to what his ego sensed or did not sense. Starting from the Renaissance, the slow reverse movement began, and the subjective pole became the center of interest. Man became interested in his individuality as subtracted from the element "Object," which eventually allowed the rise and proliferation of modern sciences, such as psychoanalysis or psychology of inner depths and modern psychiatry[2]—essentially different from the science of the soul or the spiritual psychology of the ancients—as well as sociology etc. It is as if man suddenly realized, after centuries of obscurantism, the prodigious interest of his apparently unexplored self, filled with unknown hopes, until finally lapsing into the infra-human, the pathological, and the philosophies of despair.

As Tage Lindbom states in his book *The Tares and the Good Grain: The Kingdom of Man at the Hour of Reckoning*, "We are now dealing with a secularized generation for which material existence is everything and spiritual life is nothing. This is a generation for which everything symbolical becomes ever more incomprehensible."[3]

[2] Nevertheless, an assessment of modern psychiatry calls for certain reservations. The latter is not negative in itself when it is confined to its own limits, and its applicability is retricted to the plane dictated by the nature of things, to the extant that one can "relatively" compartmentalize these planes—obviously, psychic health has in itself a non-negligible importance—but it is such when it presents itself as a totalitarian ideology: a point of view which claims to explain the whole psyche without taking into account its interpenetration by elements of a spiritual nature. Hence, it is intrinsically sympathetic to the atheist and modernist vision of the world. Sharing the same postulates with this vision, it will inevitably place the real manifestations of schizophrenia or of paranoia into the same basket with spiritual experiences or with cognitive phenomena escaping it. However, it will pass blindly over the collective paranoia affecting our society, which it will readily consider a norm. Summing up, the matter concerns the preservation of a system, and the discrediting *de facto* of every unfamiliar phenomeon, or every reaction to this system. Psychiatry has the tendency to protect to a great extent the modernist deviation from all those perceiving it, by attempting to neutralize the latter through the attribution of pathologies which they are by far devoid of. But it would be unjust not to mention the—doubtless, relatively infrequent—possibility of practitioners possessing a spiritual and traditional vision, and who, without betraying the primacy of the Intellect, are preoccupied (as other doctors do with the body) with the re-establishing and the preservation of mental health. *Mens sana in corpore sano* ("a sound mind in a healthy body"). However, in order to be fully complete, it is more than evident that there exist a large number of "progressive believing" psychiatrists who cannot enter this exceptional category of men of the elite. What impact can the "belief" of such a practitioner have, when he adopts a point of view which *de facto* negates the basis of the universal and essential *religio*, thus driving it into a fatal contradiction?

[3] Macon, GA: Mercer University Press, 1983, p. 19. Tage Lindbom, born in Sweden in 1909, was a former Marxist. He was appointed director of the library and central archives of the social-democrat party in Stockholm, a

Freedom of Expression

It is useful to point out that it is not error which is most harmful, but rather error mixed with truth. It is precisely the partial truth contained in such an error that gives the latter all of its strength. Being pure negation, absolute error cannot in fact have any kind of positive effect. And one of the signs of our times is what is rightly called the *inextricabilis error*. It has never been so difficult—at least for those who refuse or who are incapable of going beyond passional reason—to extract truth from falsehood, or gold of pure Truth from its straight jacket of impure materials.

That being said, it is true that in the relatively recent past, education authorities—both religious and secular—very often showed a rigidity and narrowness that contributed to the results we know so well: the very rejection of authority,[4] for which May of 1968 in France could be a reference point or culmination. For there is the letter that kills, and the spirit that vivifies. In principle, the spirit should always be indissolubly linked with the letter, since the latter has meaning only through the former. But the process of the loss of the spirit for the benefit of the letter is in fact a natural process of aging, and one has to ceaselessly be watchful in order for the spirit to continue to vivify the letter. Ingrained habits, together with the dangers of intellectual softening that they bring about, combined with the very narrow and unobjective reactions by those responsible for education, have very often contributed to a sort of dialogue of the deaf: education authorities not making their positions sufficiently clear with regards to new false and subversive ideas (and whose true nature no doubt escapes them in part). Among certain people, this has engendered a tension of fear which is neutralized one way or the other by a rigid attachment to the letter alone. Others feel victims of an authority which "constrains in order to constrain," and which is intolerable for this very reason. Although one obviously cannot explain everything from this angle, one can nevertheless conceive of mitigating circumstances in favor of well-intentioned people who, at bottom, have been partially misled.

Be that as it may, in the present day there exists a real loathing to submit: anything goes, except being like the generations of parents and grandparents who "dared say nothing" and who submit, without discernment, to the smallest caprice of authority. The present modern trend is particularly set on maintaining this rough caricature fostered in the spirit of students. It is certainly undeniable, as was just alluded to, that the exercise of authority has posed serious problems: not only has it given rise to abuses, but it has also waned to a considerable extent. The legitimacy of the rights belonging to authorities resides in the truth which the latter conveys and protects. However, by no longer representing principles or conformity to the nature of things, this same authority has deprived itself of a great part of its legitimacy, and today there is a clear tendency to replace a relationship of subordination by one of negotiation. These days, almost everything seems inclined to "negotiation," as if it were taken for granted that arbitrary and individual interest conflicts enter into the exercise of authority. Let us note that the relationship

position from which he resigned in 1965. From then on, he wrote numerous works in which he returned to the Truth and timeless Wisdom he had found again.

[4] Let us recall here Plato's famous remark: Democracy makes way for tyranny when freedom becomes license and when egalitarianism becomes doctrine. Parents and children, masters and students, the elderly and the young: all are equal. A father fears his own son and a son has no respect for his parents. The teacher fears the students and flatters them; the students scorn their teachers. In the end, citizens no longer tolerate any form of authority or law. They no longer tolerate any master. This is how the way is paved to tyranny. Excess of freedom leads to excess of slavery and the greater the freedom, the greater the slavery.

of subordination does not exclude suppleness on the part of authority, in domains where the human margin allows it, no more than it does generosity and magnanimity, attitudes which must not be confused with the weaknesses of modern psychologism (to which F. Schuon often alludes). It is moreover significant that the term "negotiate" is borrowed from the domain of economics. Would it not be better instead to render authority its true significance and to support it where it remains legitimate despite everything—*abusus non tollit usum* ("abuse does not take away use")—than to relegate it to the corner of harmful and outdated things?[5]

So what is this freedom that is defended with such vehemence against all intolerable outrage?

Freedom, according to the Ancients, those faithful to a valid tradition and in perfect agreement on this point, is the state of the person who is neither hindered in his search and approach to the Truth by the numerous traps which constitute the passional and highly subjective and self-serving tendencies of his own soul, nor by external influences of nature which are just as selfish and passional. This includes truth of the most basic to the most elevated, thus including all humankind of sane mind. A Principle therefore is not an arbitrary law which limits Life. Rather, it is the rendition of the nature of things and of Life itself. A Principle liberates; it only gets in the way of the passion of an ignorant soul. That certain applications of Principles can be too stringent is another problem.

In the modern Western sense of the word, freedom is the faculty to choose any thing at all, as long as it corresponds to the satisfying of a desire, or to individual performance. Freedom is not envisaged as liberating our passional ego of petrifying tendencies, but as the realization of this ego's desires. This constitutes a veritable reversal of values.

It is therefore not surprising that contemporary Western man will see in the teaching of protective principles and rules merely an intolerable attack on this form of pseudo-liberty which he cherishes so much, and that one of the first commandments of the modernist credo is to "liberate" the pupil from all restriction of the free expression of his "self."[6]

Nowadays, the question of whether desires are justified or justifiable is not even raised. Insofar as the postulate is rejected, all criticism against it is sacrilegious. The same thing plays out in the classmroom. It is highly ill-viewed to openly contradict a student who is obviously in error, except, of course, in scientific disciplines. At the very most, it is still possible to offer him a different opinion, which he will treat as he wishes anyway. And what's more, most of the time, almost all courses on religion consist of endless "discussions" from which the truth of the moment is supposed to gush forth.[7] And as in every democracy, the truth is not what follows from Principles, but the summary or amalgamations of a heap of different opinions.[8] The result is that, from one year to another—and even spatially from one classroom

[5] As Schuon has written somewhere, it is to "prefer a clean error to a sullied truth."

[6] Hence the key idea of "partnership" in education. In the form it is conceived, this partnership is strongly impregnated with sentimentalism, with a tendency to egalitarianism and the abolition of hierarchy. In other words, it is evident that a certain form of partnership has always existed, even within the most rigorous hierarchies, which follows from the nature of things, because it is a question of exchanges among beings who partake of the same human character, despite their temporary or definitive position within a hierarchy. However, the modernist partnership is essentially different, as it intends to replace all *de facto* forms of natural hierarchy.

[7] Here lies one of the after-effects of the unprecedented subversion—with incalculable dramatic consequences—of Vatican II for the Church, a Council which officially instituted the cult of the human individual. (On this subject, see the excellent writings of Rama Coomaraswamy, Jean Madiran, and Jean Hani.)

[8] Let us recall that, for Plato, the ideal government is aristocracy (cf. *The Eleventh Hour*, p. 52)—and the author of the book proposes to render this term in current vocabulary as "theocracy" (a term which corresponds the best to

to another—conclusions may be diametrically opposed. But whether this is right or not seems to disturb no one, provided that freedom of expression is safeguarded. This is really a sovereign contempt for the Truth, and this contempt is then found inevitably—and in different degrees—at all the levels of society. More often, when two individuals express contradicting opinions, it is acceptable to demand from each of them to "put in some effort" in view of reaching an "agreement" which will be called "at least objective truth," each having sacrified, so to speak, a little of their subjectivity, not to mention their pretension and pride. It all happens without regard for the dignity or the intrinsic value of the characters involved, as well as the profundity of what they utter. This attitude takes after political or commercial compromise, which must lead to an immediate and pragmatic agreement, taking into account diverging interests, thus having really nothing more to do with truth. Truth is not a question of an "arrangement" made of weakness and subtle hypocrisy. In arithmetic, for example, no one would ever dream of adopting a similar behavior. If one person maintains that two plus two is five vis-à-vis another, who claims that the result is four, no one would demand to "arrive" at four and a half in order to "arrange things" and "make everybody happy." Pure Truth also has a rigorously mathematical aspect, whether one likes it or not, and it is inviolable by definition, whether modernists who wish to drown it in artistic fuzziness and make it dependent on their open-mindedness of the moment and on their passions like it or not.

Those who act likewise in the classroom do not wish to understand that, in the same way, pupils are locked into the narrow framework of their egos and a sort of autocracy is encouraged. This tends to make young people gradually insensitive to things other than their own opinions, the expression of their own personality and individual freedom. Moreover, we are not far from the idea that the more their opinion diverges from that of the other pupils, the more they demonstrate character! And undoubtedly, the most formidable of all prisons which confine the youngster is this: his own self—a cell bound on all sides, as it is with every other individual. The student is therefore prevented from breaking out of the cell lest he lose what is called freedom, but which in reality is the worst of all slaveries. This is a fundamental teaching of Wisdom and Religions worthy of the name, since the beginning of time. This lack of traditional teaching, then, immerses youth into a most uncomfortable situation. Having no valid reference point in the face of a mass of relative contradictions, he does not possess the necessary tools to orient himself; and from the point of view of the attitude to be adopted, according to his opinion, this state of affairs can bring about certain extenuating circumstances.[9]

what Plato had in mind)—and the worst government is tyranny—for which the author proposes the current terms of "dictatorship" or "demagogy." As the same author points out on page 56: "From the point of view of modern democratic education, both the restraints in question are tyrannies"—those imposed by a theocentric system, as well as that of dictatorship properly speaking.

This explains why in our day and age religion, insofar as it does not submit to the whims of men, is considered a purely arbitrary dictatorship.

[9] "For thousands of years the best of men, men we cannot despise without making ourselves despicable, have promulgated and propagated doctrines and lived according to them or died for them. The ill certainly does not lie in the hypothetical vanity of all doctrine but solely in the fact that too many men either have not followed, or do not follow, true doctrines, or have on the contrary followed, or are following, false doctrines; in the fact that brains have been exasperated and hearts deceived by too many inconsistent and erroneous theories; in the fact that innumerable errors, both garrulous and pernicious, have cast discredit on truth, truth which necessarily is expressed in words and is always there, even when no man pays heed to it. All too many people no longer even know what an idea is, what its value and what its function is; they do not so much as suspect that perfect and definitive theories have always existed, theories which are therefore on their own level fully adequate and effective, and that there is

However, and this brings us back to the heart of the subject, man is seemingly in constant evolution towards the better, in all aspects! This in effect means that the innumerable outstanding human beings preceding us were only taking the first steps of a primitive and embryonic knowledge. Modern man, on the contrary, has finally started to become an adult, and liberate himself from all obscurantism of the past.[10] He is wrongly locked into a "closed and totalitarian system" aiming to be an explanation of the world (e.g. Aristotle or St. Thomas Aquinas).

Incidentally, not everyone is fooled, as many still relatively healthy souls aspire to the source, the original purity, and there are ever more disillusioned souls in the West who turn to the great perennial Wisdoms of humanity.

It follows from all this that for the modern student, no more than for the parents, professors do not constitute valid and definitive points of reference. In evolution, they belong to the past and they are more or less consciously regarded as less evolved beings. On the contrary, youngsters belong to the present, with the indisputable advantage of standing a little bit higher on the evolutionary ladder. No more need to listen to all these outdated people, described not so courteously as "decrepit"—and not always completely wrongly, since at present this is the reality for a "bourgeoisie" which elevates material comfort to the status of ethics. There is no longer any need to take an interest in the immense literature and heritage of the past, which are merely immature stutterings and judgments. In one of his articles from May 1992, Pierre Gauthy, an admirer of Teilhard de Chardin, feels that "what constitutes the charm of a child,

nothing to add to what has been said by the sages of old except effort on our own part to understand it. If we are human beings, we cannot abstain from thought, and if we think then we are choosing a doctrine; the lassitude, the lack of imagination and the childish arrogance of disillusioned and materialistic young people changes nothing in all this. If it is modern science which has created the abnormal and deceiving conditions which afflict youth today, that is because this science is itself abnormal and deceiving. No doubt it will be said that man is not responsible for his nihilism, that it is science which has slain the gods; but this is an avowal of intellectual impotence, not a title to glory, for he who knows what the gods signify will not let himself be carried away by discoveries in the physical realm—which merely displace sensory symbols, but do not abolish them—and still less by gratuitous hypotheses and the errors of psychology" (Schuon, *Understanding Islam* [London: Allen & Unwin, 1976], p. 134).

[10] Let us note that according to another point of view, which is corollary to the first, modern people are convinced of the miserableness and even wretchedness of the life of the majority of our ancestors; it suffices not to enjoy the privileges of the minority of the rich or the powerful to lead, according to them, a life of exploited vagabonds in rags. And yet, as F. Schuon states in his *Castes and Races*, p. 25, "In order to be able to judge of the quality of happiness in some past state of the world one would have to be able to put oneself in the place of the men who lived in it and adopt their way of evaluating things. . . ; many things to which we have become accustomed would seem to them intolerable restraints to which they would prefer the more familiar risks; just the ugliness and the atmosphere of triviality of the world of today would seem to them like the worst of nightmares. History as such cannot give a full account of the soul of some distant epoch: it chiefly registers calamities, leaving aside all the static factors of happiness; it has been said that happiness has no history, and this is profoundly true. Wars and epidemics no more reflect than do certain customs the happy aspects of the lives of our ancestors, while their literary and artistic works plainly do so."

See also note 19 at p. 112 of Ananda K. Coomaraswamy's *The Deeper Meaning of the Struggle*: "There was a time when all civilizations were so similar that a traveller could feel at home anywhere he went; Plato was understood better by Philon and Florin, Marcello Ficino and Peter Sterry that he could ever be understood by a modern nominalist, however instructed the latter may be, and 'the greater the ignorance of modern times, the more profound becomes the darkness of Middle Ages.' Archaeological discoveries and anthropological research have done little to widen our horizons, chiefly because the eyes of our understanding have been blinded by our belief in 'progress' (i.e. by the application of evolutionist concepts to culture) and by the sentimentalist error (which attributes our aesthetism to primitive man)."

or his essence, that which is the most profound in an adolescent, is the fact that their future lies ahead. They are going through this journey which we are half-way along or at the end of. There is no past to stop them, or to weigh them down, or tie them down, no closed avenue for them. Whereas we adults, we are precisely 'accomplishments,' 'inertias,' 'achievements.' We are cluttered, they are not, they can still become so, and they can still experiment. We have our feet on the ground, too much so; their feet are elsewhere, and rightly so."

But why, then, identify adult age simply with sclerosis, even though, alas, this evokes a possibility to which we have already alluded. Adult age is identified essentially and qualitatively with maturity, into which the qualitative aspect of (the healthy) childhood should be integrated. With such a cynical and unnuanced concept of adult age, one should not be surprised by the haughty contempt displayed by most of our youngsters—individual exceptions fortunately still being possible—for all that is imposed and taught as true by their elders.[11] Pierre Gauthy moreover adds: "We must . . . understand youth; we must not form preconceptions against novelties, and we must in any case believe that humanity progresses little by little. The golden age is truly ahead, despite the falls and the exile. To say 'in my time' is to truly be behind the times. When regrets take the place of dreams, man is old."

It is as if there existed no justified regrets or utopian dreams, and a lucid judgment of a novelty was nothing but a preconception! Nevertheless, let us point out that the planetary scale of pollution and the manifold deterioration of our environment no longer allow evolution and material progress to rhyme so harmoniously; but this distinction does not seem to shake off the persistence of the evolutionist credo in that which is irreversible.

To this is added the ambiguous idea defended by leading university experts (especially Mr. De Landsheere of Liège University) that 90 % of the knowledge of humanity has been acquired in the last thirty years, and that the capital doubles every seven years. This is a flagrant confusion between quality and quantity. Essential knowledge—which is adaptable to all forms of thought, of course—is intangible by definition, and unfortunately also in decline. Ancillary knowledge is very often useless, being the fruit of a Promethean curiosity, no doubt increased to unimaginable proportions. Apart from the fact that this ancillary knowledge is not mastered by our students, to say the least (apart from isolated exceptions), it comprises dissipation and dispersion which gives the illusion of knowledge. Thus, the student of thirty or forty years ago "knew" fewer things than the student of today, but he was less ignorant; whereas the present student "knows" more things, all the while being more ignorant. It is because there is no commensurability between the essential and the ancillary; "much of the ancilliary" offers nothing essential. Did Montaigne not say that "it is better to have a well-made head than a filled one"?

However, youngsters themselves no longer occupy a comfortable position on the ladder of evolution. If the past is not likely to help them, the present will help them even less so, because the present is also considered inferior vis-à-vis an inaccessible future. And this is precisely why large portions of the youth of our modern societies cling to nothing except the search for

[11] Due to their proximity to the origin, children enjoy in principle a freshness of perception, purity, and an ontological relationship with things. This relationship tends to disappear with age; they still bear the nostalgia of a lost Paradise. We say in principle, because nowadays children have all the chances of being plunged too early into the fictitious and illusory ambience of an increasingly material world, which tries to eliminate in them that nostalgia of Heaven. This world—where the disillusioned adult who was unable to keep his childhood's virtue intact tends to become a sort of norm—is often the only one with whom the child enters into contact with. It cannot not have his/her wings broken, thereby inducing a behavior characterized by disequilibrium and hence "abnormal".

immediate pleasure, resulting from the peripheral desires of their ego, desires not based on any principle. Caught between the stranglehold of a past which he does not own and a future he is ignorant of, but the superiority of which he thinks he can grasp, the youngster lets his life run adrift on the river of its own limits. The growing sense of insecurity, anxiety, the search for the artificial paradise, if not suicide, is increasingly noticed among youth, as is a sort of completely superficial reassurance, to a great extent stemming from the absence of respect for anything which he/she imagines may restrict his/her freedom.

Ignorant of the fact that he/she is the victim of a system conceived by others, and which is destined to immerse him/her into a dreadful freedom, because it is illusory, there is unfortunately no reason to trust those who say otherwise. This is what Tage Lindbolm also alludes to in his already quoted book (p. 20):

> This is a generation which stands at the point of eliminating the notion of family from its consciousness. It is an orphaned generation. This is why brotherhood loses its meaning too, for, in order to be brothers, a common father is needed. And if there is no longer a father the past will become equally absurd, since without a past there is no future. There is therefore nothing left but to lead an existence in the present without history. One must console oneself by an "involvement" in a collective world, but without identity, and return to one's vacuity under the form of symbiotic "community" where promiscuity should serve as ersatz to the lost brotherhood.

To return to the question of freedom of expression: As soon as a child masters his language, however insufficiently, he is invited to express himself freely, to give his opinion on anything and everything. And it would be unsuitable not to take his opinion seriously. At the very most, especially at a young age, one can rectify the form of expression, but very rarely the content. Invested from a very early age with such importance, once they reach secondary school, most of the time, youth are incapable of avoiding showing a total lack of a sense of proportion. They will not take into consideration the opinion of their teachers except through their narrow and immature minds. When it happens that a teacher expresses something profound or beautiful which they cannot always grasp within their immature minds, many will respond with a profane and sacrilegious insolence, "this is stupid"; and just because they say "it is stupid," it is certainly "stupid" (not hesitating, moreover, to use a much more vulgar word). This is how "limited individual perception" and "truth" are confused. The truth is not what exists on the exterior and independent of me; the truth is what *I* think and nothing else! Here is an example of the trivialization of language, which has never been the sign of the apogee of a civilization nor of its refinement. This trivialization is accompanied by an odd lack of sensitivity in human relationships, both with regards to their fellow students and to their professors. The students most often express themselves in a crude and direct language (which is much appreciated—it is better to be cheeky than timid, it seems, as if it were a question of alternatives), when it is not outright rude. Even worse still is the comfortable well being of this way of expressing oneself; souls become eventually blunted, and they consider—even according to some students—this way of speaking as completely normal and legitimate. Delicacy and tact are outdated values; rudeness and total lack of nobility have come to replace them.[12] In Shintoism, as in Islam—to

[12] In his book *To Have a Center*, Schuon writes: "All these distinctions do not prevent human language as such from being, by definition, something sacred; thus it is a real loss to neglect it or even to push it into the abyss, as is cheerfully done in our times. One of man's first duties is to speak and write correctly, hence also in a noble fashion,

quote just two examples—politeness is an integral part of religion. It is essentially a question of not stopping at the earthly accidence of the neighbor, but to become conscious of his or her celestial substance.[13]

Tage Lindbom alludes to this modernist conception of things when he writes (p. 40):

> While all values are declared relative and everybody must "save themselves in their own way," it may be tempting to make of all aspiration for truth a matter related only to individual egotism. But chaos is pointed out as a menacing possibility and no one in modern times has described this dilemma better than Thomas Hobbes: we must choose between war of everybody against everybody and submission to an organized and institutionalized egotism.

What is most suprising—at least if one can still be surprised—is the encounter with the modernist concept of the flowering of the ego where one least expects to find it, at least in principle. Father Simon Pierre of the Wavreumont monastery wrote a book some years ago called *Dieu sur Parole*, in which he expresses concepts which are surprising, to say the least. Some of these ideas stigmatize the religious mentality in particular which impregnates a large sector of believers at present, and which inevitably has an impact on schools. It is worth pausing for a moment at this point, even though it resumes the ideas already developed. Father Simon Pierre himself has made some very significant comments on the Catholic religious program "le Coeur et l'Esprit," during which he said:

> Nowadays, it is no longer a question of following rigid principles,[14] but of favoring Life; this means that that which is good is that which gives life; and that which is bad is the opposite of Life, that which withdraws into itself and shrivels up.

This opinion seems to translate into a very odd lack of discernment, because it does not take into account, or does not wish to take into account, the fact that this highly subjective concept of Life can ruin the Life of the immortal soul, because there are an indefinite number of situations which clearly make the external ego live and blossom, but to the detriment of the divine Life within us. Obviously, this is a question of favoring a subjective and essentially

always keeping one's gaze fixed on tradition, which represents and canalizes the divine origin; even profane languages, which are our own, have in themselves maintained that essential element—basically natural to man—that is dignity. The same is not true for demagogic jargons forced upon us in the name of a sincerism inspired by the real or supposed vulgarity of the masses, and in any case propagated by the mass media. On the one hand, it is decided that the people are trivial—forgetting that there are people and people—and on the other hand triviality is forced upon them, it being considered as the human norm, whereas in fact it results from irreligion, hence from the loss of the sense of the sacred" (chap. 13).

[13] See *Esoterism as Principle and as Way*, pp. 107-8.

[14] It is said that a principle is rigid, and one speaks of rigidity of principles, because just like the substantive, the adjective translates well the characteristic of the immutability as well as the inviolability of things. In the language of today, however, these terms often take on a connotation of moral reproach, which is obviously absurd, being at the opposite of the nature of a principle. One should not forget, of course, that the "total" Truth includes also "suppleness," by taking away from this term its eventual connotation of moral weakness or of abusive permissivity, since it implies an indefinite number of aspects.

human point of view about obedience to Laws which are very often judged as too restrictive and outdated. The question of knowing what God thinks about them is no longer posed; it is man (and woman) who decide in His place and that is all. It is this perspective which makes the same monk say, on pages 198 and 199 of his book, that "the Christian is neither exclusively 'no' nor exclusively 'yes.' Jesus himself fought this evangelical dilemma, although Paul insisted on the fact that he was never ambiguous about it."[15] And a few lines after that, causes him to render symbolism meaningless when he writes:

> As for the truth of this fundamental question (i.e. discerning when the Christian must say "yes"), I would like to reread here the story of the visit of the Magi or Wisemen according to Matthew (2, 1-6). It seems to me that uncounsciously, in Church, we have read this episode of the Epiphany the wrong way. In fact, if we are asked the naïve question: "Where did the light come from?" We will spontaneously reply: from the "manger," that is, from amongst us (our own tradition, religion), where the Emmanuel rests, in other words from the Church. This is not true! The "manger" remains in obscurity until the arrival of the wisemen. They have seen the star of Christ in their far off pagan Orient. . . . This parable contains a profound lesson on the "yes" of the believer to the world. Do we possess the boldness and humility to light the darkness of our ecclesiastical manger by the light of the "orients" of today called atheism, technology, political and cultural globalism, etc.? There is perhaps Good News to receive before judging and condemning, starting from our "truth" which is sometimes so obscured.

This does not stray us too much from our subject, since the modern tendency in schools is to adopt an approach by which light will be readily sought in darkness, and darkness in Light. This constitutes a characteristic Luciferian reversal.

Atheism, being a privation, even the essential or "absolute" privation, how can it light anything? If not *ab absurdo*? But then it is obscurity which emphasizes light, and this is obviously not what the author means here. What a perversion, then, in the relationship of this reverse symbolism which places the manger in obscurity. This is in order to make it be lit up by the Star of the Wisemen, which is assimilated to phenomena (one rightly asks why) which are as far removed as possible from oriental wisdom.

In order to return for a moment to the subjective morals of our times, one could refer to Descartes, the destroyer of scholasticism, who had already prepared the ground for this by saying that science followed facts. Sensing, no doubt, the danger of an almost inevitable amalgamation that could be made of his statement in the domain of morals, he nevertheless added that this "rule" was not valid for morals. But, alas, our times have consumed this amalgamation, because, in practice if not always in theory, morals very well follow facts. The present general tendency is in fact to consider a behavior as normal insofar as it is produced relatively often. This leads to our changing morals which are heading to who knows where, without anyone wondering if they are good or bad. There are doubtless few things as annoying as the reactions of certain people to the observation of the growing immorality and the flagrant lack of virtues in our times: "But this is how it is nowadays! . . . This is how the world is! . . . Our times are

[15] And one wonders with curiosity about the interpretation given by the author to Christ's word: "Your language must be yes, yes, no, no."

different! . . . One must accept it! . . . The morals of yesterday are no longer those of today! . . ." etc. This, among other things, is where the fascinating magic of evolutionism leads to. Thus, one can understand why pedagogical thought deliberately placed into a dynamic of permanent change or *aggiornamento*. Teachers are ceaselessly invited to "evaluate themselves." It is not a matter of evaluating their own adherence to virtue or to principles stemming from the nature of things, which would be normal and desirable. But the issue is to carefully avoid harboring those principles which are considered fixed ideas or *a priori* ideas; especially and above all if these ideas are the reflection of what is permanent in man, and therefore in precise conformity with the nature of things. This instability of reflection, combined with an underlying self-guilt which is required and maintained, is the best means of rendering all veritable transmission of knowledge impossible.

Translated by Eden Lohja

IV.

Solutions for Education Today?

Transdisciplinary Education: Profiles and Projects

Jean Biès

By "transdisciplinary education" we mean the appropriate rehabilitation, within schools and universities, of a tripartite anthropology, a spiritual ecology, a psychology-psychosophy, a universal metaphysics, and their respective practical applications.

Ternary anthropology envisages man in his totality of "body," "soul," and "spirit." It is this totality which is taken into account by transdisciplinary education. It does so by not contenting itself with mere cerebral hypertrophy, but by restoring lost dignity to the corporeal, psychic, and pneumatic planes of the human being. It is of a holistic nature.

A harmonious development of the body insists less on muscular exercises than on controlled respiration, on self-control, on the consciousness of the movements performed, and on the apprenticeship of acts in view of ritualization. Bodily limbering has a close relationship with a certain aquatic plasticity, a vegetal suppleness—which is that of a sensitive psyche and detached intelligence. Manual activity is not separate from it, as it shapes matter starting from personal initiative and extending to crafted and artistic works. It gives the creating hand its due importance, and it combats the prejudice which only gives deserved consideration to intellectual life.

The individual body is itself linked to the cosmos: both the body and the cosmos are rooted in the same elements and are developed in accordance with the same laws. Transdisciplinary education adopts the following equation: microcosm equals macrocosm; hence the importance given to spiritual ecology, beyond politics.

It is a question here of another view of *physis*, an awareness of its threatened fragility and willingness for protective measures, issuing not so much from decrees than from a re-educated love of the beauty of nature. Moreover, children are naturally brought to the rediscovery of the *mirabilia* abounding in fauna and flora; their power of wonder makes them spontaneously sensitive to the sacredness of these phenomenal "theophanies" which enchant the world. It is easy to underline the correspondences between the infinitely large and the infinitely small through recourse to macro-photography and micro-photography.

Reconnecting with the archetypes, transdisciplinary ecology includes in its program, without omitting necessary corrections and updates, the German philosophers of Nature: Schelling, Novalis, Schlegel;[1] the Russian sophists: Soloviev, Florensky;[2] the American transcendentalists: Emerson, Thoreau;[3] all those who, whether following or emulating a Gregory of Nyssa or a Jacob Boehme, do not adhere to a mechanistic and scientific concept of matter, but adopt the non-dualist vision of the different degrees of materiality.

* * *

[1] The *Naturphilosophen* reinterpret Nature starting from "correspondences" and "signatures"; they see in it a living All, not separating it from the Spirit.

[2] "Sophianity" recognizes in Divine Wisdom the immanence and the feminine; it identifies the original Earth, cosmic Energy, and the Mother of God.

[3] Having resulted from Germanic idealism and being the discoverer of Hindu philosophy, transcendentalism reunites into one whole: God, nature, and man.

Transdisciplinary education shatters the boundaries of knowledge, and, according to the fortunate formula of Basarab Nicolescu, it practices "jubilatory transgression." It seeks the acquisition of a transculture bringing together literary and scientific domains under the aegis of such intellects as Pascal who combined expressions of finesse and geometry, Goethe who wrote poems and carried out chemical experiments, or Bachelard exploring the imaginary without dispensing with rationality, in order to create the "new scientific spirit."

The same perspective invigorates every discipline from within. In linguistics, it opens up an unprecedented discovery of Indo-European roots: so many keys giving access to the fifty languages that were born from them. It does not reduce history to the linear sequence of the factual or to economic-social philosophy, but seeks to study the role of the sacred, not as a stage of evolution but, as Mircea Eliade pointed out, as a constant of consciousness. It restores the legendary and the mythological to botany and zoology, through decoding their symbolism. It broadens medicine to include energy therapies, which were started by Paracelsus. It adds numerical quality to quantitative mathematics, as envisaged by Pythagorism and Taoism, thus reestablishing a systemic thought where the whole of reality is more than the sum of its parts. It enriches binary logic: A is different from B, with other possible combinations existing, which are familiar to the East and which were revivified by Lupasco. By distinguishing in its wake the contradictory, which includes opposing polarities, and the contradicting, which excludes opposed polarities, it opens up and teaches a range of different viewpoints seen as so many levels of reality governed by different logics, as Husserl pointed out. Thus, transdisciplinary education wards off the dangers of conflict, which are inherent to the unilateral and the exclusive, the latter being fruits of a corrupt dualism. It opens itself to tolerance, which means respect for the other.

The individual mind is itself related to Divine intelligence. It is the seat of discursive thought, of sapience, and understanding; it is also the seat of intuition and knowledge.

Founded upon the multidimensional, transdisciplinary education inevitably brings about a system of formulations completely different from that of the more *geometrico* expositions of classical rationalism. Its utterances are not strangers to the objective, to the subjective, to the image, to that poem about which Roberto Juarroz says that it is "something without which man cannot live," and which is actually missing from the *voie sèche* of technocrats.

In addition, it is necessary to introduce new researchers to the polysemy of symbols, to the figurative and the suggestive opening onto their meanings, beyond impoverished literalism; but they should also be introduced to the paradoxical, which is intolerable only to a rationalism folded up on itself into definite categories. Researchers should also be introduced to apophasis, which subtracts instead of adding, reduced not to the trifling but to the quintessential, a free and vast space where an intermediary forest stands; but also, and going beyond cataphasis and apophasis, they should be introduced to the silence reigning in the most secret of its cave.[4]

This return to hermeneutics allows *expansion*, in the commentaries on poems, stories, myths, and sacred texts; it does not exclude a completely Delphic ambiguity, which stimulates creative inventiveness by making it function on several frequencies. If the specialist and compartmentalizing scholars strive hard for definitions, which confine and rigidify, the transdisciplinary researcher, who strives for openness, likes *in-finitions*.

[4] The cataphatic, or affirmative path, enumerates the attributes of God through its energies; the apophatic, or negative path, eliminates them successively in order to retain only the inexpressible Essence.

* * *

Transdisciplinary education also encompasses psychology. It becomes difficult, with regard to Freudian reductionism, to act as if Jung did not exist, in whom alchemy and the I-Ching were mutually fertilized before even meeting this transhumanist wisdom whereby one ceases to *believe* because one *knows*.

Although the *nigredo* explores the dual world of antagonisms and becomes aware of the analytical, and the *albedo* governs and reconciles them, the *rubedo* will transcend within through a superior unity.[5] If two functions proclaim their antinomy, analytical work will favor the appearance of a third, transconflicting function. If man and woman are opposed in the war of prerogatives, the examination of dreams will regulate the emergence of the anima and the animus. If, on a first level of reality, the encounter of an external fact and of an inner state arises from the unpredictable, another event will be named, at a more elevated level, coincidence, or even synchronism. Each time, the third element at work in such and such a competing function reduces the conflict, and vibrantly proclaims its perfection.

The individual soul is in itself related to the great community of souls. Just like the nutritive elements of "homeomeres" each of whom contains the others, every human being possesses the diverse components of humanity.

Transdisciplinary education can only favor the fecund relationship and interaction of dualities in the encounter of two subjects, in each of which there is something of the other. Transdisciplinary education becomes, in this instance, a school of brotherhood. It appeals to Martin Buber, for whom the encounter is placed beyond the "I" and "You," and for whom the human face-to-face prefigures the human-divine Face-to-Face. In a true relationship, the experience of reciprocity is in the nature of Being; it resolves opposites within this *conciliatio oppositorum* which, for Nicholas of Cusa, is God Himself. The former can also quote Berdiaev, who considers that "the essence of love is to transcend," and that communion raises each self to the status of "person."

Damaged by solitude, wounded by the impoverishment of metaphysical knowledge, youth, given to spontaneous get-togethers, ask for nothing more than this apprenticeship of community, which is neither solipsism, nor collectivity, but a peculiar situation where the person before us is not a wall but a mirror. Already, a first attempt of comprehension between student and professor—who teaches less with what he knows than with what he is—lays the ground for this type of authenticity.

* * *

Transdisciplinary education will not banish from its field the domains of the sacred, in so far as the sacred is precisely that which links the object and the subject, thought and experience, the

[5] Editor's Note: terms used in traditional alchemy. The *nigredo* refers to blackness, putrefaction, or decomposition. In the soul, it refers to the difficulties man has to face in the underworld and/or on the spiritual journey. *Albedo* refers to whiteness and is a scientific word used in astronomy, where it is the fraction of solar energy reflected back into space. Alchemically it signifies an ever deepening descent into one's deepest unconscious center, which might suddenly become illusion from above. *Rubedo* is redness adopted by alchemists to define the fourth and final major stage in the Magnum Opus. It signaled alchemical success, the end of a great work. It signifies the total fusion of spirit and matter, achieving enlightened consciousness.

effective and the affective; it defies dualities and carries out transmutations.

An example of the transdisciplinary focus is the following phrase of Saint Paul: "One God . . . , who is *above* all, and *through* all, and *in* all"[6] which could serve as an introduction to the exploration of the great spiritual traditions. In other words, what is involved here is to simultaneously take into consideration Transcendence—the Absolute, the Beyond-Being, the Empty-Plenitude—, the standpoint of all standpoints going beyond everything; the intermediary space—the plane of archetypes, the place of reconciliation of heavenly and earthly opposites, a third imaginary domain; and immanence—the plane of elements as yet not organized.

Such an exploration brings back the isomorphism and analogies which bring together these traditions towards the subtle point of the Infinite where the ultimate convergences are founded upon Unity. It is situated at the antipode of a false dissolving syncretism, and in complete respect for every tradition attached to a common primordial ground. This means that such a discipline is less open to the sociology of religions than to their metaphysics, and that its ideal library is honored to gather the transdisciplinary masters of non-duality such as Dionysius the Areopagite, Meister Eckhart, Ibn Arabi, Shankaracharya, Chuang Tzu, to cite but the most illustrious of them, as well as, among the contemporary ones, the most authoritative guides of the *philosophia perennis*: René Guénon, Frithjof Schuon, Henri Corbin, Ananda Coomaraswamy and others.

The individual spirit is in itself linked to the Spirit. According to a well-known comparison, it is, *qua* human individuality, like the reflection on water in relation to the sun, which designates the Transcendent Personal Divinity, the two being united by the luminous ray: the supreme Intellect, the link between the divine and the human. All human vocation lies in the return to the sun of one's reflection. Just as in other domains, there should not be an imbalance between the speculative and the operative, between the exposition of principles and their lived integration. Transdisciplinary education does not stick to an object of experimentation; it gives rise to an experimenter, and to their fusion in inner realization.

Transdisciplinary education cannot dispense with being a school of wisdom.

* * *

The advent of the transdisciplinary among us seems rather like the avataric appearance of an unusual presence, giving rise to interest, astonishment, enthusiasm, or awe. It is certain that it leads to a profound upset of consciences and mentalities, a complete ontological reversal. But is it not during a change of worldview that the world begins to change?

It would be superfluous to specify that transdisciplinary education does not imply a question of a nostalgic return to a past in the modes of interpretation or expressions gone by, but to find the basic structures and the reference points, the permanence of which allows one to navigate the successive walls of time without fading.

The transdisciplinary vision alone is in a position to prevent, through its vocation to reconciliation and rising above events, the advent of new totalitarian forms of political, intellectual, or religious orders, to encourage the emergence of the one in the many and of the many in one, to put an end to the absolutization of objectivity—and objectivization— to speculations and outrageous fragmentations, to revaluate the role of the corporeal, of awareness,

6 Ephesians IV, 6.

of the imaginary, of intuition, of the feminine, and to substitute a globalization from below with an ecumenism from above.

The gap left by nihilism can deviate into a cradle of new inspiration, a germinating concavity where the opposite becomes the different, the separated becomes the connected, and antagonisms become complementarities. Resistances to transdisciplinary education are not lacking and will not be lacking, due to the slowness of the human mind in requestioning, in getting rid of habits, as well as the fear of the unknown. The accusation of utopia will be launched like every time there exists a maturity to pronounce and an immaturity to do.

In this twilight age populated by dawning ambiguities, the transdisciplinary, whose overhanging signs and predicates are already noticeable, will come into its own time.

Patience in the lit darkness!

Translated by Eden Lohja

The Once and Future College:

Rose Hill in Theory and Practice

James S. Cutsinger

The Body of a College

The body of a college, like the body of a human being, is of course its most outward dimension—the part that takes up a certain amount of space in the world and lasts for a certain period of time.

Located about 160 miles east of Atlanta in the small but surprisingly cosmopolitan city of Aiken, South Carolina—nationally known for its fox hunting, polo, and other equestrian activities—the body of Rose Hill College was a five-acre, turn-of-the-twentieth century estate occupying an entire block in a beautifully wooded residential area near the city's downtown. The grounds included a newly renovated 32-room manor house, two additional cottages, an art studio, and a chapel, all set in the midst of immaculately groomed Victorian gardens. The manor house fulfilled a number of purposes. The upstairs functioned as the women's dormitory, while the downstairs included the college kitchen and dining room as well as a seminar room and small library. One arm of this body reached out to embrace three additional buildings, all within a five-minute walk from the central campus: a small house that served as the men's dormitory and another larger, two-building complex where administration and faculty offices, classrooms, and a recreation area were located.

Since my own undergraduate days, I have been keenly interested in what John Henry Newman called "the idea of a university," and no doubt like anyone who has given serious thought to this subject, I had more than once contemplated what I would do if I were given the opportunity to design a college curriculum and implement a pedagogy. From the start I could see that my work at Rose Hill had afforded just such a chance, and soon after arriving in Aiken I began voicing support for the idea of trying to start a new college. Here, I proposed, we might endeavor to do full-time what we had been doing part-time in the summer seminars: provide young men and women with an education rich in both spiritual and intellectual nourishment—one in stark contrast to the "fast food" variety offered by most of our country's institutions of higher learning, public and private alike. During Father Hopko's visit, I participated in a brainstorming session with several of the visiting scholars. They were generally supportive of the idea and agreed it was an auspicious moment to attempt a transition from Anglican retreat center to Orthodox Christian college. Within a few weeks a mission statement had been drafted and an advisory board assembled, headed by Metropolitan Philip Saliba of the Antiochian Orthodox Christian Archdiocese.

The next two years, leading up to the formal opening of the college, were a blur of activities, which included designing a curriculum, composing a catalogue, developing promotional materials, placing advertisements in selected journals and magazines, combing through College Board and other lists for the names and addresses of promising students, and of course hiring a faculty. We also consulted extensively with educators at other small liberal arts colleges we hoped to emulate and visited Orthodox and other churches around the country in order to make our plans known to as broad an audience as possible. At last things were in place, and with a faculty of five, Rose Hill College opened its doors on August 28, 1996 to an entering class of 17 adventurous freshmen, ten men and seven women, ranging in age from 16 to 26.

Needless to say, funding is to the body of an educational enterprise what food and drink are to our own bodies. Without money a college dies, and this is what was to happen all too soon to Rose Hill. The financial resources our principal benefactors thought would materialize failed to do so, and by the spring of 1997, in only our second semester, it was evident that the college was in trouble, though it did manage to limp into a second year—with nine new students to balance nine who had left—before finally closing in the early spring of 1998.

The Soul of a College

If the buildings of a college and its location in space and time are its body, then its soul is its educational program.

As mentioned already, I have been interested throughout much of my adult life in the nature and art of higher education. I have for many years been especially enamored of the great books model, where the curriculum consists entirely of classic texts, and of the Socratic or dialectical method of teaching, where the instructor's aim is not to dispense facts or express opinions but to ask questions, questions designed to lead his students to clearer thinking and a deeper understanding of principles. My undergraduate alma mater, Cornell College in Mount Vernon, Iowa, was not a great books college, but I had the rare blessing of studying there with a classics professor who was himself a living, breathing Socrates—a master of the western intellectual tradition, who used only primary texts in his classes and who seemed to know at least 50 moves in advance where we his often bewildered but always fascinated interlocutors would find ourselves when we had finally encountered the truth![1]

I spent considerable time examining the philosophies, polities, histories, and curricula of two other great books institutions: St John's College, a secular school with campuses in both Annapolis and Santa Fe, whose program of instruction, inaugurated in the early 1930s, has served as the model for a number of other similar ventures; and Thomas Aquinas College, a Roman Catholic institution in Santa Paula, California, which was established in 1971 and which itself borrowed rather freely from the St John's curriculum. A Rose Hill colleague and I visited both of these schools, sat in on classes, and talked with students, teachers, and administrators about their accomplishments and experiences.

First a few words about what is meant by "great books". A great book or a classic, as we understood these terms at Rose Hill, is any text that has had a defining impact on man's view of himself and his world: religiously, scientifically, politically, or artistically. This impact, let us add, may have been for better or worse. In other words, *great* books are not necessarily *good* books—books a traditional Christian might regard as spiritually nourishing or even "safe". Nonetheless they have so deeply and lastingly affected the world within and around us that we are obliged to understand them if we wish to make deep and lasting sense of that world. It was therefore determined from the start that the Rose Hill curriculum would not be limited to authors whose views could be easily accommodated within an Orthodox, or even generally

[1] The professor was the late John M. Crossett, and I am very happy to have this opportunity to discharge my debt of thanks to him. Another of his former students writes that Crossett "taught by a method as close to Socratic dialectic as the English language allowed.... Although students may at first have been wary of [his] methods, those who eventually realized the effect of his teaching would not have traded Crossett's class for any other.... No method could compare with dialectic for forcing a student's mind to grasp and keep a true idea" (James A. Arieti, "John M. Crossett: A Memoir", *Hamartia: The Concept of Error in the Western Tradition: Essays in Honor of John M. Crossett* [New York: The Edwin Mellen Press, 1983], 285).

Christian, frame of reference. As I point out in the Catalogue,[2] many of the ideas that have brought us to our present moment of history have been anything but pious and godly, and yet this does not mean they should be ignored. On the contrary,

> the Christian who wishes to lead an effective life in this age must come to grips with those ideas, not simply in their effects, but at their roots, and this means that alongside of the Bible and the patristic tradition, and ancient writers like Plato, who have traditionally been called upon to help support the Christian worldview, he must also study the works of such figures as Descartes, Hume, and Kant, and Darwin, Marx, and Freud (8).

One of the marks of a great book is that it cannot be easily classified: in fact the greater the work the less susceptible it will be to placement in a single category. Great books theorists are nonetheless obliged in practice to bring some organizational pattern to their reading lists. At Rose Hill my plan was to follow the example of both St John's and Thomas Aquinas College by requiring that certain books be read for tutorials and others for seminars. Tutorials were intended for a focused and guided study of more demanding materials, where mastery of a particular system of symbols or specialized vocabulary was deemed essential. Texts to be studied in these settings were arranged under six headings: Language, Mathematics, Natural Science, Theology, Philosophy, and Religion. Seminars on the other hand were reserved for discussion of works that are less technically difficult and require a somewhat less exacting investigation, including various literary, political, and historical classics. I should note that the Rose Hill curriculum differed from that of the other great books schools in two ways: first, in the emphasis it placed, not surprisingly, on Orthodox authors, including the Cappadocians, Maximos the Confessor, Symeon the New Theologian, and Gregory Palamas; and second, in its incorporation of sacred texts from other religious traditions, including the *Upanishads*, the *Tao Te Ching*, and the *Koran*, as well as non-Christian spiritual classics, such as Dogen's *Shobo-Genzo*, Ibn al-Arabi's *Bezels of Wisdom*, and the *Zohar*.

One other distinctive feature of the program was the chronological arrangement of the curriculum. The list of books was laid out over the course of four years in such a way that students would be reading historically both forward and backward in any given semester—generally forward in the tutorials and backward in the seminars. In their freshman year, for example, while they were learning Greek in their Language tutorial and studying such ancient authors as Plato and Aristotle in Philosophy, Euclid and Nicomachus in Mathematics, Archimedes and Galen in Science, and Irenaeus and Athanasius in Theology, our students were at the same time reading modern literature by Solzhenitsyn, Camus, Twain, Tolstoy, Melville, Dostoyevski, Thoreau, Goethe, and Austen. On the other hand, by the time they were seniors, the plan was to have them examining such modern authors as Kierkegaard and Wittgenstein in Philosophy, Lobachevski and Cantor in Mathematics, Maxwell and Einstein in Science, and Newman and Theophan the Recluse in Theology, whereas their seminar readings would include ancient literary classics by the likes of Aristophanes, Aeschylus, Sophocles, and Homer.

My aim in formulating this admittedly idiosyncratic, and no doubt controversial, schedule was to help underscore the numerous differences between traditional and modern thought and

[2] The Rose Hill College Catalogue can be found on my website: http://cutsinger.net/teaching/index.shtml. See in particular the sections entitled "Rose Hill College" and "The Curriculum". In what follows, page numbers have been placed in parentheses after quotations from the Catalogue.

culture by bringing representative texts from widely divided periods into a kind of collision with each other. Reading in one direction alone, from the past to the present, can create the illusion that worldviews are the result of blind historical fatalism, and it is easy for young people, even the best and brightest among them, to fall prey to what C. S. Lewis called "chronological snobbery"—that is, "the uncritical acceptance of the intellectual climate common to our own age and the assumption that whatever has gone out of date is on that account discredited".[3] This I was determined to avoid.

The second aspect of our collegiate soul was its pedagogy. If the great books curriculum was the matter of a Rose Hill education, the form of this education was Socratic *elenchos*—the dialectical method of teaching by questioning. To quote again from the Catalogue:

> At Rose Hill, the role of the faculty is primarily to guide discussion. They do not teach the great books. They make it possible for the books themselves to do the teaching. Rather than serving as experts or specialists in particular subjects, with the responsibility of promulgating the fruits of their scholarly research, the Rose Hill faculty are tutors and Socratic interlocutors, whose task is to stimulate reflection and inquiry and to foster intellectual community and the fruitful exchange of ideas (9).

Unless one has experienced a class run on these principles, it is difficult if not impossible to understand its dynamics. I tell other professors who are interested in trying their hand at dialectic that what they must do is prepare a lecture on the assigned reading for the day but then "swallow" it, converting its sentences from indicative to interrogative mood, so as then to enter their classroom with nothing but a series of questions in mind, the answers to which, supposing they are able to ask them all, may or may not prove to be the main ideas of their undelivered lecture.

The words "may or may not" are crucial here. Like Socrates himself, the practitioner of Socratic *elenchos* commits himself to following the argument wherever it leads.[4] This means being sensitive to the shifting currents of a given dialogue and the needs and insights of individual students as well as to the actual content of the text at hand. Critics often suppose that the Socratic method is less rigorous than a more didactic and typically professorial style, but in fact its rigor is simply of another kind. In the serious cross-examination of a great book, the course of the argument is often unpredictable, and it is certainly less "linear" than that of the lecture hall. But the intellectual commitment required of both teacher and students, together with the continual vigilance, demand a preparation and in my experience yield a mental fitness not promoted by other forms of learning.

I distinguished above between two elements, the matter and the form of our educational program. Insofar as this program was the *soul* of the College, it might be more appropriate, however—and certainly more in keeping with the Eastern Christian tradition—to say instead that there were *three* distinct factors or forces at work. I have in mind the psychology we would find if we followed the example of the Fathers and looked for inspiration once again to Plato's *Republic*.[5] Using Platonic and patristic terminology, one could say that the rational element—

[3] C. S. Lewis, *Surprised by Joy: The Shape of my Early Life* (New York: Harcourt, Brace, Jovanovich, 1955), 207.

[4] "I certainly do not yet know myself, but we must go wherever the wind of the argument carries us" (*Republic*, 394d).

[5] Book IV, 434d-441c.

the *logistikon*—in the soul of Rose Hill was the curriculum, the great books themselves, which provided a pattern or structure for study and reflection. The incensive or "spirited" aspect—Plato's *thymos*— could be seen in the thrusts and counterthrusts of Socratic *elenchos*, as we endeavored to wield our questions in such a way as to overcome premature interpretations and unexamined assumptions. And the appetitive or passionate aspect of the soul—*epithymia* for Plato and the Fathers—came into play in our efforts to disperse a lustful desire for mere information by arousing in its place a deeper longing for genuine wisdom, a longing too often suppressed, or only superficially satisfied, by the ingestion of lectures.

In remarks he prepared for the matriculation-day ceremonies, my colleague Vincent Rossi warned our new charges, "Knowledge is not a quantity that can be weighed or measured but a potentiality of being that must become a noetic act through ethical habit".[6] Much of the spirit as well as the soul of Rose Hill is captured in this powerfully succinct admonition. But here I would focus on the single word *act*, for intellective *activity*—and of course the *activation* it presupposes—are without doubt the distinguishing marks of a genuinely Socratic education. To quote the poet and philosopher Coleridge, a good teacher's aim should be

> not to assist in storing the passive mind with the various sorts of knowledge most in request, as if the soul were a mere repository or banqueting-room, but to place it in such relations of circumstance as should gradually excite the germinal power that craves no knowledge but what it can take up into itself, what it can appropriate, and re-produce in fruits of its own.[7]

The dialectician's job is clear. He must continually challenge his interlocutors, provoking them in every way possible to move from a state of passive acquiescence to one of active engagement. But this he can do, fallen human nature being what it is, only if he works by attraction and not compulsion alone—only if he succeeds in conveying something of the delight his students may expect to experience when, by virtue of their own burgeoning powers, they have broken through the dark underbrush of a difficult argument and re-emerged into sunlight, *seeing* not just being *told* what is so.

This was the ultimate goal of our educational program. But I need to be careful lest I end up painting too rosy a picture of the Rose Hill classroom. No teacher, and certainly no Socratic teacher, can expect every class to go well: so much depends on so many imponderables—including how well his interlocutors might have slept the night before!—and I would be guilty of grossly misleading you if I failed to admit that our short history was marked by its share of frustrations and disappointments. I do not believe, however, that the great books curriculum or the dialectical pedagogy were themselves the cause of these disappointments. Of course, you need to take my assessment with a few grains of salt: no parent wishes to admit his own child may be the problem! But based on the evident success of St John's and Thomas Aquinas College— colleges whose experiences now span several decades—I am confident that a Socratic

[6] Vincent Rossi, "The Three Principles of Rose Hill Pedagogy in the Light of St Isaac the Syrian's Three Degrees of Knowledge" (unpublished lecture delivered at Rose Hill on 14 September 1996). I had said in the Catalogue that "the Rose Hill program is liberal, it is classical, and it is Orthodox" (3). Rossi connects these three dimensions with what St Isaac called knowledge of works, knowledge of faith, and knowledge beyond knowledge (see especially Homilies 52 and 53).

[7] Samuel Taylor Coleridge, *The Friend*, ed. Barbara E. Rooke (Princeton: Princeton University Press), Vol. I, 473.

approach to classic texts can work, and indeed work very well.

In fact I remain convinced that this is the ideal form of education for an Orthodox college, much more so than for its secular or Catholic counterparts—or rather that it *would* be ideal if everyone, students and faculty alike, were prepared to honor, if not accentuate, the apophatic or Dionysian current of our Eastern Christian tradition. I shall return to this important qualification below.

The Spirit of a College

The microcosmic *collegium* called a man embraces three distinct parts, we have said with Saint Paul: a body, a soul, and a spirit. It stands to reason—or so at least I have claimed—that the macrocosmic *anthropos* we call a college should exhibit the same basic structure and be describable in the same basic terms. It too will have somatic, psychic, and pneumatic dimensions. I use the word "dimensions" advisedly, for it is important to stress that the third of these elements, the spirit of Rose Hill, was to be much more than just another piece of some puzzle. Intersecting the length of its body in Aiken and the width of its soul in the Socratic classroom, the Eastern Orthodox spirit of the College was intended to provide us with a vertical axis, giving depth and height—and thus solidity— to what would otherwise have been a merely secular surface.

We had agreed from the start that Rose Hill would be an Orthodox college. But we were also agreed that students from a variety of religious and non-religious backgrounds would be welcome. As noted earlier in my brief historical sketch, our efforts to advertise the College had included making visits to both Orthodox and non-Orthodox churches, and promotional materials were distributed to prospective applicants based as much on their standardized test scores and the likelihood of their attending the College as on their religious affiliation. We also took advantage of the mailing lists we had compiled when Rose Hill was still a retreat and conference center. For example, we had orchestrated several symposia for university students in cooperation with the Intercollegiate Studies Institute, an organization dedicated to politically conservative issues and values. Announcements about the College were sent to the students who had come to these conferences, even though none were Orthodox and some had no significant religious background at all.

Daily life at the College was deliberately and very carefully structured around worship and prayer. Weekday services in the chapel included First Hour at 7:15 a.m., Third and Sixth Hours at 11:15 a.m., Ninth Hour and Vespers at 5:00 p.m., and Compline at 9:00 p.m. Wednesdays began with Orthros and the Divine Liturgy at 7:00 a.m. No services were scheduled on Saturdays, and on Sundays students would either attend the Antiochian liturgy in the chapel or visit other nearby Orthodox Churches. In keeping with our policy of accepting applicants from a variety of backgrounds, attendance at these various services was not required, but it was strongly encouraged. Every class began with prayer, and meals were occasionally eaten in silence so as to allow for a reading from the lives of the saints or another edifying text. The Antiochian priest whose local mission shared the chapel had primary responsibility for the spiritual needs of the College community, but he was assisted by two additional chaplains: a Greek Orthodox priest and a priest of the Orthodox Church of America, both of whom served churches in Columbia.

The Orthodox ethos of the College was also reflected in subtler ways, not least in our insistence that the education we offered was intended for the whole human being, body, soul, and spirit. One of the ways we made this point was by requiring that everyone participate in a weekly horticulture class and assist in caring for the grounds as well as by providing occasional opportunities for instruction in iconography and Byzantine chant. Emphasis was also placed on thinking of ourselves as a Christian family.

The Rose Hill chapel was blessed to have a relic of Saint Severinus, better known among scholars by his family name, Boethius. Like Catherine of Alexandria, the patron saint of the College and herself a dialectician of great renown, Boethius stood for precisely the unity or harmony we hoped to achieve between worship and intellectual inquiry—between the *spirit* of the Orthodox tradition and the *soul* of a classical education. Martyred for his faith in the early sixth century by the Arian king Theodoric the Ostrogoth, Boethius was one of the most brilliant and learned men of his time, and perhaps of all time.[8] A master of both the *trivium* and the *quadrivium*, he was a translator and enthusiastic transmitter of Plato and Aristotle, and the author of a Socratic-style dialogue called *The Consolation of Philosophy*, which was written while the saint was awaiting execution and which appears on nearly everyone's list of great books.

Needless to say, a truly Boethian unity of faith and scholarship, let alone of sanctity and sagacity, is not something that just comes about of its own accord. It must be deliberately and repeatedly struggled toward, with the help of God. As I have hinted already, there were certainly days at Rose Hill when our own struggles seemed particularly painful and unproductive, and this was notably the case when it came to integrating the liturgical and community life of the College with our work in the classroom. Of course, we were but a fledgling institution, and it was inevitable that a variety of anxieties, financial and otherwise, would have been on nearly everyone's mind, adding to the tensions one naturally encounters in the daily life of any small community. This no doubt contributed to our pedagogical challenges. But setting these historical and psychological facts to one side, it is clear in retrospect that there was something about the educational program itself that served to impede us in our efforts to unite spirit with soul. As I approach my conclusion, I would like to focus on this obstacle in hopes that Orthodox Christians with their own college-building aspirations may be able to draw some useful lessons.

I said earlier that I do not think either the great books curriculum or the Socratic method of teaching were themselves the problem. But to be more precise what I should have said was that neither of these elements—neither the matter nor the form of the program—would necessarily have been problematic on its own. Looking back, however, I can see that I had been rather naïve in supposing that the combination of these potentially volatile elements within the crucible of a self-consciously Orthodox institution would not result in at least the occasional explosion!

By the end of the first week it was obvious that some of our students would benefit from these detonations more than others. For some they came as sudden flashes of insight as they began to see more deeply into the origins and implications of differing views of the world. But for others it was the painful force of the explosions themselves, not the light they released, that proved more decisive in shaping their classroom experience. As far as I can tell, religious demographics had little to do with these differences: there were Orthodox and non-Orthodox in

[8] Even the atheist Bertrand Russell was obliged to concede that Boethius "would have been remarkable in any age; in the age in which he lived he is utterly amazing" (*History of Western Philosophy* [London, 1961], 366). Given our emphasis on the Christian East, it is worth mentioning that Boethius's martyrdom was owing at least in part to the sympathetic contacts he had established with the court of the Byzantine Emperor, Justin I, a staunch defender of Orthodoxy.

both groups. Nor do I think inequalities in intelligence or academic preparation were at issue. It seems to me that these widely divergent responses were rooted instead in the students' varying expectations as to how academic work and religious life would—or would not—intersect at Rose Hill. I am eager for correction if you think me mistaken, but I submit to you that these different expectations flowed in turn from competing currents within the Orthodox tradition itself.

The students who were best suited for what we were trying to do pedagogically— whether they were Orthodox or not, and whether they knew it or not—were those who were most deeply attuned to what I called earlier the apophatic current of the Christian East. This first group was by no means indifferent or uncommitted to the traditional teachings of the Church or uninformed as to their history and meaning. But they seemed better able than their peers to follow the risen Lord's injunction to Mary Magdalene, "Do not cling to me, for I have not yet ascended to the Father" (John 20:17). In other words, they regarded dogmatic formulations not so much as *saying* what is so as *unsaying* what is not—as a means for pointing the mind, emptied of what it may have supposed to be true, toward a final participation in What Truly Is. As a result these apophaticists—if you will permit me this shorthand—seemed from the start more at home in the fluid medium of dialectical discussion, and they were correspondingly less wary than their fellows of giving careful attention to the arguments of non-Christian authors. They seemed instinctively to be of one mind with Saint Justin the Philosopher, who informed them in the freshman Theology tutorial that "those who lived in accordance with the *Logos* are Christians, even though they were called godless, such as, among the Greeks, Socrates and Heraclitus and others like them".[9] Although the writings of Bishop Nikolai Velimirovich, a scholar and canonized saint of recent times, were not on our reading list, I believe these same students would have readily embraced his claim that Krishna, Lao Tzu, Zoroaster, and the Buddha are to be numbered among "all the prophets".[10]

On the other hand, the students who had the greatest difficulties with the program were those who had arrived in expectation of receiving an education more catechetical and cataphatic in form. They were clearly troubled at the prospect of having to enter seriously into the minds of the pre-Christian pagans—to say nothing of such anti-Christian authors as Feuerbach and Freud, to mention just two of their freshman seminar readings. But I do not think the curriculum itself would have seemed nearly so perilous to them had it not been for the dialectical method with which it was paired. It was when they realized we teachers would not be offering them the safety net of an officially Orthodox interpretation of the books that they seemed to become especially unnerved. I realize in hindsight that we had probably done a less than adequate job of explaining the nature of a pedagogy that would prove so relentlessly interrogative and so demanding of the active mental engagement I was describing above. Part of the problem, in other words, was a certain amount of natural, and perfectly understandable, resistance to the peculiar demands of the Socratic method—resistance to which we faculty were by no means

[9] "First Apology", *Early Christian Fathers*, ed. Cyril C. Richardson (New York: Macmillan, 1978), 272.

[10] *Prayers by the Lake* [Grayslake, Illinois: Free Serbian Orthodox Diocese, n.d.], 86-87). A survivor of Dachau, Saint Nikolai (1880-1956) held earned doctorates from both the University of Berne and Oxford. Our students never reached the already mentioned *Consolation of Philosophy*, which had been scheduled for late in the sophomore year, but the apophaticists would not have been surprised to discover that our holy father among the saints Severinus—Boethius himself—could write, "I agree fully with Plato" (*The Consolation of Philosophy*, trans. Richard Green (New York: Macmillan, 1962), 70 (Book 3, Prose 12).

immune, but which in our case took the form of not always practicing what we preached, or rather of giving in to the temptation to *preach* and opine in the usual way of professors instead of *practicing* the more difficult art of dialectic!

But there was another factor at work here as well. The wariness these cataphaticists brought to their studies was not just a function of the Rose Hill pedagogy. It reflected in many ways a second current in Orthodox tradition, one more characteristically focused on dogmas as propositional truths—more concerned, in other words, with the said than the Unsaid—and therefore *a priori* mistrustful of competing verbal formulations, even those that might actually complement or corroborate the formulations of the Church. If saints Justin and Nikolai were precedents for the eagerness with which the first group of students approached their education, the anxieties of the second group were also clearly prefigured among the holy Fathers. One thinks, for example, of Gregory Palamas, who likened the paltry benefits of non-Christian writings to the "therapeutic value" one obtains from the "flesh of serpents".[11] Is there anything to be gained from such "secular wisdom"? Yes, he replied, but "you must first kill the serpent". These students could also have easily looked for support to those who compiled the *Synodikon*, which is read in many of our churches on the first Sunday of Great Lent, the "Sunday of Orthodoxy", and which contains this dire warning:

> To those who study pagan philosophies and do not take them as tools of instruction only but follow their futile theories, being so thoroughly convinced of their truth that they shamelessly introduce them and teach them to others, sometimes secretly and sometimes openly, *anathema*! *anathema*! *anathema*![12]

As you know, such statements are not uncommon. On the contrary, there exists within our tradition a very powerful and persistent current of mistrust regarding philosophical speculation and an often-unreflective dismissal of what are perceived to be "worldly", or even "demonic", forms of wisdom. A born apophaticist myself—in case you couldn't tell!—I am nonetheless obliged to admit that the more anxious and frustrated of our young people were perfectly within their Orthodox rights in feeling that the soul of Rose Hill College was, on occasion, in conflict with its spirit, or at least one current of that spirit.

Concluding Questions

During a pilgrimage last summer to the Holy Mountain of Athos, I was told by one of the fathers that the contemplative and ascetical life consists in placing the Prayer of the Heart in the spirit, the spirit in the soul, and finally the soul in the body. This he said is the key to

[11] Gregory Palamas, *The Triads*, ed. John Meyendorff (New York: Paulist Press, 1983), 28, 29.

[12] Cited by John Meyendorff, *Byzantine Hesychasm: Historical, Theological, and Social Problems* (London: Variorum, 1974), 64. The phrase rendered here as "pagan philosophies" appears in Meyendorff as "Hellenic sciences". Let us note that this was one of nine anathemas added to the *Synodikon* in the eleventh century and directed against the scholar John Italos, who was tried and condemned for his Platonic sympathies and use of dialectic. Saint Basil the Great is more temperate, but he too would have sided with those who might have preferred we avoid certain authors altogether: "If we are wise, having appropriated from [pagan literature] what is suitable to us and akin to the truth, we will pass over the remainder" (*Advice to Young Men on the Proper Use of Pagan Literature*, trans. Roy J. Deferrari, Martin R. P. McGuire [Cambridge, Massachusetts: Harvard University (Loeb Classical Library), 1934), 391 (Book 4, Chapter 8).

unifying and transfiguring the pneumato-psycho-somatic reality we call a man. Had we been granted more time, could Rose Hill have attained a correspondingly transfigured unity? God alone knows. What is clear, however, is that the difficulties we faced in trying to bring about this union give rise to a host of questions bearing upon the relationship between Orthodoxy and higher education. With just a few of these I shall conclude my remarks.

- First, can an Orthodox spiritual life, a penetrating study of classic texts, and a pedagogy of Socratic questioning be linked in a way that bears spiritual and intellectual fruit for all concerned, or was my supposing they could be a serious mistake from the start?

- Second, how does the Orthodox educator go about teaching books that are undeniably great but not necessarily good? Where exactly is the line to be drawn between using these texts as "tools of instruction only" and "shamelessly introducing and teaching them to others"?

- Third, are the dogmas of the Orthodox faith like icons, which we look *along* and not *at*? Or are they verbal enclosures beyond whose limits our minds trespass at peril? Do they *point* to the Truth or *contain* it? Or do they do both simultaneously? And if so, what would it mean to teach accordingly?

- Fourth, is it enough for an Orthodox college to rely on its liturgical and community life in providing its students with a "vertical axis", or should the classroom itself be safeguarded in ways we had not deemed necessary at Rose Hill?

- Fifth and finally, what should I say to the various individuals, both priests and laity, who continue to approach me for advice about creating an Orthodox institution along the lines of Rose Hill? Is our once-upon-a-time College deserving of some future resurrection, or should we leave it to rest in peace?

I do not have ready answers to these questions. So in good Socratic fashion, I shall simply leave them with you, inviting you to join me in thinking our way toward the Light.

Educating Young Children Today:

An Interview with Elena Lloyd-Sidle

Gray Henry-Blakemore

Elena Lloyd-Sidle: Can religious values and tradition be transmitted to children within the modern, secular education system?

Gray Henry-Blakemore: Formerly, England had a program called Christian Education (CE) which they devised for their entire school system thinking that this was the only way that the children could get religious values, as their parents no longer went to church (just like here in America). Then England became "multicultural" (like here) and had immigrant populations from Trinidad to Bangladesh living all over the country. Then there were some race riots such as the one at Brixton and they came up with a system called Religious Education (RE) in which all the world's religions would be taught very objectively to the young people with an idea of transmitting universal values and respect for others' cultures with whom they lived, based on an appreciation of their festivals, eating habits, and so on.[1]

There was an RE journal to which I subscribed as I was at that time doing a masters degree in education. A particular article struck me. "Whatever happened to the sacred in RE?" My thought was "how could you bring the sacred back into these multicultural classrooms?" I found in my own self that knowing about the festivals, foods and customs of other religions did not bring me any closer to these people as human beings. I did not find understanding and respecting their various traditions—on the purely mental plane—helpful in breaking down barriers. These people were still "foreigners."

The thought that I had which arose from considering the article's question "Whatever happened to the sacred in RE?" was as follows:

First, what is something that could be commonly held as sacred for young people of different traditions, or for anybody for that matter? The exploration of this could take place in the context of the accrual of basic universal virtue. There is absolutely no point in having an intellectual grasp of other faith traditions and have it remain merely in one's thought and mind. How, in fact, could one cultivate young children from the outset into virtuous, ethical, moral people of value?

My suggested plan was the following:

Let us suppose, for example, that there is a classroom of seven or eight year olds (obviously the idea I am suggesting would vary in complexity according to the age group). On the first day, the teacher could have a child from each of the represented faiths read out from their scripture their own version of "honor thy father and mother." It would then become apparent that all traditions share this value. The same would be done with other precepts.

But this is not enough. How do we engage the students to not only honor their parents, but to come closer together with one another as sympathetic and dear friends?

The students would be asked to keep a notebook with them and during the week record

[1] Elena Lloyd-Sidle: this is comparable to the Religious Literacy work being done in America by Diane Moore (Harvard Divinity School) and Stephen Prothero (Boston University). See D. Moore, *Overcoming Religious Illiteracy: A Cultural Studies Approach to the Study of Religion in Secondary Education* (New York: Palgrave, 2007), or the online article with the same title which is a synopsis.

10 instances when they did something in which they honored their father and mother and 10 instances in which they failed to do so (such as disobedience, talking back, etc.). Then at the end of the week, each child would read out his list. What would then happen is that the children of each tradition would conclude "we're all in the same boat." At the same time, these children would come to respect others for the ways in which they creatively honored their parents, and at the same time appreciate their honesty and objectivity in identifying and admitting their own failure.

What we have asked of these students during that week is to *watch* themselves, catch themselves, and correct themselves.

But this is only the beginning.

Then the teacher would say, "Ah, this next week, let us look at passages regarding patience, or anger, or envy, etc., etc." So on the second week, they would still keep writing about honoring the parents. Maybe five or so instances of honoring and dishonoring, and then add to this list the ten accounts of being patient or failing to be so, etc. The point of this exercise is mainly to create the habit in the young person of *self-observation* and *self-correction*, to the point that this approach to acquiring the virtues would become second-nature. So this is one idea which could be in fact tailored to the secular classroom, if the specific and universal values and virtues were identified. Whether or not it is pointed out that they all originate equally in all the world's faiths would not be absolutely necessary if the school were anxious about introducing other faiths. This exercise could be used in ethics courses if schools are hesitant to teach faith. Etiquette is taught in schools anyway, to a certain degree, so one might as well make ethics training explicit and methodic.[2]

Elena Lloyd-Sidle: What should be the underlying principles of a primary level curriculum in the Western secular context?

Gray Henry-Blakemore: Character development of children. What is very important is the positive approach to forming character, that is, addressing one another at our highest level. This exists linguistically in the Japanese way of speaking to people. When you add "*sen*" to a phrase, you are speaking to the Divine within a person. This is why you bow your head. We have to be able to, when we address people, address who they are in their highest potentiality and always expect the best.

Today in teacher training courses they tell the story of once telling a teacher "these are the dumb kids" on one side of the room, and "these are the smart ones," but they reversed it, so that the teacher then turns to the "dumb" ones thinking they are the smart ones and says, "would you please tell the class." The point of this is that people rise up to what people believe them to be and expect them to be.

In my MA classes, the most interesting things I learned were from the other school teachers about being positive. One teacher worked in the inner city of New York with big tall black boys who never even brought a pencil to school. Not knowing what to do, she realized these young people had given up and they already imagined that they would never in their lives ever

[2] Elena Lloyd-Sidle: see *The Book of Virtues*, which is a compilation of stories for children that is divided into sections on respective virtues, so that children may observe examples through literature of patience, courage, other-centeredness, etc. See also P.M. Forni, *Choosing Civility* (New York: St. Martin's Press, 2002), which traces 25 points of basic etiquette which are found in religious, philosophical, and moral traditions throughout the world and history.

be able to struggle enough to get good grades, and an A certainly never. So what she did was say to all these boys, "Everyone that is in the class has an A, and this is how you can keep it: you get points for bringing a pencil to school, points for turning in homework, even if it is wrong. . ." and so on. Her philosophy was, everyone already has excellence and they just have to learn to struggle to keep it.

In another case, a kindergarten teacher in the group was sad that as soon as school began there were the children who were left out and not popular, and as sometimes happens, those children were the more interesting ones. They may read or have interesting hobbies. So she asked everyone in the class to draw a name out of a hat so that everyone in the class was picked by someone else. The assignment was that each student would be a secret detective and find out all of the positive, unusual, interesting things they could about the student whose name they had drawn. The result was that things of great interest were discovered about the unpopular children, and this helped to finally make them more included in the class.

We were also taught as teachers that the only way to really learn is to fail. It is only when you make a mistake, and then must realize it and correct it, that you really have learned something. The sad thing in education is that when students get things wrong, it is a negative thing, rather than positive. Like a big, red, bad grade on their paper. What should be said is "isn't it wonderful that you got all this wrong, because now you can actually learn and go up!" Therefore, the student—by seeing the failure as a wonderful and necessary step—is able to transmute the failure, which he could so easily *identify with*, into a feeling of self-esteem and getting somewhere.

Related to this, I feel very strongly that teachers should not put the grades on a paper. Rather they should first show where all the mistakes are. Only when the student has corrected all those mistakes, should the teacher give the grade. Otherwise, the teacher has spent hours marking those mistakes, but when the student sees the grade, that is all he is interested in, so he simply throws the paper in the waste basket. He does not learn from his mistakes this way and no further learning occurs.

When my son was young, he always suffered: "I didn't get on the team," "I didn't, etc. etc." What the parent/teacher can do is say, "Isn't this wonderful? Now you can practice the attitude of detachment!"

Another example of how ideas like this could be used with older youth and again perhaps pulled out of the context of world religions would be the following: when I taught world religions at Centre College, I told the class that I would not be grading them on what they knew of facts, but on another form of effort. After a religion was taught, I asked all the students to write an essay for my eyes only describing how they could use ideas and principles found in the particular faith under study to solve any problem or suffering current in their own lives. The grades I gave them were for the effort they made to do this.

In the process, I watched many lives change because they were actually *using* the material to observe themselves. I can't imagine why people teach in any other way. Finally, human beings do not live by bread alone. It is their capacity to transform their inevitable trials and sufferings into a greater state of permanent being which is important and the point of education. The word "education" comes from the Latin *educare*, which does not mean to add facts or data into the mind, but *to draw out* that which is already there. It is interesting that in the history of education in Europe, all the schools and universities originally had chapels at their center and Latin was taught because education was for the greater glory of God. Today the pendulum has swung to the direct opposite goal: for getting a better job and more money for the most part.

Elena Lloyd-Sidle: Do you think this generation of children can still learn from books?

Gray Henry-Blakemore: I do. I really think children love books. A book is an archetype, so the soul is attracted naturally.

Elena Lloyd-Sidle: What essential knowledge can be transmitted to children by books?

Gray Henry-Blakemore: How to become better people. If children are given story-books of fairy tales, perhaps books could be developed for the parents, if they don't know the moral of the story and its deeper dimensions, to direct the parents so that they can explain to the children. At the end of the story, children could be asked what they had learned to make them better people. Or, before the story is read, tell them to be on the look-out for what lessons are to be gained from the tale.

Elena Lloyd-Sidle: How can children today be brought up with faith and be inclined to prayer?

Gray Henry-Blakemore: Children should be told the truth. First, they should be told about the various parts of the self. A simpler version (than the three selves: lower, conscience, and highest) is what I did with my oldest granddaughter, Sophia when she took a toy away from her younger sister, Layla. I said, "Did you know that you have two selves, the pure, beautiful, luminous self that is kind and generous, which is the Real Self, and then the mean, nasty, ugly, False self which takes the best for itself." So I asked Sophia "who took Layla's toy away?" and she said with great certainty and without missing a beat, "not my *real* self." There should be a book of metaphysics for children. One of their greatest problems is they think if they do something bad, which they do, that they are in fact bad people. I thought like this for years until I was introduced to the traditional breakdown of the levels of the self, so that they don't identify with the lower self.[3]

Secondly, if the religious point of view is permitted in the school, one could speak about final accountability, which is central to all faith traditions. Children can be told that they know about this ultimate judgment because they are already taking account of themselves continuously by thinking quietly to themselves, "I shouldn't have done that, it would be good to do that." So they already know about this in their secret lives as children.

Mythology could be used, which is non-threatening, and stories of heroic trials and feats to introduce ideas of noble qualities. Another course which could be taught would be about lives of people who are exemplary. One of my favorite stories goes back a few years ago to a local school which was honoring the mother of one of my childhood friends, Mrs. Serpell. When I was little, she used to make peanut butter sandwiches for her daughter Cornelia and me, and she seemed to be a typical mother. What a surprise to come to the school gymnasium, set with little luncheon tables and have Mrs. Serpell, now an older lady, being honored by the governor of the state and the commissioner of mental health for Kentucky. Apparently Mrs. Serpell, while being a mother and wife took one thing on and never gave up.

She began to investigate all the mental health facilities throughout Kentucky and make

[3] Elena Lloyd-Sidle: there is the story of the Cherokee grandfather who sits with all of the children of the tribe and says to them, "There is a battle going on in each and every one of you. It is between two wolves. One of the wolves is beautiful and kind and generous and helpful and luminous; the other wolf is ugly and awful and dirty and mean and selfish and hurtful. Even right now they are battling." One of the children asked, "Oh Grandfather, but which one will win?" Grandfather answered, "The one that you feed."

recommendations in the capital. As new commissioners came and went, changing every four years or so, not one of them had the long-term careful eye of the system as Mrs. Serpell had. At the honoring ceremony, the governor mentioned, "When I took over this job, I assumed Mrs. Serpell was on the staff. I had no idea she was simply a private citizen." He concluded, "It finally became easier to do what Mrs. Serpell suggested at the outset rather than trying to oppose her and then end up doing it anyway." The moral to this story is, if you take one thing and stick with it, you can make a major change in some field.

Book Reviews

L'Ecole à la Derive: L'Enseignement Actuel à la Lumière de la Tradition Universelle
by Ghislain Chetan
Paris: Publibooks, 2007

A preliminary translation of the first part of the title of this succinct yet illuminating book might be "Schools Gone Adrift." However, other translations of the French phrase "à la derive" include "floundering" and "going to rack and ruin," which more aptly describe the current state of most national education systems, both in the Western world, the framework for this book, and in most so-called "developing" countries. Following independence, Middle Eastern and African countries have patterned their national education systems on the Western model and have fallen into the same pitfalls as described in Ghislain Chetan's summary analysis of the current state of education in most of the world. The author, a Traditionalist, is one of the first modern educators to dissect the essential, underlying deep-rooted ills that have befallen schools in the West. His in-depth examination is based (as indicated in the sub-title of the book, "Present-Day Education in the Light of Universal Tradition") on the outlook of the world in the light of universal Tradition and perennial values.

In justifying his intriguing title, Chetan says in his preface, "Schools are adrift as if floating on the surface of water, pushed here and there by the disordered winds of passion, revolt, fashions, caprices. Schools resemble boats that have had their compasses and rudders cast off to facilitate navigation." And then he bluntly states: "Schools are ill because modern civilization is ill."

As the author points out, a classroom is a mirror of the society in which it is placed and thus the values of that society are refracted and perpetuated within the classroom. Modern society has lost its center; it has lost its access to the Perennial Truth vehicled by Divine revelation and the values refracted from religion. The knowledge conveyed to our students no longer contains the wisdom which addresses the higher level of the intelligence. In past eras this perennial wisdom assisted students in rising above themselves, giving young people meaning to their present life and guiding them towards preparing them for the eternal life. We now inculcate students with vast quantities of information, filling and cluttering their minds, entertaining them with countless "activities" but we no longer nourish their souls.

Chapter One of the book describes what he calls the fundamental "prejudices" which poison educational systems. The prime "prejudice" which ultimately produces the distortions in modern education is, he says, the Darwinian theory of evolution. Modern pedagogical principles take the Darwinian theory of evolution as a given premise, that is, that matter can evolve into a human being. The human soul and the presence of the Spirit in the human heart is obviously dismissed in the theory of evolution, thereby by-passing the fundamental *raison d'être* of the human state, i.e. to be both a vice-regent and slave of God in this world. Based on an evolutionary, developmental vision of manifestation and humankind, Divine Truths thus become inconvenient and are left out of modern, secularized education systems. The individual, not God, becomes absolute Object, and a disproportionate emphasis is placed on the individual in Western societies and educational systems. Love of individuality has led to those false values so cherished in Western societies: freedom of expression, human rights, the "democratization" of institutions as a result of the revolt against hierarchical principles, and the need and "right" to satisfy the individual whims and desires of the moment at any cost.

After clarifying the destructive influence of the evolutionary theory on modern education, the next chapters describe values that have derived from this recent vision of the world and that have long been taken for granted in Western school systems. These fundamental but illusory values have led to a constant, ever-changing parade of innovative pedagogical theories and applications in an attempt to understand what has gone wrong with educational systems and why young people are less educated, both in mind and soul, than previous generations. Chetan hits the mark when he says in Chapter Two that "students no longer enjoy any viable reference points in the face of masses of relative contradictions. Students do not have the necessary tools to situate themselves. . .". This is because the eternal Truths are no longer passed on to students or because Truth is consistently watered down with error.

Without referring to any particular one of the multitude of student-centered approaches in education, our author is ruthless in denouncing the practices of: 1. investing students with excessive self-aggrandizement, 2. taking their "interests" into consideration above all objectivity, 3. constantly encouraging critical thinking, 4. placing students' "rights" at the center of educational planning, 5. promoting "tolerance" and anti-elitism. These disproportionate foci on students' individual interests result in excessive student self-evaluation which leads to a complete lack of objectivity and sense of proportions on the part of young adults leaving the educational systems and entering the real world.

In our egalitarian-based education programs (*Education For All, No Child Left Behind*) a total rejection of authority at all levels, ultimately reflecting a rejection of Divine authority, has had devastating results ranging from undisciplined, disrespectful students in the simplest of cases, to the unfathomable violence witnessed recently in Western educational systems. Chetan not only explains the results of eliminating authority; he also wonders why, in current analyses of education, the "quality of the receptacle," i.e. the student, is never taken into consideration. Egalitarianism assumes that all students are equal in all capacities, which any classroom teacher will contradict. Education policy-makers and administrators take it for granted that any "good" teacher can create miracles with "bad" students, because all are equal and should have equal access to education. The right of every child to a quality education is defendable, but Chetan points out that there may be students who, because of their attitudes and/or character, may not *deserve* a quality education.

The following are selected excerpts of Chetan's book that I have, with the assistance of the author, attempted to translate from the original French (chapters one and two are not included as they are translated in full in this special volume):

From the Preface

Schools are "ill" because modern civilization is ill; and the cause of the malady of present day education undoubtedly lies in the philosophy upon which modern civilization thrives, or rather in the absence of any philosophy so-called.

* * *

One could truly speak of schools being "adrift," because they have disavowed their very raison d'être as well as almost everything that they were originally meant to be. Modern schools "float" on the surface of water, tossed from side to side by indiscriminate winds of passion, revolt, fashions, and whims. For some time now, schools have resembled a boat which, trying to facilitate navigation, (mistakenly) threw out its compass and rudder.

* * *

We should also mention that modern philosophy, especially French philosophy, holding sway in Paris from the sixties on by avant-garde philosophers such as Michel Foucault, Levi Strauss, and Derrida, attack the very notion of "human nature." This is why someone like Foucault, for example, is called a philosopher of the death of humankind, echoing the death of God proclaimed by Nietzsche at the end of the nineteenth century. In fact, these philosophers attack the very notion of the universality of human nature, reducing humankind to a set of relative cultural data, depending on their location in time and space. Tage Lindbom alludes to this same heresy when he writes: "We certainly do not contradict the fact that in our secularized world there exist both true and false affirmations. However, that which is declared as true is not recognized as absolutely valid. The dominating outlook is that truth is relative and that 'each should save himself or herself however possible. That which is a truth in Halle and Iena is a joke in poor taste in Heidelberg.'"

From Chapter Three: The So-called Critical Mind

Indicating a truth to someone and inviting him or her to submit to it, means, for modernists, a manipulation and restraint on his or her individual freedom. On the other hand, telling a person that truth does not exist outside his or her ego and desires, means, for modernists, to liberate a person. This is a curious paradox: on the one hand, the modernist claims to "liberate" the individual, but, in fact, effectively "imprisons" individuals within the limits of their egos. On the other hand, modern people consider true "freedom," that is, freedom from the individual limitations of the ego and the ability to go beyond oneself, which is precisely the goal of all Religion and of all Wisdom, as an "imprisonment."

* * *

In our days, there is a clear tendency to consider youth as "good" by nature and generally even "better" and more "open" than their elders. This illusion of moral superiority over ancient peoples is a sort of pseudo-religion, corresponding to the principle of compensation. This means that one retrieves on a lower plane what has been lost on a higher one: the emptiness left by abandoning spirituality having to be compensated for in one way or another. This is why young people's humanitarian movements and charity are admired, and could be labeled "long distance charity." Indeed, a very real humanitarian commitment may exist on the part of some young people, and may be even more widely practiced than that of the preceding generation. However, almost no one asks how it is possible to show generosity and real charity from a distance, when one proves oneself incapable of showing generosity or charity to one's parents, teachers, or peers. It is easy to be generous with the strength and money of others, as this does not commit one to very much, and above all does not require a change in one's self.

From Chapter Four: Students' Interests are Sovereign

It is said that the end will be near when, hierarchically, the lowest category of humankind become the most numerous. This category concerns *homo economicus*. Now, are we not witnessing today an ever-growing economic factor governing the world? This explains why a student left to his or her own devices has every chance of not going beyond himself or herself.

Subjected more than ever before to their individual centrifugal tendencies, students are denied a framework which, with the aid of grace, would be capable of re-centering them.

* * *

There is a blatant trend in our days to "absolutize" or "render as absolute" the traumatisms of a child's upbringing with a view to completely excusing him or her, as if the child were, by definition, a fated mechanism incapable of virtues.

From Chapter Five: Do Not Criticize Young People

In the past, Kings received their authority, or their temporal power, from Heaven. It is true that they were not always worthy of it, but this is another question. In every traditional society, the authority of parents, of the Emperor and of conveyors of knowledge, i.e. teachers, was always considered as God-given, representing the Authority of God before a certain people or community.

* * *

At the present time, all forms of authority are more or less tainted with suspicion. One commonly speaks of a "nice crook" and a "vile policeman." In our world, there is the latent psychological tendency to eliminate all forms of constraint (cf. May '68 in France: "it is forbidden to forbid"). It is the role of civil authority to enforce constraints, and since nothing is more feared than insecurity, forces of order are tolerated. However, obstacles are put up against them wherever possible. Moreover, whenever a tragic error is committed by civil authority, be it real or imagined, it is blown out of proportion and civil authority becomes stigmatized by society.

In modern analyses of education, the quality of the receptacle, the student, is almost never taken into consideration, as if the quality of the student were simply obvious, or a very secondary matter. It is a "given" that a "good" teacher can work miracles with a "bad" student.

From Chapter Seven: Tolerance

The concept of tolerance as understood by modern people is so unanimously recognized, imposed, and invoked as a golden rule that this notion alone could make up the contents of a whole chapter.

The following saying by Voltaire is often cited as the key expression of the meaning of tolerance: "I'm not in agreement with what you say, but I shall fight so that you can say it." This is the very negation of Truth, of its most blatant disdain, as F. Schuon has noted in one of his books. "There is no right superior to that of the Truth" said a sage of Benares. The modern notion of tolerance places rights on individual claims, even the most false ones. To paraphrase Voltaire, it is as if he had said: "I recognize no right higher than the expression of your individual claim, even if it is an error. However, this is of little importance because I am more ready to fight for your claim than for the manifestation of the Truth."

From Chapter Eight: Anti-elitism

Egalitarianism is also found in the endeavor to efface all qualitative differences amongst individuals over the course of their academic education. A child's academic career unfolds from birth as if everyone possessed *grosso modo* the same chances. Differences are seen to arise primarily from the social class to which an individual belongs. Differences can even take on a proclaimed "sexist" attitude when one takes into consideration differing academic careers of boys and girls. The egalitarian outlook has resulted in the unquestioned policy of maintaining an integrally mixed form of education throughout the school age years. Yet, it behooves us to recognize that it was during the eras of their decadence that ancient civilizations adopted policies of mixed education, and introduced the concept of a common curriculum where all students are thrown together to follow the same type of instruction. This fact is, alas, ignored by modern educators. The notion of a qualitative selection of students (of sifting the more gifted from the less gifted with a view to the students' best interests) is seen as not offering equal opportunities to all students.

Jane Casewit

A Spirit of Tolerance: The Inspiring Life of Tierno Bokar
by Amadou Hampaté Bâ
Introduction by Louis Brenner. Edited by Roger Gaetani. Translated from French by Jane Casewit. Bloomington, IN: World Wisdom, 2008

The rainbow owes its beauty to the variety of its shades and colors.
In the same way, we consider the voices of various believers
that rise up from all parts of the earth as a symphony
of praises addressing God (p. 126).
(Tierno Bokar)

With the unremitting bombardment of news and media coverage depicting contemporary Africa in a state of total disarray—ridden with famine, disease, genocide, war—we are blessed for this profound testimonial of Amadou Hampaté Bâ's extraordinary Sufi master of Africa, Tierno Bokar. It is through the universal message of this African mystic that the world's spiritual traditions, not only Islam, can honor what has been regarded as the "religion of the heart," or "the transcendent unity of religions"[1]—fearlessly affirmed in *The Tarjuman al-ashwaq*[2] of Ibn 'Arabi, *al-Shaykh al-Akbar* (the Greatest Master). Considerable interest has come about regarding this great spiritual teacher of Mali via the acclaimed play *Tierno Bokar* by renowned director Peter Brook, which was adapted for the stage from Bâ's book by Marie-Hélène Estienne. It is with the hopes of the editors and publisher that this volume will accompany other key contemporary works, such as that of Martin Lings' book on Shaykh Ahmad al-Alawi.[3]

During his youth, Amadou Hampaté Bâ (1900-1991) became a disciple of Tierno Bokar while attending a Koranic school under Bokar's direction in Bandiagara, Mali. Bâ was to become a well-known Malian diplomat, writer, and influential voice of Africa—providing information and insight into its history, religion, literature, culture, and life. He is the author of the following celebrated quote: "In Africa, when an old person dies, it is as if a library has burned down" (p. xvii). Without Hampaté Bâ's efforts to put this testimony into writing, the modern world would perhaps know nothing of this great master, Tierno Bokar, since this work contains most of the only recorded words of this man of remarkable spiritual insight.

This new translation, *A Spirit of Tolerance: The Inspiring Life of Tierno Bokar*, is divided into a tripartite discourse—Part 1: *His Life*; Part 2: *His Words*; and Part 3: *His Teachings*. There are also two important appendices—Appendix I: *The Pearl of Perfection* and Appendix II: *Sufism and Brotherhoods* (*Turuq*) *in Islam*, offering a broad overview of the different Sufi orders, including relevant photographs depicting the ambience of where Tierno Bokar lived, his disciples, the mosque of Bandiagara, his tomb, as well as illustrations of present-day Malian life. The book also contains significant biographical notes on the authors and those who helped prepare the book. Louis Brenner, who provides the Introduction, is arguably the most knowledgeable scholar in

[1] Frithjof Schuon, *The Transcendent Unity of Religions* (London: Faber and Faber, 1953).

[2] *The Tarjuman al-ashwaq*, or "The Interpreter of Desires," trans. Reynold A. Nicholson (London: Theosophical Publishing House, 1978).

[3] *A Sufi Saint of the Twentieth Century: Shaikh Ahmad Al-Alawi, His Spiritual Heritage and Legacy* (Cambridge: Islamic Texts Society, 1993).

the English-speaking world on the writings of both Hampaté Bâ and the life and thought of Tierno Bokar.

Part One, *His Life*: Tierno Bokar Salif Taal (1875-1939) was known as "the sage of Bandiagara" in Mali, West Africa. From an early age his life was infused with the spirit. His maternal grandfather was Seydou Hann, a great Sufi mystic of the Qadiri order, and later the Tijaniyya. In addition, Tierno benefited from the innate wisdom of his other family members, which provided a pivotal support to his traditional education. And yet his education took place in juxtaposition to a social milieu that was characterized by an atmosphere of turmoil: with the seething combination of compulsory modernizations and foreign occupation, tribal and sectarian differences were escalating. From an early age he learned to find peace within himself and to converse regularly with God. Bokar provides us with some advice offered by his mother to guide him in "the greater *jihad*":

> Write the Divine Name *Allah* on a wall, next to your bed so that when you awaken the Name will be the first image that your eyes fix upon. When you get up, pronounce it with fervor from the depths of your soul, so that it is the first word to come out of your mouth and to enter your ears. At night when you go to bed, fix your eyes on the Name so that it is the last image contemplated before being taken off into the temporary death of sleep. If you persist, the light contained in the four letters will spread over you and a spark of the divine Essence will enflame your soul and illuminate it. (p. 14)

By the age of fifteen, Bokar had virtually memorized the Koran, the rituals and laws of Islam, and the lives of the saints such as al-Ghazali, Muhyiddin Ibn 'Arabi, and Muhammad ad-Dabbar, and yet his knowledge was in no way restricted to only this. Readers will be interested to note that "the *Meccan Revelations* [*al-Futuhat al-Makkiya*] of the great Andalusian spiritual master Ibn 'Arabi was his [Tierno Bokar's] favorite book" (p. 21).

Tierno Bokar was tremendously unassuming and did not wish to be addressed with any titles, even that of spiritual master or teacher—"We are all teachers and we are all students"—referring to his students as "brother" (p. xv). Tierno Bokar received initiation (*al-bay'a*) into the secrets of the Tijani Sufi order by Amadou Tafsir Bâ. At the age of twenty-six, Bokar's *shaykh* informed him, "I have nothing more to teach you" (p. 23). By the age of thirty-three, Tierno Bokar was the director of the Bandiagara *zawiya*, which was called "the refuge of love and charity."

A central and unforgettable element of Tierno Bokar's life has to do with the disagreement that emerged in the Tijani order over certain ways of reciting a particular Tijani prayer, known as *The Pearl of Perfection*. There were those who practiced the "eleven beads" and those who practiced the recitation of "twelve beads." The disagreement came about when the founder of the order, Ahmad al-Tijani, arrived late on one occasion:

> One day he was delayed, and the students started the *wazifa* [a Tijani litany] without him. They had already finished the eleventh recitation of *The Pearl of Perfection* when the Shaykh was at last able to join them. Spontaneously, and so that the Shaykh could give them his benediction as was the custom, they repeated the prayer a twelfth time, after which the Shaykh blessed them. (p. 44)

Without any observation, positive or negative, from the Shaykh, some of his disciples began to practice the "twelve beads," a practice that was later adopted by the Umarian branch of the Tijaniyya found in Mali and Niger.

Later in his life, having received a crucial letter from Alfa Hashimi Taal (brother of the king of Bandiagara), Bokar traveled to meet with Shaykh Sharif Hamallah, a clan rival, in order to better comprehend this dispute between the two practices. During his stay Bokar had a *metanoia*, or "change of mind," and asked to receive *tajdid* (renewal of his *wird*) into the "eleven beads." On Bokar's return to Bandiagara, the news had spread quickly of the renewal of his *wird* into the "eleven beads" with Sharif Hamallah. It was from this point on that Tierno Bokar experienced extreme hardships: he was essentially ostracized by his clan and family and forbidden to teach or pray publicly. Tierno Bokar's school was destroyed and he and his two wives and children were placed under house arrest. He spent the remaining years of his life in sheer solitude and yet he never lost confidence in God's benediction nor did he cease to be a spiritual light to all those who dared to visit him under such adverse conditions.

Part Two, *His Words*: Tierno Bokar taught in the traditional method that was known and used throughout Africa, which was oral rather than written. Contrary to the modern bias against oral traditions, the "word" was perceived as being potentially sacred, originating from what was transcendent and divine, and was referred to as the "life-giving word." The author points out that, "In Islam, as in many other religious traditions, esoteric knowledge is taught by word of mouth" (p. 111).

In this section of the book, "the sage of Bandiagara," Tierno Bokar, expresses a universal truth regarding the ineffable nature of the Absolute or the Divine Reality which is beyond all conceptualization:[4]

> God is the bewilderment of human intelligence because on the one hand, if you affirm His existence, you cannot, in any case, prove it materially or mathematically. On the other hand, if you deny His very existence, you deny your own existence, which is merely the effects of His existence. Of course, you do exist. And even if one cannot prove God materially, it is nonetheless necessary to remember that the non-visibility or non-tangibility of a thing is not absolute proof of its nonexistence.
>
> Finally, God is the bewilderment of intelligence because everything that you conceive in your thought and give form to in your speech as being God ceases by this very fact to be God. It becomes no more than *your own way* of conceiving Him. He escapes all definition. (p. 135)

Throughout this book readers will notice that Tierno Bokar continuously acknowledges and affirms the underlying significance of the world's religions:

> With all my heart, I desire the coming of the era of reconciliation amongst all religions of the earth, the era in which these united religions will support each other to form a spiritual and moral canopy, the era in which they will be at peace in God by resting

[4] Given Tierno Bokar's unanimous recognition of the inherent truth pervading the world's religious traditions, it is appropriate to point out that the terrestrial inability to conceptualize the Absolute is reminiscent of the sacred formula of the (first) *shahadah*: *La ilaha illa 'Llah* (There is no divinity but God), the "Tao that can be named is not the Tao" of the *Tao Te Ching*, *neti-neti* (not this, not that) of the Upanishads or *negatio negationis* (negation of a negation) which is central to Meister Eckhart's teachings.

> upon three supports: Love, Charity, Brotherhood.
>
> There is only one God, and there can be only one Way that leads towards Him, one Religion of which its various worldly manifestations are like branches spreading out from a single tree. This Religion can only be called Truth, and its dogmas can only be three: Love, Charity, Brotherhood. (p. 159)

Part Three, His *Teachings*: one of the principal methods of Tierno Bokar's instruction was to meet the seeker at his or her own level of receptivity, which was in accordance with the Prophet's instruction: "Speak to people according to the level of their understanding" (p. 110). Tierno Bokar often made use of the potent symbol of the river that was widely used by the different Sufi *turuq* when describing stages of the spiritual path:

> There are three ways to know a river: First of all, there is the man who has heard the river spoken about and becomes capable by imitation and repetition to describe it without having seen it himself. This is the first degree of knowledge.
>
> Then there is the man who has undertaken the journey and who has arrived at the banks of the river. Seated on the banks of the river, he contemplates it with his own eyes and is a witness to its majesty. This is the second degree of knowledge.
>
> Finally, there is the man who throws himself into the river and becomes one with it. This is the supreme degree of Knowledge. (p. 199)

This book stands out as a traditional testimony to the universal spiritual heritage of all people *qua* the life of a twentieth-century African saint, Tierno Bokar. In addressing the diverse readership we hope that this testimony may be instrumental in leading more people, especially the younger generations, to reconnect to their own spiritual traditions. "The sage of Bandiagara" provides this astute aphorism for the modern world: "Do not go seeking fortune by begging in far-off places, you who are seated upon a sack of gold. Make use of this fortune, make it grow by trading in it with others" (p. 155). Readers will find that Tierno Bokar, like his fellow Sufi companion Ibn 'Arabi, affirms the religion of the heart.

Samuel Bendeck Sotillos

Notes on the Contributors

Jean Biès is the author of more than 20 books on philosophy, comparative religion, poetry, and travel. He was formerly a professor of Greek literature at the University of Pau, France. He was decorated with the chevalier of the French Legion of Honor and recipient of the High Prize of the Society of French Poets.

Titus Burckhardt (1908-1984) is one of the leading perennialist writers of the twentieth century. He wrote books and essays on pure metaphysics as well as traditional art and sciences. He also translated many prominent Islamic esoteric works from Arabic. An authority on traditional town planning and architecture restoration, he wrote highly celebrated books on Fez and Siena, as well as the cathedral of Chartres.

Ghislain Chetan took a degree in Greek and Latin at a Jesuit college and has more than 30 years experience teaching French and Latin in secondary schools. He carried out research at the University of Indiana for teaching French as a second language and has had a lifelong interested in Eastern and Western traditions.

William Chittick is a professor in the Department of Comparative Studies at the State University of New York, Stony Brook. He is one of the most important contemporary translators and interpreters of Islamic mystical texts and poetry. His work includes *The Sufi Path of Love: The Spiritual Teachings of Rumi*, *The Sufi Doctrine of Rumi*, and *The Sufi Path of Knowledge: Ibn al-'Arabi's Metaphysics of Imagination.*

Ananda Kentish Coomaraswamy (1877-1947) was a multi-talented Anglo-Sri Lankan researcher, scientist, linguist, art and culture expert, philosopher, museum curator and author. Born in the late nineteenth century, he was the first to expound the importance of traditional arts, culture and thought as more than simple relics of a bygone past. A prolific scholar, he was the first to reintroduce Perennial Philosophy to the West through art and handicraft.

James S. Cutsinger is an author, editor, and teacher focusing on Perennialism and the theology and spirituality of the Christian East. A prolific writer, he is professor of theology and religious thought at the University of South Carolina. His numerous works include *Not of This World: A Treasury of Christian Mysticism* and *Paths to the Heart: Sufism and the Christian East.*

Charles Alexander Eastman (Ohiyesa) (1858-1939), also known as Ohiyesa, was the first great American Indian author, penning eleven books. He was the spokesman of the day for Indian affairs and was presented with a prestigious award at the 1933 Chicago World's Fair for distinguished achievements on behalf of American Indian culture.

Anne Fitzgerald-Lo has spent much of her life in Africa and taught African studies at City University of New York. She did post-graduate work in African history in Tanzania focusing on Islam in Africa South of the Sahara. Her career as a freelance writer for newspapers and journals on African women and development took her to 19 African countries. She is currently retired in Morocco, writing her memoirs.

Gray Henry-Blakemore is founder and director of Fons Vitae Publishers in Louisville, Kentucky. She holds a postgraduate degree in education and taught comparative religion for many years in Egypt before founding the Islamic Texts Society in England. She has devoted her life to promoting traditional texts and teachings through publishing, film-making, lecture tours, conferences, and travel.

HRH the Jagadguru Sri Chandrasekharendra Sarasvati Swamigal (1894-1994) of Kanchipuram is known as Sankaracharya, or the great teacher of the Sankara tradition. He was installed at the age of 13 as pontiff in Kanchi of the hallowed line of succession going back to Sankara. More than 87 years of his life was dedicated to preserving and perpetuating traditional Hindu dharma. Those Westerners fortunate enough to meet him were in awe of his sanctifying presence.

Enes Karić served as Minister of Education, Science, Culture, and Sports in the Government of the Republic of Bosnia and Herzegovina from 1994 to 1996 and was dean of the Faculty of Islamic Studies in Sarajevo between 2003 and 2007 where he still lectures today. He is widely published on various aspects of Islam, modernity, and modern ideologies and also serves as a UNESCO expert in Islamic cultures.

Ali Lakhani graduated from Cambridge University in England and moved to Vancouver, Canada, where he has practiced law as a trial lawyer for 25 years. In 1998 he founded the Sacred Web Journal, devoted to traditional metaphysics and modernity for which he regularly contributes. He organized the Sacred Web conference in 2006.

Martin Lings (1909-2005) was a leading representative of the Perennialist school and an acclaimed author, editor, translator, scholar, and poet. He was also an authority on Shakespeare. A well known scholar of Islam, his biography of the Prophet, *Muhammad: His Life Based on the Earliest Sources* and *Splendours of Islamic Calligraphy and Illumination* won international acclaim.

Elena Lloyd-Sidle has a Masters Degree in Religion from Yale Divinity School where she studied Historical Theology. She and Gray Henry-Blakemore co-produced the film interview *Death and Transformation: The Personal Reflections of Huston Smith*, and co-edited the volume, *Water: Its Spiritual Significance.*

Joe Medicine Crow is a recipient of the Presidential Medal of Freedom, the highest civilian honor given by the United States. He is the last living Plains Indian war chief, and is the author of seminal works in Native American history and culture. A veteran of World War II, Medicine Crow accomplished during the war all of the four tasks required to become a 'war chief'. He was the first member of his tribe to attend college, receiving his master's degree in anthropology in 1939, and is the Crow tribal historian.

Sachiko Murata is professor of religion at the State University of New York at Stony Brook. She holds an undergraduate degree from Chiba University in Japan and was the first woman to study Islamic jurisprudence at Tehran University in the 1970s. She holds a doctorate degree in Persian literature and is best known for her book, *The Tao of Islam.*

Seyyed Hossein Nasr is University Professor of Islamic Studies at the George Washington

University. The author of over fifty books and five hundred articles, he is one of the world's most respected writers and speakers on Islam, its arts and sciences, and its traditional mystical path, Sufism. He is the leading spokesman for universality and the Perennialist school in Islamic academia. A volume in the Library of Living Philosophers series has been dedicated to his thought.

Lord Northbourne (1896-1982) was the fourth Baron Northbourne. He was educated at Oxford and was provost of Wye College for many years. He was an agriculturist, educator, translator, and writer on agriculture and the environment as well as comparative religion. His works include *Look to the Land*, *Religion in the Modern World*, and *Looking Back on Progress.*

Marco Pallis (1895-1989) was a gifted musician, composer, mountaineer, and translator, as well as being a renowned authority on Tibetan Buddhism and Perennialism. His books *Peaks and Lamas* and *The Way and the Mountain* came from his experiences traveling in the Eastern Himalaya region and his exposure to Tibetan Buddhism. Pallis also wrote many pieces for the important traditionalist journal *Studies in Comparative Religion*, some of which are included in his last publication, *A Buddhist Spectrum.*

Frithjof Schuon (1907-1998) is the foremost spokesman of the Perennialist school and a philosopher in the metaphysical current of Shankara and Plato. He wrote more then two dozen books on metaphysical, spiritual, artistic, and ethnic themes and exerted the greatest influence on Perennialism in the twentieth century. He was also a prolific poet and gifted painter of images that portrayed the beauty and power of the Divine and the nobility and virtue of primordial humanity.

Samuel Bendeck Sotillos has received graduate degrees in Education and in Psychology. He has traveled throughout the world to visit sacred sites, and had contact with noted spiritual authorities. He currently works as a mental health clinician in California. He is preparing a future issue of Studies in Comparative Religion entitled *Psychology and the Perennial Philosophy.*

William Stoddart has spent his life leading others to the understanding of the writings of the Perennialist School, especially the writings of Frithjof Schuon and Titus Burchkhardt. He is the greatest authority on the works of the latter. His books *Outline of Hinduism* and *Outline of Buddhism* were highly acclaimed and he is also the author of *Remembering in a World of Forgetting.*

Note on the Editor

Jane Casewit is an educator, translator, and writer with a deep interest in religious education, religious studies, interfaith understanding, and metaphysics. She has many years of teaching experience in North Africa and the Middle East and held key positions in girls' education and community mobilization projects in that region as well as consulting in sub-Saharan Africa. In Morocco she worked for the United States Agency for International Development as an education and workforce development advisor. She translated the "Tibetan Caravans" parts of *Islam in Tibet* (Fons Vitae, 1998), and *A Spirit of Tolerance: The Inspiring Life of Tierno Bokar* (World Wisdom, 2008) and has written extensively on Islam and femininity. She presently designs education and workforce training programs for North Africa and the Middle East.